For Sylvia Darley

Diana von Welanetz

1977

BOOKS BY

Diana and Paul von Welanetz

THE PLEASURE OF YOUR COMPANY (*1976*)

WITH LOVE FROM YOUR KITCHEN (*1976*)

THE PLEASURE
OF YOUR
COMPANY

THE PLEASURE
OF YOUR
COMPANY

Diana and Paul von Welanetz

NEW YORK *Atheneum* 1976

Illustrations by Kurt Welanetz

Library of Congress Cataloging in Publication Data
von Welanetz, Diana.
The pleasure of your company.
Includes index.
1. Cookery, International. I. von Welanetz, Paul,
joint author. II. Title.
TX725.A1V66   1976   641.5'9   75-41855

ISBN 0-689-10724-2

Published simultaneously in Canada by
McClelland and Stewart, Ltd.
Manufactured in the United States of America by
H. Wolff, New York
Designed by Kathleen Carey
First Edition

FOR OUR PARENTS,

Mimi, Papa, Marge and Kurt

AND FOR

Mary Dean Erpelding

CONTENTS

II *Menus for the Four Seasons*

III   *Menus with a European Influence*

Contents

VI *Menus for the Holidays*

THE PLEASURE
OF YOUR
COMPANY

Introduction

$\mathcal{D}$IANA WAS ALREADY an extraordinary cook by the time I found her at 8:15 in the morning on November 2, 1962. I stepped off the elevator into the lobby of the Ambassador Hotel in Hong Kong, and there she was, the most beautiful girl I had ever seen.

We were married exactly one year later to the day, after I had chased her completely around the globe. First to France, where she had returned to study classic *haute cuisine* and where we took long, frosty winter walks through the parks of Paris. Then almost everywhere else, holding hands under tables in small candlelit restaurants, or watching the gentle sway of Chinese sampans at dusk. All pretty heady stuff which finally worked its inevitable magic. At last she said yes, and she has been enchanting me ever since.

Because Diana loved to cook, it was often difficult to pry her loose from the kitchen. As a bridegroom I found this frustrating at times, but one enormous plus emerged—*I became a cook*. After following her all over the world it was only a few more steps into her kitchen, and my conversion occurred almost imperceptibly. At first I was asked to remove hot dishes from the oven. Or, if guests were expected and Diana was running late, she would ask me to prepare a Roquefort salad. From there it was only another step to boning chicken breasts for Chicken Kiev or creating a decoration for the pastry case of a Filet of Beef Wellington. We have been working harmoniously together in the kitchen, experimenting, discussing, helping each other—for twelve years now. And our "togetherness" has in no way diminished my appreciation of this exciting woman. She still remains my greatest pleasure.

Our cooking classes began almost by accident, without any indication that they would ultimately occupy so much of our time. It all started the day Diana quit smoking. She wanted a diversion to keep her hands busy, so she started making crêpes to store in the freezer. Two friends dropped in and were intrigued with the process. Hundreds of crêpes later, they decided, with great enthusiasm, to meet the next day for a class in omelette-making and the following week for soufflés. They had so much fun that word spread quickly, and soon total strangers began calling to inquire about lessons. The classes grew rapidly until Diana was teaching four and five times a week. She loved the involvement and the enthusiasm of the students.

It was also a time of adjustment to having a new baby daughter, and the classes provided an answer to Diana's need for personal expression and creativity. We couldn't know then that the tremendous success of these classes and the eventual writing about them would lead to an exciting new career for both of us.

We have never intended to have a large commercial cooking school, though it is a struggle to prevent it from happening. We do not advertise—all our students are referred and recommended by other students—and our classes are kept intimate and elegant. Celebrities, socialites, novice and advanced cooks alike gather in our kitchen to learn about food, its preparation, and how to serve it imaginatively. Some even come from as far away as Chicago for private lessons.

Because of the intimacy of our classes, we have time to develop a close rapport with our students and still retain our own freedom and creativity. During a typical class, the students watch us prepare a complete party menu. They sample all the dishes, along with appropriate wines selected especially for the menu by our wine authority. Students are encouraged to ask questions, share their own knowledge and participate in the serving. The accent is on elegant entertaining and all that it involves—timing, advance preparation, and glamorous presentation.

During the years that we have been teaching, we have traveled extensively to explore the cuisines of our own as well as other countries. We enjoy searching out unusual restaurants and discovering new ideas. When we are not teaching or traveling, we can be found researching, writing, experimenting in the kitchen, and corresponding with cooks all over the world who take the time to write to us and share recipes.

We are tremendously excited about what is happening with food in America today. People are becoming more sophisticated about cooking, paying more attention to the quality of what they eat and how it is served. Among young people there is great interest in nutrition, fresh foods, lighter meals, and the foods of other countries. Entertaining has become a creative activity, a way of expressing one's individuality that is so much more personal than dining in restaurants. In short, Americans, in their newly found leisure, are discovering the joys of cooking and entertaining, and we are delighted to be involved.

This book is not a simple collection of recipes—it is a treasury of well-orchestrated menus complete with wine selections and timetables for advance preparation. The menus have been thoroughly kitchen-tested and demonstrated to countless discerning cooks throughout our years of teaching. We are grateful that we will now be able to share these menus with those of you who cannot be cooking with us in class.

Paul von Welanetz
Los Angeles, California

Words on Wine

DENNIS OVERSTREET

A LOVE AFFAIR with wine, like a fairy tale, always has a happy ending—both loved one and lover improve with age. Certainly, the drinking of wine has a moral edge over other hobbies and pleasures, for it promotes companionship, sharing and good conversation. I have yet to meet a miserly wine lover; in fact, I find most oenophiles to be urbane, witty, elegant, sociable, learned and even a bit better-looking than most other people.

Wine has left its mark on every major civilization; it has been praised by poets, painters and philosophers. An early discussion of wine glows with Plato's praise, "Nothing more excellent or valuable than wine was ever granted by the gods to man." The Greek dramatist Euripides wrote, "Where there is no wine, love perishes, and everything else that is pleasant to man." With Christianity came more praises of wine—we find countless references to it in the Bible. During the Renaissance, wine again came to the forefront. William Shakespeare said, "Give me a bottle of wine; in this I bury all unkindness."

The eighteenth century, which brought developments that blossomed into one of the greatest intellectual revolutions in the history of mankind, brought this observation by Ben Franklin: "Wine is constant proof that God loves us and wants us to be happy." Arriving in the twentieth century, we find the words of Ernest Hemingway: "Wine is one of the natural things of the world that has been brought to perfection, and it offers a greater range of enjoyment and appreciation than possibly any other pure sensory thing which may be purchased."

The art of dining well is within the reach of practically anyone who cares enough to make the effort of complementing flavors. It should be emphasized in this age where erosion of quality is, to me at any rate, as much of a worry as the current concern over ecology.

THE HOW-TO OF WINES

When you go to buy wine, the most important selection you will eventually make is not the wine itself, but your choice of a wine merchant. Through his diversified knowledge he will be able to recommend wines to you. He will be more impressed with quality than with widely advertised labels or profit margins—and he can guarantee that the wines he sells have been stored properly.

If you are to appreciate wines fully, you will have to learn what to look for. The first step is to look at the wine in the glass. Compare the different shades of the reds, which range from brilliant ruby to purple hues. In older wines, you will usually detect brownish shades. It is sometimes helpful to look at the wine against a white background, such as a tablecloth or a white card. The white wines vary from pale yellow (even greenish) to rich, deep gold. The color is one of the characteristics of the wine. A Chablis, for example, is very pale yellow and cannot be mistaken, even at first sight, for a golden Sauterne.

The second step is to swirl the wine in the glass. This is done in order to allow the wine to "breathe." Contact with the air develops its wonderful bouquet, which is like a rose unfolding. It is for this reason that a small amount of wine is poured into a large glass—so that there is room for the perfume of the wine to expand and develop in the glass. Now, smell the wine. This is one of the greatest pleasures of wine tasting, because the bouquet gives a foretaste of the wine itself.

The third step is to sip the wine—but do not swallow it immediately; it is with our mouths that we taste! Let a small amount of wine roll to the back of the tongue, where the taste buds are located (the tip of the tongue is sensitive only to temperature). Try to take air in through the mouth; this will cause the esters of the wine to fill the mouth and nasal area. Now swallow the wine.

There are still two phases of wine tasting left to discuss. One is to concentrate on the aroma which lingers in your mouth. The last, and most enjoyable phase, is the conversation which ensues about the wines which have been tasted. Exchange of opinions helps a great deal in the fixing of impressions in one's own mind. For example, detect fragrances, such as a bouquet of peaches and apples in white wine, or the fruitiness of raspberries and taste of oak in the reds.

Gourmets, wine lovers and wine experts agree that there are certain marriages of food and wine which are pleasant to everyone. The marriages which meet with general approval are the following; when in doubt one should abide by them.

Hors d'Oeuvres:	light, dry white wine
Fish:	dry white wine and some sweet white wines
White Meat and Poultry:	dry white wine, light red wine
Red Meat:	full-bodied red wine
Cheese:	red wine best with pungent cheese, but all wines (except sweet ones) excellent with all cheeses
Sweet Dessert and Fruit:	sweet white wines and champagne

Red wines should be served at about 65°, which is considered room temperature. Red wines generally improve greatly if uncorked about an hour before the meal to let them "breathe." White and rosé wines are served slightly chilled, about 50°. Champagne and sparkling wines should be chilled slightly more.

I

A Culinary Tour of the United States

A Southern California Supper

Hot Pepper Cocktail Jelly
with Cheese and Crackers

Marinated Mushroom Salad with Avocado

Cioppino

SOAVE

Toasted Garlic Cheese Bread

Souffléed Cheesecake von Welanetz

*S*OUTHERN CALIFORNIA is an extraordinary place to live. We enjoy rich, golden sunshine nearly all year round. Almost everywhere we look there's a soft, shiny greenness scattered with colorful and exotic flowers. The land has such an inviting warmth that most houses here are designed with picture windows and sliding glass walls that lead to rambling terraces. Southern Californians are a cult of sun-worshipers who feel a basic need to move outside in the evening and watch the day put itself to bed.

Since we are favored with such an outrageously fine climate, patio entertaining for all occasions has become a way of life, from the casual barbecue to the ultra-formal wedding reception for two hundred guests.

But all of us from time to time, wherever we happen to live, have unexpected guests drop in. For such pleasant occasions we have designed this simple and elegant dinner which we enjoy serving on the terrace. But it is equally suited to warm weather or cold, inside or outdoors. It is an exceptionally versatile menu and one we often fix just for ourselves and our seven-year-old daughter, Lisa.

The Italian-American fishermen of Fisherman's Wharf in San Francisco have invented a magnificent fish stew called Cioppino. Diana's version of this savory, lusty dish is always delicious and easily prepared without notice. So, it is unnecessary to have hushed conversations away from surprise visitors, wondering if they are going to stay for dinner. We just start feeding them immediately!

While I am mixing the drinks, Diana is taking the base for the stew out of the refrigerator or freezer. If we have had any prior notice, I will have purchased some fresh seafood; otherwise frozen will do very nicely indeed. While the Cioppino warms slowly on the stove, Diana prepares an hors d'oeuvre tray featuring a crock of cream cheese, crackers and a jar of her special, sweet and fiery Hot Pepper Cocktail Jelly. One word describes the jelly: terrific! Guests have been known to take a bite, weep, slap their thighs and ravenously go back for more.

While our guests are enjoying this easiest of all hors d'oeuvres and visiting with Diana while she slices mushrooms for a salad, I mix a second round of drinks before dinner. Then, when we decide we are hungry enough, Diana adds the seafood to the stew and I uncork a chilled bottle of Soave. Toasted Garlic Cheese Bread goes under the broiler at the last minute.

A very special dessert, which we almost always have in the house, provides a perfect conclusion to the evening. It is a cheesecake, but no ordinary cheesecake. Light and airy, it is really more like a soufflé. A taste of this delicate confection is a wonderful way of saying to friends, "Thank you for dropping by . . ."

T I M E T A B L E : Hot Pepper Cocktail Jelly makes such a great hostess gift that we always have it on hand. It will keep indefinitely on the pantry shelf if vacuum-sealed in canning jars. We seldom bother to do that, though, because it will keep a month or more in the refrigerator. So make it months, weeks, days or only hours before serving.

Prepare the dressing for the Marinated Mushroom Salad any time you think of it to have on hand as a basic salad dressing. It will keep indefinitely in the refrigerator.

The tomato-wine sauce base for the Cioppino is easy to make. Prepare a large quantity to have in the freezer. Then making the dish is simply a matter of purchasing fresh fish on serving day and thawing the base before cooking. So here again, choose your own time.

The cheesecake may be made up to 5 days in advance. Store as directed.

The Toasted Garlic Cheese Bread may be made in the morning and reheated, wrapped in foil, in the oven.

Slice the avocados for the salad and add the seafood to the Cioppino just before serving.

HOT PEPPER COCKTAIL JELLY

(ABOUT 6 ½ CUPS)

This is our favorite hostess gift, and an unusual hors d'oeuvre when served with Cheddar cheese spread or cream cheese and crackers. It is essential to make this jelly in the quantity specified here. Use the extra for other occasions or for gifts.

1 cup seeded and chopped green bell peppers
¼ to ⅓ cup canned jalapeño peppers, rinsed and seeded
1 ½ cups apple cider vinegar

6 cups sugar
1 bottle Certo (fruit pectin)
4 or 5 drops green food coloring
Cheese spread, or cream cheese and crackers

Place both kinds of peppers in the container of an electric blender with 1 cup of the vinegar and blend until smooth. Pour into a 4- or 5-quart heavy-bottomed saucepan. Rinse the blender container with the remaining vinegar and add that to the peppers. Stir in the sugar. Over medium-high heat bring the mixture to a rolling boil that you cannot stir down. Remove the pan from the heat and allow it to stand for 5 minutes. Skim the foam off the top and discard. Stir in the Certo and the green food coloring. Pour the jelly immediately into containers, let cool to room temperature, then cover with plastic wrap and refrigerate. Serve with cheese and crackers.

To Make Ahead: If you are making the jelly for your own use, it is easiest to pour it into serving dishes, cover it with plastic wrap and refrigerate. It will keep for several months in the refrigerator, but it will probably disappear long before that! If sealed in canning jars according to manufacturer's directions, it will keep for months without refrigeration.

MARINATED MUSHROOM SALAD WITH AVOCADO

(4 SERVINGS)

MARINADE:

¼ cup olive oil
¼ cup vegetable oil
2 tablespoons red wine vinegar

1 tablespoon fresh lemon juice
1 clove garlic, crushed but left whole

2 heaping teaspoons Dijon mustard
Several dashes Worcestershire
   sauce
Pinch of salt

Pinch of sugar
Several grindings of black pepper
2 tablespoons finely chopped
   parsley

SALAD:

1 pound large, fresh mushrooms
4 leaves Bibb lettuce
1 avocado, peeled and cut into 8
   wedges

Juice of ½ lemon
2 tomatoes, each cut into 8 wedges
2 tablespoons chopped parsley
Several grindings of black pepper

To prepare the marinade, combine all ingredients in a medium-size stainless or ceramic mixing bowl and blend thoroughly. Leave the garlic whole but be sure to remove it before serving the salad.

Wash the mushrooms under cold running water, holding them stems down. Do this quickly so that the mushrooms will not have time to absorb any water. Rub your fingers over the surface to remove any grit. Dry immediately, and slice the mushrooms ¼ inch thick—they must not be too thin or they will soften and become limp. Mix them gently into the marinade to coat them completely. Refrigerate no less than 1 hour and no longer than 3 hours; 2 hours is perfect. Stir occasionally.

To serve, place a leaf of lettuce on each of four salad plates. Top each with 2 wedges of avocado sprinkled with the fresh lemon juice to prevent discoloration. Lift the mushrooms from the marinade with a slotted spoon and place them in the center of each plate. Garnish each salad with 4 tomato wedges. Sprinkle with chopped parsley and freshly ground black pepper.

To Make Ahead: The mushrooms must marinate for 1 to 3 hours. The dressing can be made ahead of time and stored in the refrigerator. Any leftover marinade can be used again for the same purpose or for salad dressing. The avocados darken quickly, so slice them as close as possible to serving time.

CIOPPINO

(4 SERVINGS)

Our own version of a San Francisco seafood stew.

TOMATO-WINE SAUCE:

⅛ cup olive oil
1 large clove garlic, pressed
3 shallots, minced
1 one-pound can whole tomatoes
2 cups canned tomato-vegetable
   juice (V8)
2 cups dry white wine
1 teaspoon dried oregano

1 teaspoon dried Italian herb
   seasoning
Cayenne, to taste
1 teaspoon Worcestershire sauce
¼ fresh lemon with peel
2 bay leaves
Salt to taste

STEW:

12 fresh clams (optional)
About 1 cup fresh or frozen
   scallops
8 large raw shrimp, unshelled
About ¾ pound fresh fish (sea
   bass, red snapper, halibut, etc.),
   cut into 4 pieces

1 ten-ounce can whole baby clams
   and their liquid
½ cup parsley, chopped fine
4 slices toasted cheese bread or
   Garlic Cheese Bread (page 17)

To make the sauce, heat the olive oil in a heavy-bottomed saucepan. Briefly sauté the garlic and minced shallots, taking care not to burn the shallots. Add the rest of the sauce ingredients and bring to a boil. Lower the heat and simmer, uncovered, for 45 minutes, stirring often. (If you are doubling or tripling the recipe, simmer 1 to 1½ hours.) Discard the lemon and bay leaves. If preparing the sauce in advance, refrigerate or freeze until needed.

To finish the stew, scrub the clams well, then soak them in cold water for at least an hour so they will spit out all their sand. Place the scallops in a colander in a bowl of cold water for at least 30 minutes so that they, too, will give up their sand. Rinse the shrimp and other fish. Fifteen minutes before serving, pour the sauce into a stew pot and bring to a simmer. Add the fresh clams, the juice from the canned clams, the chopped parsley, shrimp and fish pieces. Cover and simmer for 10 minutes. Add the scallops. Simmer, covered, 5 minutes longer until the pieces of fish are done and all the fresh clams are open—discard any clams that do not open after 10 minutes. Stir in the canned whole baby clams.

Serve the stew right from the stew pot or in a tureen. Ladle it over slices of Toasted Garlic Cheese Bread in large individual soup bowls. Provide plenty of napkins!

To Make Ahead: The sauce should be made ahead of time because it freezes beautifully and the flavor is much improved when reheated. All the seafood should be purchased fresh the day of serving.

TOASTED GARLIC CHEESE BREAD

(4 SERVINGS)

We have tried many different methods of making garlic toast, but think this one is easiest and best.

1 small loaf French or Italian bread
¼ pound (1 stick) soft butter or margarine
⅛ teaspoon garlic powder (or more for garlic enthusiasts)

2 tablespoons fresh or dried chopped parsley
⅓ cup grated Parmesan cheese
A sprinkling of paprika (optional)

Split the bread lengthwise. Beat the butter or margarine until fluffy and mix in the garlic powder. Spread the halves generously with this mixture. Sprinkle generously with the chopped parsley, followed by the Parmesan. Top with a very light sprinkling of paprika for color, if desired.

Arrange the loaves, cut side up, on a baking sheet or a piece of heavy foil. Toast the bread under a preheated broiler, about 6 inches from the heat, for a minute or two until well-browned. Cut diagonally or crosswise into 1½-inch slices and serve immediately. Allow at least 2 slices per serving.

To Make Ahead: After broiling the bread let it cool, then put the loaves together again and wrap tightly in foil. Fifteen minutes before serving, place the loaves, still wrapped, in a 375° oven and heat thoroughly.

SOUFFLÉED CHEESECAKE VON WELANETZ
(8 TO 12 SERVINGS)

This may very well be the best recipe in the book. You will need a 9- or 10-inch spring-form pan—if you don't already own one it is well worth purchasing.

1 ½ pounds cream cheese	*1 teaspoon lemon juice*
6 eggs, separated	*1 teaspoon vanilla extract*
1 cup sugar	*1 ½ teaspoons grated lemon rind*
1 tablespoon all-purpose flour	*1 ½ teaspoons grated orange rind*
1 cup sour cream	*¼ teaspoon cream of tartar*

Preheat the oven to 325°.

Using an electric mixer, beat the cream cheese with the egg yolks until the mixture is completely smooth. Beat in the sugar, flour, sour cream, lemon juice, vanilla extract, lemon and orange rinds. Place the egg whites in a clean, grease-free mixing bowl. If they are not at room temperature, set the bowl in warm water and stir to take the chill off—cold egg whites will not whip up properly. Add the cream of tartar to the whites and beat them, using an electric mixer or large wire whisk, until they do not slip when you tilt the bowl. Continue beating cautiously until they hold short, distinct peaks. Fold about one-third of the whites into the cheese mixture thoroughly, to lighten it, then carefully fold in the rest.

Pour the mixture into an ungreased 9- or 10-inch spring-form pan. Bake at 325° for 1 hour and 10 minutes, or until the center no longer appears soft. (During the cooking the cheesecake will puff up like a soufflé but will shrink and crack a bit as it cools.)

Let the cake cool at room temperature for at least 2 hours before removing it from the pan. If you keep the cheesecake at room temperature, it will have a light and airy texture. If you like a creamier cheesecake, simply refrigerate it. It is especially delicious served with any kind of fresh or thawed frozen berries.

To Make Ahead: This cheesecake will keep for at least 2 days if stored, tightly covered, at room temperature. If may be stored in the refrigerator for up to 5 days. Do not freeze.

A San Francisco
Fondue Dinner for Four

Scampi Sharif

SOAVE

Fondue Bourguignonne

RED BURGUNDY or PINOT NOIR

Béarnaise Sauce

Easy Bordelaise Sauce

Basic Curry Sauce†

Canlis' Special Salad

Poires au Vin

† Daggers denote recipes that appear in a different chapter; please check index.

*T*HIS IS A MENU in the San Francisco style—friendly and informal. It does, however, call for some special equipment (see note below). For the main course, your guests gather congenially around the fondue pot and do their own cooking. It's fun for them and easy for you because you can prepare the sauces before your guests arrive. We serve an assortment of sauces—some our own, and some bottled—in tiny dishes at each place setting. The fondue pot will, of course, be your centerpiece. Since the dinner is informal, we sometimes serve it on the terrace. There is a reason for this—the smoke from the hot oil used in cooking the Fondue Bourguignonne tends to settle on the light fixture over the dining table. If serving inside, you would be wise to do so the day *before* cleaning your chandelier.

Our appetizer, Scampi Sharif, is very special and lends itself to being served dramatically in a chafing dish with cocktails. Although there are no true scampi to be found outside the waters of Venice, our own jumbo shrimp or even larger prawns provide an excellent substitute for the traditional Italian crustacean.

Scampi Sharif acquired its name the first time we served it. Carole Wells Doheny and her escort were stopping by our house for cocktails before a night on the town. We were delighted when Carole's escort turned out to be Omar Sharif—delighted not only because he is as handsome, charming, witty and entertaining as one would expect, but also because he enjoys fine food and is a recognized gourmet. We named our scampi after him, and he enthusiastically returned the compliment by adding his mother's favorite recipe for eggplant to Diana's scrapbook.

The salad is our version of one we sampled at Canlis' Restaurant in San Francisco. Their salad is world-renowned and deservedly so. It is a splendid variation of a Caesar Salad and is inviting to even the most devout garlic-hater. Constant requests inspired this famous restaurant to print the recipe, much to the good fortune of those of us who are not San Francisco–dwellers. As usual, we have added a few flourishes of our own. For the purposes of this menu, the salad is best served with the entrée and complimented by a California red wine—we prefer a Burgundy or Pinot Noir.

San Francisco lies in the heart of California's beautiful wine country; hence the fresh pears poached in red California Burgundy are an appropriate and enjoyable finale to the meal.

It is possible to be informal and gracious at the same time—and here's the menu that proves it.

Note: We see fondue sets being sold almost everywhere these days. A good set will include two pots, one for cheese and one for meat, both of which fit onto one burning stand. The pot for Fondue Bourguignonne should be of thin metal, with the somewhat closed-at-the-top shape of a brandy snifter. This will provide the high heat necessary for cooking a meat fondue, and it will prevent the oil from spattering.

TIMETABLE: The pears may be poached in wine 3 to 4 days ahead of time. They'll improve in flavor as they wait in the refrigerator. Turn them in their syrup several times—whenever you think of it.

All the sauces for the Fondue Bourguignonne (except the béarnaise) and the salad dressing may be made the day before serving. Press plastic wrap into the surface of the sauces to keep a skin from forming, and refrigerate until time to reheat.

On the morning of your party, cut the meat into bite-sized chunks and refrigerate it in a plastic bag until ready to arrange it in the serving bowls. Assemble and prepare all the salad ingredients as specified in the recipe so that all you will have to do to finish the salad is toss it with the dressing at the table. Arrange the shrimp in the pan in which they will be cooked and refrigerate. Reduce the wine and set out the other sauce ingredients for the Scampi. The shrimp should be cooked and the sauce finished just before serving.

SCAMPI SHARIF

(4 FIRST-COURSE SERVINGS)

12 raw jumbo shrimp, unshelled
3 cups dry white wine
1 tablespoon minced shallots
¼ teaspoon salt
6 tablespoons butter or margarine
½ cup heavy cream

1 tablespoon cornstarch, dissolved
*   in 2 tablespoons cold water*
1 tablespoon fresh lemon juice
Salt to taste
Dash of cayenne
Lemon wedges and parsley sprigs
*   to garnish*

Wash the shrimp and remove the shells. Place the shells in a saucepan with the white wine, minced shallots and the salt. Place the saucepan over high heat and boil the mixture until it is reduced to ¾ cup (one-quarter of the original volume). Meanwhile, devein the shrimp and cut them lengthwise through the center (as illustrated), taking care not to cut through the heads or tails. This method of cutting will make the shrimp stand up with both ends curled upward (see illustration). When the wine has reduced, remove from fire, strain out the shells and the shallots and cover the wine to prevent further evaporation.

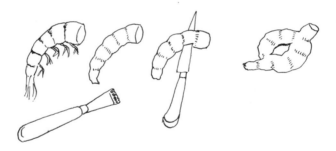

Lightly butter a heavy skillet (or a chafing dish, if you wish to prepare this at the dinner table). In it arrange the butterflied shrimp, with heads and tails pointing upward. Cover and refrigerate until ready to cook.

To complete the scampi, pour the reduced wine over the shrimp and bring to a simmer over medium heat. Cover, reduce the heat to low, and cook for 2 or 3 minutes until the shrimp are just tender and have turned pink. Remove the shrimp from the cooking liquid with a slotted spoon and place them on paper towels to drain. Cover them to keep warm while you prepare the sauce.

Add the butter or margarine and the cream to the cooking liquid in the pan and bring to a boil. Reduce the heat under the pan. Stir together the cornstarch and the cold water until smooth and pour into the slowly simmering sauce, whisking constantly until the mixture has thickened. Turn the heat as low as possible, then blend in the lemon juice. Season to taste with salt and cayenne pepper. If the sauce is not thick enough, continue to simmer it over very low heat until it is the desired consistency—a minute or two should do it. Turn off the heat. Return the shrimp to the pan and spoon the sauce over them. Serve 3 to each guest, spooning extra sauce over the shrimp on the plates. Garnish each serving with a lemon wedge and a sprig of parsley.

To Make Ahead: Reduce the wine in the morning and set aside, covered, until needed. Arrange the shrimp in the skillet and refrigerate. Cook the shrimp and finish the sauce just before serving.

FONDUE BOURGUIGNONNE

(4 SERVINGS)

2 pounds beef filet or sirloin
3 to 4 cups vegetable oil
Béarnaise Sauce (page 24)
Easy Bordelaise Sauce (page 25)

Basic Curry Sauce (page 41)
Other sauces for dipping, such as Escoffier, barbecue sauce, horseradish sauce, etc.

Trim the meat of all fat and cut it into 1-inch cubes.

To serve, fill your fondue pot half full of vegetable oil (or a combination of oil and clarified butter). Heat it to about 375° on top of the range, or until it sizzles when you insert a piece of meat. Then, carefully transfer the pot of oil to the burner of your fondue set on the dining table. Serve each guest a bowl containing 8 ounces of cubed raw beef.

Each guest may have his own assortment of sauces, or the sauces may be passed at the table. Have each guest spear a meat cube with a fondue fork and place it in the hot oil, letting it cook to the desired doneness. As soon as one cube is removed, it can be replaced with another.

To Make Ahead: The meat can be cut into cubes in the morning and refrigerated, covered, in the serving bowls. Make all the sauces except the béarnaise ahead of time; refrigerate them until needed, at which time they will reheat beautifully. Béarnaise sauce must be made within 2 hours of serving time.

BÉARNAISE SAUCE
(4 GENEROUS SERVINGS, ABOUT 1 ½ CUPS)

½ pound butter or margarine
1 ½ teaspoons dried tarragon, or 1
   tablespoon fresh tarragon leaves
1 teaspoon dried chervil (if not
   available, use more tarragon)
1 tablespoon minced shallots
4 whole black peppercorns

¼ cup tarragon-flavored white
   vinegar
¼ cup dry white wine
3 egg yolks
1 tablespoon water
Salt
Pinch of cayenne

Divide the butter or margarine into three equal parts and allow it to come to room temperature. Combine the tarragon, chervil, shallots, peppercorns, vinegar and wine in the top of a double boiler (preferably glass) and reduce the liquid over direct heat (not over water) until almost completely evaporated. Remove the peppercorns and allow the mixture to cool slightly. Beat in the yolks and water with a small whisk or a slotted spoon until the mixture is frothy. Add the first third of butter or margarine.

Place the pan over hot, not boiling, water. If your double boiler is glass, you should be able to see slowly rising bubbles in the water below. Stir the sauce constantly until it has thickened to the consistency you want it to be when finished. Be sure the water below doesn't start bubbling too fast. Add the second portion of butter and continue stirring over hot water until the butter is completely incorporated. Stir in the third portion in the same manner. Turn off the heat; season with salt and cayenne and, if you like, a little more tarragon.

Cover the top of the pan of sauce with plastic wrap and leave off the heat, over the hot water, until ready to serve.

To Make Ahead: The sauce will keep warm for 2 hours over the hot water. It is best not to reheat it, as the risk of curdling is very great.

Note: If by chance you should curdle the sauce from too much heat at any point, simply beat it gradually with a whisk into another egg yolk—this will bring it right back to its proper consistency. Do not return the sauce to the pan in which it curdled because the heat from the pan will cause the sauce to curdle again.

EASY BORDELAISE SAUCE

(4 SERVINGS, OR 1 CUP)

2 tablespoons butter or margarine	*2½ teaspoons cornstarch*
2 tablespoons minced shallots	*½ cup canned beef broth or bouil-*
1 bay leaf	*lon, undiluted*
½ cup red Burgundy wine	*2 teaspoons chopped parsley*

Melt 1 tablespoon of the butter or margarine in a small skillet. Add the minced shallots and sauté until soft but not browned. Add the bay leaf and Burgundy and simmer over medium heat until the wine is reduced to about one-third its original volume.

Stir the cornstarch into the beef broth and add it to the reduced wine mixture. Continue to cook, stirring, until the sauce boils and thickens. Add the remaining butter and the chopped parsley. Heat until the butter is melted.

To Make Ahead: The sauce may be completed ahead of time and carefully reheated. Press plastic wrap into the surface to prevent a skin from forming, and store it at room temperature. Reheat slowly while stirring. *Add the last tablespoon of butter and the chopped parsley just before serving.*

OUR VERSION OF CANLIS' SPECIAL SALAD

(4 TO 6 SERVINGS)

SALAD:

Olive oil	*1 peeled tomato**
Salt	*1 small head romaine*
1 large clove garlic	*½ cup fresh bean sprouts*
Salt and pepper	*(optional)*

* To peel a tomato, spear it with a fork and plunge it into boiling water for 15 to 30 seconds. The skin will slip off easily, even after refrigeration.

DRESSING:

2 tablespoons olive oil
2 to 2½ tablespoons fresh lemon
   juice
¼ teaspoon cracked pepper

½ teaspoon chopped fresh mint
⅛ teaspoon dried oregano
1 coddled egg*

CONDIMENTS:

2 scallions, sliced thin
½ cup freshly grated Romano or
   Parmesan cheese

½ pound bacon, chopped fine
   and cooked crisp
1 cup croutons**

Prepare a large, preferably wooden, salad bowl by pouring in a little olive oil, sprinkling with salt, and rubbing firmly with a large clove of garlic—the oil will act as a lubricant and the salt as an abrasive. Remove the garlic.

In the bottom of the bowl, first place the tomato, cut into eighths, then the romaine, sliced into 1-inch strips. (You may add any other salad vegetables you choose, but remember to place the heavy vegetables in first with the romaine on top.) Refrigerate until needed.

Combine all the dressing ingredients and set aside (but do not refrigerate) until needed—salad dressing has more flavor if it is served at room temperature.

To serve, place the salad condiments on top of the romaine, pour the dressing over the top, and toss well.

To Make Ahead: The salad vegetables, dressing and condiments may be prepared in the morning and stored separately. Dress and toss the salad just before serving.

* To coddle an egg, drop it into boiling water for 30 seconds. Store in the refrigerator until needed.
** To make croutons, cut stale white, wheat, or French bread into ½-inch cubes. Heat about ⅓ cup olive oil in a small skillet over medium heat until it begins to smoke. Toss 10 or 12 cubes at a time into the hot oil, moving them about constantly until evenly browned. Remove with a slotted spoon and drain on paper towels. Store them in an airtight container until needed.

POIRES AU VIN

(4 SERVINGS)

This is a typical French dessert, often served in California's wine country. Serve it cold in the summertime and warm during the winter.

4 medium pears, ripe but firm
2 cups red Burgundy wine
2 tablespoons fresh lemon juice

1 cup sugar
1 small stick cinnamon, or ½ teaspoon ground cinnamon

Peel the pears with a vegetable peeler, leaving the stems intact. Trim a bit off the bottoms so the pears will stand up.

In a large saucepan combine the Burgundy, lemon juice, sugar and cinnamon. Bring to a boil over medium heat, stirring until the sugar is dissolved. Add the pears, partially cover the pan, and reduce the heat. Simmer slowly for about 15 minutes, turning the pears occasionally, until they are barely tender when tested with a knife point. Cool them in the syrup until lukewarm, or, if serving them cold, refrigerate them in the syrup until thoroughly chilled.

To serve, stand each pear up on a dessert plate, and spoon some of the sauce over it. Each guest will require a knife, fork and spoon.

To Make Ahead: The pears will keep 5 days or longer in the refrigerator, during which time they continue to improve in flavor. Turn them over in their syrup whenever you think of it.

An Elegant Dinner Party
in the New Orleans Manner

Oysters Rockefeller

WHITE WINE FROM THE LOIRE VALLEY

Coq au Vin

FINE RED BURGUNDY

French-Style Baked Peas

Croissants

French Quarter Ice Cream Torte

with Fudge Sauce

Café Brûlot

*H*ERE IS THE perfect menu for an intimate group of six or eight very special people. This is an elegant occasion in itself, calling for your finest serving pieces, candlelight, and a floral centerpiece: camellias, in the Southern tradition, might grace your table if available. Some of these recipes are rather time-consuming to prepare, but here is the true beauty of this New Orleans menu—everything can be made ahead of time! Your evening will be all the more enjoyable because you will be able to relax on the day of the party.

Oysters Rockefeller, the spectacular first course, was invented by Jules Alciatore of Antoine's restaurant in 1899; the sauce was named after America's wealthiest citizen because it was so "rich." Ours is somewhat different from the original, which, according to our sources, did not contain the now-traditional spinach. The recipe included here is our version of one taught by chef Gregoire le Balch, our great friend and teacher for many years. Gregoire, once the head chef of the Escoffier Room at the Beverly Hilton in Beverly Hills, now owns a restaurant and cooking school in the San Fernando Valley section of Los Angeles. We think this recipe is divine. It is superbly complimented by a chilled white wine from the Loire valley.

Coq au Vin is an elegant ragout. The flavor of its rich brown sauce, a combination of beef broth, cognac, red Burgundy, garlic and thyme, is improved when the dish is made ahead and reheated. To enhance it even further, we sprinkle crisp pieces of salt pork over the top of the

Coq au Vin just before serving. Naturally, the wine you serve should also be a fine red Burgundy. It is unnecessary to serve anything more than a simple vegetable such as French-style Baked Peas on the plate with the entrée.

Flaky croissants (crescent rolls), available frozen at all markets, are light, delicious, and easy—a welcome addition to the meal.

Paul's French Quarter Ice Cream Torte is as simple to make as it is delightful to eat. It will wait for a month in the freezer, so it is a lovely treat to have on hand for emergencies. Simply cut off slices whenever needed and return the rest to the freezer.

And Cafe Brûlot is a flaming success, flavored with orange rind and spices. It is flamed and ladled into demitasse cups at the table. Sensational!

With this menu, you are sure to enjoy an evening of elegance. All the trouble is out of the way before the day of the party, and you have only the pleasure of serving your beautiful meal.

TIMETABLE: The ice cream torte may be made weeks ahead and stored in the freezer. Its sauce may also be refrigerated or frozen indefinitely.

Two days ahead (or longer if you are going to freeze it), make the Coq au Vin, undercooking it by about 10 minutes. Refrigerate or freeze it until needed. Like most ragouts, this dish truly improves in flavor with reheating. At the same time, assemble the peas in their baking dish with all other ingredients *except the lettuce*. Set the dish in the freezer until you are ready to bake, then add the lettuce, and slide it directly into the oven. No last-minute fuss! Also, this is the day to call your favorite fish market to order the oysters for the next morning. Have them open the oysters and put them on the half shell for you.

The day before the party, completely assemble the Oysters Rockefeller, keeping the sauce and grated cheese separately. Press some plastic wrap into the surface of the sauce to prevent a skin from forming, and refrigerate it.

Set the table the night before—you will congratulate yourself for this the next morning. Use your best china, silver, wine glasses, attractively-folded napkins and, if you wish, place cards for a formal evening.

To mix and serve the Café Brûlot, you will need a chafing dish, brûlot bowl or fondue pot, and a ladle, as well as demitasse cups.

Everything simply needs heating and a few finishing touches on the day of the party. Arrange the floral centerpiece a few hours before your guests arrive. Your evening will be a triumph!

OYSTERS ROCKEFELLER

(8 SERVINGS—*they are
"rich as Rockefeller," so
allow only 3 per serving*)

*24 oysters, freshly opened, on the
"deep" half shell (or save the
shells and use frozen oysters)
¾ cup dry white wine
¾ cup bottled clam juice
2 cups (1 pint) heavy cream
2 to 3 tablespoons* roux *to thicken**
*1½ to 2 teaspoons fresh lemon
juice
Cayenne and salt, to taste*

*2 ten-ounce packages frozen
chopped spinach
3 tablespoons butter or margarine
Salt and pepper to taste
2 tablespoons Pernod (an anise-
flavored liqueur)
2 tablespoons grated Parmesan
cheese
Sprigs of parsley, to garnish*

To serve Oysters Rockefeller, you will need some sort of serving plates
—oyster plates if you have them (very unlikely) or pie tins filled with
rock salt (ice-cream salt).

Remove the oysters from the shells. Scrub the shells well and lay
them on a bed of salt, either on a cookie sheet or in the individual pie
tins used for serving. This will hold the shells steady during the cooking
process.

Place the oysters in a small saucepan with the white wine and clam
juice. Bring just to a boil, and remove the pan immediately from the
heat. Remove the oysters from the liquid with a slotted spoon and set
them aside to cool. Strain the liquid through a clean kitchen towel to
remove any sand. Rinse the skillet and return the liquid to it. Bring to a
boil and let simmer until reduced to ⅜ cup of liquid (about one-quarter
its original volume). Stir in 1½ cups of the cream (save the rest for
later use), and bring to a boil. Add the *roux*, a little at a time, while
stirring with a wire whisk. Be sure the sauce returns to a boil after each
addition. Keep adding *roux* and beating until the sauce is smooth and
just thick enough to coat the top of an oyster without running off.
When the sauce seems to be the right consistency, season it to taste
with lemon juice, cayenne and salt. It should be highly seasoned, as

* *Roux* is a mixture of butter and flour cooked together to remove any raw
floury taste. It is used for thickening sauces. Combine in a heavy saucepan ½ cup
butter and 1 cup all-purpose flour. Cook the mixture over very low heat, stirring
often, for 15 minutes. Be careful not to scorch the flour or it will not perform
properly. Make it ahead of time and store it in the freezer so it is ready whenever
you want it. It is not necessary to thaw it before adding it to boiling liquid as
directed.

31

the addition of more cream later will dull the flavor somewhat. If you are making this sauce early in the day, press some plastic wrap into the surface to prevent a skin from forming, and refrigerate until ready to use.

Cook the spinach according to package directions and drain it very well. Chop it coarsely. Melt the butter or margarine in a skillet and sauté the spinach for a minute or so. Season it to taste with salt and pepper and stir in the Pernod. Let the spinach cool a bit, then place a spoonful of the mixture in the bottom of each prepared oyster shell and top with an oyster. If making ahead of time, simply cover the whole thing with foil and refrigerate.

About 20 minutes before serving, place the foil-covered oysters into a preheated 350° oven for 15 minutes, or until they are heated through. Remove from the oven and turn your broiler unit to high. Warm the sauce in a saucepan. Whip the remaining ½ cup cream only until it holds a shape. Fold this into the warm sauce. This French process, which creates a puffy and delicately browned sauce, is called *glaçage*. With a spoon, put a coating of this sauce over the top of each oyster. Sprinkle lightly with grated Parmesan cheese, and place under the broiler for 5 or 10 seconds, until the sauce is lightly browned and bubbly. Garnish each serving with a sprig of parsley.

To Make Ahead: The oysters may be poached and placed on their bed of spinach in their shells the day before serving. The sauce, except for the *glaçage*, may also be made and then stored in the refrigerator. Reheat and finish the oysters and the sauce as directed in the recipe.

COQ AU VIN

(8 SERVINGS)

½ pound salt pork, cut into
   ¼-inch cubes
24 small white onions, peeled and
   left whole
4 whole chicken breasts and 5
   whole chicken legs and thighs,
   cut apart, or 2 whole fryers, cut
   up
Salt and pepper

Vegetable oil
1 bottle fine red Burgundy
½ cup cognac or brandy
6 tablespoons flour
1 ten-ounce can condensed beef
   broth or bouillon
4 sprigs parsley and 4 celery tops,
   tied together with string
2 bay leaves

1 teaspoon dried thyme

2 teaspoons salt

¼ pound (1 stick) butter or margarine

¼ cup minced shallots, or the white part of scallions if shallots are unavailable

2 cloves garlic, pressed

1 pound medium mushrooms, washed quickly, dried, and cut into quarters through the stems

Finely chopped parsley to garnish

Use a large, attractive earthenware or ovenproof casserole in which the chicken will be both cooked and served.

Place the diced salt pork in a saucepan and cover it generously with water. Bring to a boil and simmer for 5 minutes—in other words, "blanch" it. Rinse the pieces in a strainer under cold running water and dry well with paper towels. In a heavy skillet (an iron one is perfect) cook the pieces of salt pork over medium-high heat, stirring often, until they have rendered their fat and are lightly browned. Remove the pieces with a slotted spoon and drain on paper towels. Set aside at room temperature until needed.

Brown the onions, as evenly as possible, in the hot pork fat. Remove them to a small baking dish, pour a little of the fat over them, and bake at 350° for about 15 minutes, or until they are tender when pierced with a sharp knife. Set aside.

Meanwhile, brown your chicken, as follows, in the remaining fat. Dry the chicken pieces well with paper towels and sprinkle with salt and pepper. Add vegetable oil to the skillet to make a depth of ⅛″. Heat the fat until it begins to smoke. Add the chicken and brown on all sides.

While the chicken is browning, pour the Burgundy into a saucepan, boil it over high heat until it has reduced to 2 cups (approximately one-half its original volume), and set it aside.

When all the chicken has been browned, remove as much of the fat from the pan as you easily can, and return the chicken to the pan. Heat the cognac or brandy in a ladle over a flame, ignite it with a match, and pour it over the chicken; shake the pan until the flame dies. Remove the chicken to the casserole in which the Coq au Vin will be served. Off the heat, stir the flour into the juices remaining in the skillet and add the reduced wine and the beef broth. Bring to a boil over medium heat, stirring with a whisk or a slotted spoon until thickened. Let the sauce cook for a minute, then pour it through a strainer over the chicken in the casserole. Add the parsley and celery tops (tied together), bay leaves, thyme and salt.

Rinse the same skillet you were using and in it melt the butter or margarine. Stir in the shallots and the garlic and cook while stirring for

33

30 seconds. Add the quartered mushrooms. Cook for 2 minutes longer and add this mixture to the casserole with the chicken. Stir the contents of the casserole gently.

Preheat the oven to 350°. Bring the contents of the casserole to a boil on top of the stove, then place the casserole in the oven. Bake at 350° for 30 minutes, or until the chicken is tender (if making ahead of time, bake only 20 minutes). Add the onions about 5 minutes before the chicken has finished cooking to heat them through.

Before serving, remove the celery and parsley and sprinkle the crisp pieces of salt pork decoratively over the top, along with some chopped parsley.

To Make Ahead: This dish truly improves in flavor (and is much easier for you) if made a day ahead and reheated. Keep the onions separate until reheating. Have the casserole at room temperature, then place it in a preheated 350° oven for about 20 minutes, or until hot through.

FRENCH-STYLE BAKED PEAS

(8 SERVINGS)

3 ten-ounce packages frozen peas
1 shallot, or the white part of 2
   scallions, finely chopped
1 teaspoon salt
4 teaspoons sugar

4 tablespoons (½ stick) butter or
   margarine in a chunk
1 leaf iceberg lettuce, cut into ¼-
   inch strips

Place the frozen peas in a 2- to 3-quart casserole with a tight-fitting lid. Top with all the other ingredients. Bake covered at 350° for 1 hour. Stir and serve right in the casserole.

To Make Ahead: Assemble all the ingredients except the lettuce. Store in the freezer until ready to bake. Top with lettuce 1 hour before serving and bake as directed.

FRENCH QUARTER ICE CREAM TORTE
WITH FUDGE SAUCE

(AT LEAST 8 SERVINGS)

*35 to 40 chocolate wafers, crushed
with a rolling pin, or 1½ cups
crushed macaroons*
1 quart dark chocolate ice cream

*1 quart mocha ice cream, or any
other flavor of your choice*
*½ pound English toffee candy
(Almond Roca), chopped
coarsely with a knife*

FUDGE SAUCE:

*8 ounces semisweet chocolate
(either squares or bits)*
1 cup (½ pint) heavy cream

½ teaspoon dry instant coffee
*1 tablespoon dark rum, cognac or
brandy*

You will need an 8- or 9-inch spring-form pan to make this dessert. Set out both quarts of ice cream to let them soften slightly while you make the sauce.

Melt the chocolate with the cream and the coffee in a small, heavy saucepan over low heat, stirring until smooth. Remove from the heat and stir in the rum, cognac or brandy. Set aside until needed. This sauce may be served warm or at room temperature.

Oil the spring-form pan and spread half the crushed cookies on the bottom. When the ice cream is soft enough to be workable, spread the chocolate ice cream carefully on top of the crushed cookies. Drizzle some of the chocolate sauce over the ice cream. Spread the rest of the cookie crumbs over this. Then spread the mocha (or other flavor) ice cream over all, drizzle more chocolate sauce on top (reserve some sauce to serve with the torte), then distribute the crushed English toffee evenly over the surface. Place the torte in the freezer for at least 3 hours until hardened.

Remove the spring-form sides of the pan about 5 minutes before serving and let the torte rest at room temperature so it will be easier to slice. Gently reheat the chocolate sauce if desired.

To Make Ahead: This torte will keep for a month in the freezer if well wrapped. Cut off the necessary number of slices whenever you need a quick dessert. The sauce will keep in the refrigerator for weeks.

CAFÉ BRÛLOT
Demitasse

(8 servings)

2 sticks cinnamon
6 whole cloves
A very long strip of orange peel
A long strip of lemon peel
¼ cup Curaçao, or other orange-
  flavored liqueur

6 sugar cubes
½ cup cognac or brandy
2 cups hot, strong black coffee
  (regular or decaffeinated)

Place all the ingredients except the sugar, cognac and coffee in a chafing dish, brûlot bowl, or fondue pot. Soften the sugar cubes with a few drops of cognac and mash them into the orange and lemon peels. Set aside.

Just before serving, warm the cognac and ignite it. For an especially dramatic effect, hold the orange peel with a fork over the pan and pour the flaming liquid down the peel. Let it blaze for a few seconds, then pour in the hot coffee in a slow stream. When the flame dies, ladle immediately into demitasse cups.

To Make Ahead: Assemble the ingredients as directed in the serving dish, in the morning. Add the flaming cognac and coffee just before serving.

A Tropical Feast from Hawaii

Peach Smash

Salted Macadamia Nuts

Island Curry in Pineapple Shells

POUILLY-FUMÉ

Oven Rice

Exotic Salad

Perfect Popovers

Chocolate Angel Food Cake

with

Cocoa-Rum Icing

ERE IS A MENU for a special luncheon or a warm-weather dinner. Shiny leaves and fresh flowers make an easy centerpiece and lend a Polynesian atmosphere to your party.

The festivities will be off to a roaring start if you serve each guest a luscious Peach Smash, our favorite summertime party drink. The recipe was given to us by June Van Dyke, the beautiful and talented fashion authority. A word of caution is called for—the drinks are deceptively potent, so two per guest will be more than ample. Serve them with salted macadamia nuts, available now at most markets in cans or jars, to nibble on.

Island Curry can be served in hollowed pineapple halves. (We like to weave fresh daisies into the fronds of the pineapples just before serving—it's a sensational way to create a garden atmosphere.) It should be served with a full-bodied white wine, such as a chilled Pouilly-Fumé, which can stand up to very spicy foods.

Our unusual Exotic Salad is the perfect complement to this meal. It combines tender lettuce, hearts of palm, and white grapes with a light olive oil dressing. If possible, serve it from a wooden salad bowl.

Steaming hot popovers are wonderful with this menu. They always remind us of happy Sunday brunches at the Halekulani, the oldest hotel on Waikiki beach. Our always successful, mistake-proof version is much easier to make than the standard popover recipe. They are old stand-bys in our home—we serve them often for breakfast.

A great deal of research and an embarrassing number of failures have gone into perfecting the recipe for our Chocolate Angel Food Cake. It was Diana's favorite cake as a child, when it was available from a local bakery. A high-rise office building now stands in the place of the charming old bake shop, so we accepted the challenge and set out to duplicate the light, airy texture of the cake and its cocoa frosting. Perhaps the addition of dark rum to the icing makes our own version even better than the original.

We hope you enjoy our Hawaiian Feast—it will lend an exotic, informal flavor of the South Seas to your entertaining.

TIMETABLE: Up to 3 days before the party, make the cake and frost it. It keeps beautifully if tightly covered. Make the salad dressing as well, and refrigerate it.

Make the curry sauce at least 1 day before serving. Store it in the refrigerator, or freeze it for storage of more than 3 days.

The day before serving, cook the chicken or turkey breasts, if that is what you are using for the curry. If you are using some leftover cooked meat from your freezer, take it out to thaw. Pour cognac or brandy over the raisins and allow them to marinate. Wash the lettuce for the salad and store it as directed in the recipe. You would be wise to mix the popover batter a day ahead and refrigerate it until you are ready to use it. Just remember to whir it again in the blender for a few seconds before pouring it into the popover pan for baking. If you will be using your blender to make Peach Smashes, you should pour the popover batter into another container to store it. If you are lucky enough to have two containers for your electric blender, no problem.

The morning of your party, prepare the pineapple shells and set them aside to drain. Chill all the canned salad ingredients. Chop the scallions and set out all the condiments for the curry. Grease the popover or muffin pans and cover them with a towel to keep them clean. Set the table, except for the fresh flowers.

Several hours ahead, wash the stems of the flowers you have chosen to decorate the pineapple boats under cold running water and set them near your work area in a vase. Put the macadamia nuts out in a serving dish. Set out the recipe for making the Peach Smashes near the blender. It is a good idea to ask somebody to take over the job of making and serving these for you. Decorate the center of the table with fresh flowers and leaves just before your guests arrive.

If you are preparing all this with only one oven, you will have to use the oven for the popovers and heat the meat or seafood for the curry some other way (perhaps right in the sauce). We like to time the popovers to come out of the oven after everybody has been served the main course. That way they will be steaming hot and still fully puffed.

PEACH SMASH

(4 TO 6 DRINKS)

Be careful with these—they are potent!

1 six-ounce can frozen, unsweet-ened pineapple-juice concentrate, undiluted
½ to ¾ cup rum, vodka, or gin
1 fresh peach, pit removed, or ½ a ten-ounce package frozen peach slices*

1 tablespoon Cointreau or Triple Sec
4 or 5 ice cubes
Mint sprigs, if available, dipped in powdered sugar to garnish

Place all ingredients except the mint sprigs in the container of an electric blender. Blend at high speed until smooth and slushy. Pour immediately into champagne glasses or old-fashioned glasses. Garnish each drink with a sprig of mint dusted with powdered sugar.

To Make Ahead: This drink must be blended just before serving. Dust the mint sprigs with powdered sugar just before adding them to the drinks.

ISLAND CURRY IN PINEAPPLE SHELLS

(6 SERVINGS)

3 small pineapples, slightly under-ripe (optional)**

6 cups cooked chicken, turkey, or lobster, cut into ¾-inch cubes, or 6 cups cooked shrimp
Oven Rice (page 43)

---

* Fresh peaches are best if available because their skin lends a sunset color to the drink.
** It is not mandatory to serve this curry in pineapple shells. It can be served in simple curry style with rice and condiments.

BASIC CURRY SAUCE:

¼ *pound (1 stick) butter or mar-*
garine
1 large, tart apple, peeled and
minced
1 medium onion, minced
1 whole clove garlic, crushed but
left whole
2 tablespoons curry powder
½ *cup all-purpose flour*
2 fourteen-ounce cans clear
chicken broth (not condensed)
1 cup dry white wine

1 teaspoon chicken stock base
(Spice Islands), or 1 chicken-
flavored bouillon cube
Pinch of thyme
1 bay leaf
1 cup heavy cream, or half and
half
1 to 2 teaspoons fresh lemon juice
(to taste)
Cayenne pepper (to taste, for a
hotter flavor)

CONDIMENTS:

Shredded coconut, plain or toasted
Toasted slivered almonds or pea-
nuts
Chutney of your choice

1 cup raisins soaked in ⅓ *cup*
cognac or brandy
6 scallions, sliced very thin

DECORATION:

12 to 18 fresh white daisies or
other flowers, if using pineapple
shells for serving

If you do use pineapple shells, you will want to freshen them. The small green tag on a Hawaiian pineapple will tell you it has been picked "plantation-ripe." That means it was picked green. The grower is depending on the time the pineapple will spend in a crowded boat, wholesaler's warehouse, truck and market for it to ripen before you select and buy it. All that crowding may seem to have damaged the green fronds of your pineapple beyond repair. Not so. You can make it perky once again by holding the fronds upside down under hot running water. They will then be soft enough to reshape with your hands. Finally, run cold water over them and trim away any brown parts. As if by magic, your disheveled pineapple, after its long trip to you, will look as fresh as the day it left the iron-red fields of Hilo.

If using fresh pineapple boats for serving the curry, cut the pineapples in half lengthwise, right through the fronds. Using a grapefruit knife or a paring knife, cut the fruit out of the pineapple halves, leaving a ½-inch-thick shell. Turn the shells over to drain off any excess juice. Remove the core from the fruit you took out of the shell and discard it. Cut the remaining fruit into ¾-inch chunks and set aside.

To make the sauce, you will need a large, heavy skillet—not iron because it can discolor the sauce. Melt the butter in the skillet. Sauté the minced apple, onion and the garlic clove for 3 or 4 minutes, stirring often, until the onion is transparent. Stir in the curry powder and continue cooking the mixture for 2 more minutes—this will prevent the curry from having a raw taste. Next, add the flour and let it cook for 2 minutes, stirring often. Remove the pan from the heat. Stir in the chicken broth, wine, chicken stock base or bouillon cube, thyme and bay leaf. Return the pan to the heat and bring the mixture to a boil, stirring constantly with a wire whisk. Lower the heat and allow to simmer slowly for 30 minutes. You should stir it often, especially toward the end of the cooking time, because it will become quite thick and could burn easily.

Press the sauce through a coarse kitchen strainer into another pan. Stir in the cream and the lemon juice. Taste the sauce for seasoning and add more lemon juice if desired and cayenne pepper if you like a hotter flavor. It is best to wait a few seconds before adding more cayenne because the aftertaste of curry is delayed! If the sauce seems too thick, thin it slightly with milk. If you are not using the sauce immediately, press some plastic wrap into the surface to prevent a skin from forming on top and store in the refrigerator.

About 20 minutes before serving, wrap whatever meat or seafood you are using in aluminum foil and heat it in a 300° oven. Reheat the sauce over very low heat. Weave the daisies decoratively into the fronds of the pineapple shells (see illustration).

Just before serving, place the meat on a bed of Oven Rice (page 43) inside the pineapple shells or on serving plates. Spoon the sauce over each serving. Top with some of the reserved pineapple cubes, coconut, almonds, chutney, raisins and scallions. Or you may pass these condiments at the table, which is easier, but not as decorative.

To Make Ahead: The pineapple shells may be hollowed the day before serving, wrapped in plastic wrap, and refrigerated. Be sure to have them at room temperature before filling. Weave the daisies into the fronds no longer than 1 hour before serving so that they will stay fresh. The sauce may be made ahead of time and stored in the refrigerator or freezer. It will keep for up to 3 days in the refrigerator or a month in the freezer. The final assembly must, of course, be done at serving time.

OVEN RICE

(6 TO 8 SERVINGS)

2 cups uncooked white rice, rinsed
   with cold water
2 teaspoons salt
2 teaspoons vegetable oil

½ teaspoon vinegar, or lemon
   juice
4 cups boiling water, or clear
   chicken broth

Place all the ingredients in a casserole with a very tight-fitting lid. Bake at 375°, covered, for 45 minutes. If you are making half this recipe, cook slightly less time. If doubling the recipe, check the rice after 45 minutes and cook longer if necessary.

Fluff with a fork before serving.

To Make Ahead: Set out the ingredients in the morning. Wash the rice and heat the liquid to boiling just before baking. Leftover rice may be wrapped in foil and reheated in the oven.

EXOTIC SALAD

(6 OR MORE SERVINGS)

SALAD:

4 to 6 heads Boston or Bibb lettuce
1 bunch watercress, leaves only
1 eleven-ounce can lichee nuts,
   chilled and drained

1 fourteen-ounce can hearts of
   palm, chilled, drained, and
   sliced into rounds
1 eight-ounce can fine-quality
   white grapes (not "spiced"),
   chilled and drained

DRESSING:

2 tablespoons sugar
⅓ cup white "champagne" or
 white wine vinegar
¾ cup light olive oil
1 clove garlic, peeled and bruised,
 but left whole

Salt and white pepper to taste (be
 rather generous)
2 teaspoons chopped fresh chives,
 or 4 teaspoons dried chives (or a
 mixture of the two)

Wash and shake the excess moisture from the lettuce. Discard the tough outer leaves and tear the hearts into bite-sized pieces. Wrap the lettuce in paper towels along with the watercress leaves and refrigerate these in a plastic bag until ready to serve. Drain and chill all the canned ingredients.

To make the dressing, dissolve the sugar in the vinegar in a small saucepan over medium heat. Remove from the heat and add the other dressing ingredients. Refrigerate until ready.

Just before serving, remove the garlic clove, assemble the salad ingredients, combine with the dressing and toss.

To Make Ahead: The dressing may be made up to 24 hours in advance and stored in the refrigerator. Wash and chill all the salad ingredients in the morning. Toss just before serving.

PERFECT POPOVERS

(10 TO 15 POPOVERS)

Solid vegetable shortening
 (Crisco) to grease the baking
 pans
2 cups sifted all-purpose flour

1 teaspoon salt
4 large eggs
2 cups milk
2 tablespoons vegetable oil

Generously grease iron popover pans, muffin tins or Pyrex custard cups with shortening. If using custard cups, arrange them on a cookie sheet for easier handling.

Combine all the other ingredients in the container of an electric blender and blend at high speed for 10 to 15 seconds. Turn off the motor to scrape down the sides with a rubber spatula. Blend at high speed for 10 to 15 seconds longer, until the batter is completely smooth.

Preheat the oven to 400°. Fill the greased containers half full of the batter and place them in the preheated oven. Bake for 30 to 35 minutes if using an iron popover pan or muffin tins, or for 40 minutes if using custard cups. They should be well browned and crisp when done. To be sure they are firm and will stay puffed, remove the popovers from the oven and, while they are still in the pan, pierce the side of each one with a sharp knife. This will allow the steam to escape. Return them to the turned-off oven for 2 to 3 minutes to dry the insides.

To Make Ahead: The batter may be mixed and stored in the refrigerator for a day or two, but be sure to reblend it for 10 to 15 seconds just before using. Leftover popovers can be reheated on a baking sheet, not touching, at 350° for 5 minutes.

CHOCOLATE ANGEL FOOD CAKE

(10 TO 12 SERVINGS)

¾ cup sifted cake flour
⅓ cup cocoa
1½ cups sifted confectioner's sugar*
13 egg whites**

1½ teaspoons cream of tartar
¼ teaspoon salt
1½ teaspoons vanilla extract
Scant ½ teaspoon almond extract
1 cup extra-fine granulated sugar

Preheat the oven to 375°.

Sift the cake flour, cocoa and powdered sugar together three times (some sifters have three layers, in which case you need only sift once) into a medium-size mixing bowl. If the egg whites are not at room temperature, set the bowl containing the whites into some lukewarm water for a few minutes, stirring often, to warm them slightly. Add the cream of tartar, salt, vanilla and almond extracts and beat at high speed (or use a wire whisk to beat them by hand) just until the whites do not slide when you tip the bowl. Add the fine sugar gradually as you continue beating—the mixture will now be much thicker. As soon as the

* If you open a fresh box of confectioner's sugar for this purpose, it will have fewer lumps, so the first sifting will be easier. Use a kitchen strainer for this rather than a regular flour sifter.
** Egg whites which have been frozen will accept more air when beaten than those which have not—so when you are making a dish calling for yolks only, freeze and label the whites to use for another purpose, such as this cake, meringues, etc.

sugar is all in, stop! Transfer the beaten whites, which have now turned into a meringue with the addition of the sugar, to a very large mixing bowl, or remove half of the mixture to another bowl for easier handling. Sift about a quarter of the flour mixture over the whites and fold it in carefully. Then sift and fold in the rest, one-third at a time.

Have ready a 10-inch tube pan which is completely grease-free, because the slightest bit of grease will keep an angel food cake from rising. It is a good idea to have an extra tube pan that you use just for angel food cakes—mark it "angel food only" on both parts with a sharp nail, so you can identify it easily. Pour the batter into the tube pan and cut straight down through the batter several times with a knife to help release any large bubbles.

Bake the cake at 375° for 30 to 35 minutes or until it is firm to the touch. Turn the pan upside down onto the neck of a bottle for at least an hour to cool thoroughly. Remove the cake from the pan by running a knife around the edges to loosen it. Frost with Cocoa-Rum Icing (see below).

To Make Ahead: The iced cake keeps beautifully in the refrigerator for several days, and perhaps even improves with waiting. If you want to freeze it, the easiest method is to cover the uniced cake tightly with plastic wrap. But if you would prefer to freeze the cake after it's iced, then you must take a precaution to prevent the icing from being bruised: put the iced cake in the freezer unwrapped first. When it has frozen, wrap it carefully and replace in the freezer. To use, thaw at room temperature for 3 to 4 hours. You can freeze leftover slices individually (on paper plates inside plastic bags) for fast thawing.

COCOA-RUM ICING

(FOR 1 TEN-INCH TUBE CAKE)

¾ cup cocoa

4 cups confectioner's sugar

¼ pound (1 stick) butter or margarine

1 ½ teaspoons vanilla

5 teaspoons rum (preferably dark)

½ cup evaporated milk

Mix the cocoa and confectioner's sugar together in a small mixing bowl. Using an electric mixer, cream the butter or margarine (in other words, beat it until creamy). Beat in half the cocoa-sugar mixture. Add the vanilla, the rum, and half the evaporated milk and beat thoroughly. Add the remaining cocoa-sugar mixture and beat well to blend. Last, add the remaining evaporated milk and beat for several minutes until the icing reaches the desired spreading consistency. If it is too thick, add just a little more evaporated milk.

A New England Family-Style Dinner

Iced Cream of Cucumber Soup

-or-

Boston-Style Clam Chowder

New England Corned Beef Bouquetière

BEAUJOLAIS

Mustard Sauce

Sour Cream Muffins with Blueberries or Currants

Betty Lou Port's Hot Apple Dumplings with Cream

I T I S A R A R E M A N who doesn't mentally click his heels at the thought of a hearty New England boiled dinner. This menu, featuring Corned Beef Bouquetière, is welcome all year round. In warmer weather, Iced Cream of Cucumber Soup is as cool and fresh-tasting as it sounds. On more bracing evenings, however, you would be wise to substitute a steaming Boston-Style Clam Chowder for the Iced Cream of Cucumber Soup to ward off the chilling effects of those blustering nor'easters—white Clam Chowder, of course; New Englanders consider the addition of tomatoes a sacrilege.

Although we have included the chowder in this menu as part of a lusty New England meal, it can now and then be the star attraction by itself, served with hot, crusty bread and a green salad. By definition, a chowder is a thick fish and vegetable soup. Most consider it to be originally American. We do not believe that it is. We suspect it came from the French word *chaudière*, meaning "kettle." Our recipe, which ironically was given to us by a California friend, is a breeze. It calls for canned clams rather than fresh ones, which must be carefully cleaned.

Corned Beef Bouquetière is a one-pot celebration—meat and vegetables, simmered together, all finished at the same time—easy to fix and fun to serve! This savory dish derives its name from the stone kegs in which New Englanders preserved their beef, kegs which held a mixture of sugar, salt and "corns" of saltpeter. Just before serving, the meat is sliced and arranged on a huge platter surrounded by carrots, green beans, cabbage, potatoes and sprigs of parsley. There is a delicious mustard sauce to serve with it, and a Beaujolais will complement the menu perfectly.

Sour Cream Muffins are flavored either with blueberries or with fresh or dried currants. Bring them to the table steaming hot from the oven. They will be devoured immediately.

Sweetened tart apples, folded into a simple short crust, become Betty Lou Port's Hot Apple Dumplings. They are then baked with a pink-tinted sauce spiced with cinnamon and nutmeg and served in soup bowls with cream. And, as a bonus, you can save and reheat any left-over dumplings for the best breakfast imaginable.

This menu is a treat any time—for family or friends. Enjoy yourself New England style!

TIMETABLE: A day or two before your dinner is scheduled, make the cucumber soup. Press plastic wrap into the surface to prevent a skin from forming and store in the refrigerator. Mix the mayonnaise-mustard sauce and store it, covered with plastic wrap, in the same manner.

The morning of the party, prepare the apple dumplings for bak-ing and refrigerate them until they are scheduled for the oven, or if you prefer, bake them in advance and reheat them before serving. Their flavor will, in fact, improve with reheating. At the same time, prepare the carrots, potatoes, and green beans. Place the potatoes in cold water to cover—they turn brown quickly after peeling. Store in the refrigera-tor until needed. Cut the cabbage into wedges and cover until needed. If serving clam chowder rather than cucumber soup, make it now, but don't add the reserved clams until the soup is reheated before serving.

About 4 hours before serving, start cooking the corned beef as directed. Next, set out the muffin ingredients: the wet ones in one bowl and the dry in another. Cover both with plastic wrap and leave them at room temperature until you're ready to mix them together.

Time the muffins to go into the oven just as everybody is sitting down to enjoy the soup. We think it's a wise plan to serve biscuits or muffins steaming hot after your guests have finished helping themselves to the main course.

The apple dumplings can be baked after the muffins are removed from the oven. Simply take them from the refrigerator, pour the sauce mixture over them, place them in the oven and set the timer. It is much better and easier, though, to bake them in the morning and reheat them briefly before serving.

There should be wonderful leftovers from this dinner. After cooling, wrap individual servings of sliced meat and any leftover vegetables in aluminum foil, and spoon just a little of the corned beef cooking broth over them before sealing. Store in the refrigerator or freezer. To serve, simply heat, still wrapped, in the oven. Or keep the thinly sliced meat for delicatessen-style sandwiches made with any remaining mustard sauce. Reheat leftover Apple Dumplings for a very special breakfast treat!

ICED CREAM OF CUCUMBER SOUP
(8 SERVINGS)

4 large cucumbers
3 tablespoons butter or margarine,
  melted
3 whole shallots
3 bay leaves
2 sprigs fresh mint, or a generous
  pinch of dried mint
2 tablespoons flour
5 cups strong chicken broth

1 teaspoon salt
1 ½ cups half-and-half
3 tablespoons fresh lemon juice
2 teaspoons fresh dill, or ½
  teaspoon dried dill
Salt and white pepper to taste
2 drops green food coloring
½ cup sour cream

Peel the cucumbers and chop coarsely all but half of one, which will be used later for the garnish. Wrap the half cucumber in plastic wrap and store it in the refrigerator until needed. Place the chopped cucumber in the container of an electric blender with the melted butter and the whole shallots. Blend on medium speed while forcing the mixture down into the blades with a rubber spatula. Pour this purée into a heavy saucepan. Add the bay leaves and mint and simmer, covered, for 20 minutes over very low heat.

Remove the bay leaves and the mint, if using the whole sprigs. Stir in the flour, followed by the chicken broth and salt. Bring to a boil while stirring, then pour the mixture back into the blender container. Blend at high speed until it is completely smooth. Pour it into a bowl and chill thoroughly. When the mixture is cold, stir in the half-and-half, lemon juice and dill. Season to taste with salt and white pepper. Color with green food coloring. Chill until ready to serve.

Just before serving, cut 8 thin slices off the remaining half cucumber for the garnish. Cut the rest in half lengthwise and remove the seeds with the tip of a spoon. Grate the cucumber fine and stir it into the chilled soup.

Serve the soup in chilled cups. Top each serving with a dab of sour cream and a cucumber slice.

To Make Ahead: The soup may be made up to 3 days ahead. Store it, covered, in the refrigerator. Do not grate and add the fresh cucumber until just before serving.

BOSTON-STYLE CLAM CHOWDER

(8 SERVINGS)

2 7½-ounce cans minced clams
1 ten-ounce can whole baby clams
¼ pound salt pork, diced fine
2 medium onions, minced
2 tablespoons flour
1 teaspoon Beau Monde seasoning
¼ teaspoon black pepper
½ teaspoon MSG (optional)
1½ teaspoons salt

¼ teaspoon dried summer savory
¼ teaspoon dried thyme
2 cups milk
1½ cups half-and-half
2 dashes Worcestershire sauce
2 large potatoes, diced fine
Salt
1 tablespoon butter or margarine
1 tablespoon chopped parsley

Drain the juice from all the canned clams and reserve the liquid.

Use a very heavy-bottomed pot to make chowder because thick soups or sauces are very easily scorched! In the soup pot, sauté the diced salt pork over medium heat until it has rendered most of its fat and is slightly crisp. Add the onions and sauté until transparent. Meanwhile, combine in a small bowl the flour, Beau Monde, pepper, optional MSG, salt, summer savory and thyme. When the onions are transparent, stir in the flour and herb mixture, allowing it to cook for a few seconds, then stir in the milk, half-and-half, the reserved liquid from the clams, Worcestershire sauce and diced potatoes. Bring the soup to a simmer over medium heat, then lower the heat and continue to simmer until the potatoes are tender when tested. Stir in the clams and additional salt to taste—it will probably require an additional teaspoonful, depending on the saltiness of the clams. If you prefer a thinner chowder, add more milk or half-and-half. Do *not* cook the chowder much after the addition of the clams or they will toughen.

Just before serving, stir in the 1 tablespoon butter or margarine and the chopped parsley. Serve immediately.

To Make Ahead: Chowder will keep for 3 or 4 days in the refrigerator or may be frozen if desired. But if preparing it in advance, do not add the clams until you are about to reheat it for serving. Reheat it very gently, then stir in the butter and chopped parsley.

NEW ENGLAND CORNED BEEF BOUQUETIÈRE
(8 SERVINGS)

4 to 5 pounds corned beef brisket
1 clove garlic
2 whole cloves
10 peppercorns
2 bay leaves
1 pound fresh green beans, tied in
   8 bunches

8 medium potatoes, peeled and cut
   into quarters, or 16 to 24 new
   potatoes, scrubbed but not
   peeled
8 small carrots, peeled and left
   whole
1 medium-sized head of cabbage,
   cut into 8 wedges
Chopped parsley, to garnish
Mustard Sauce (page 54)

About 4 hours before serving, place the corned beef in a large kettle and cover it with cold water. Add the garlic, cloves, peppercorns and bay leaves. Bring to a boil, reduce the heat and simmer for 5 minutes. Skim the surface, then simmer, covered, for 3 to 4 hours or until the meat is tender when pierced with a fork. Add the green beans and potatoes and simmer 10 minutes more, then add the carrots and cabbage by laying them over the top. Cover and simmer slowly 10 to 15 minutes longer, cooking just until the vegetables are tender.

Remove the cabbage from the water gently with a slotted spoon to prevent its falling apart. Slice the meat across the grain so it doesn't shred. An electric knife is the most efficient way to do this. Arrange the sliced meat on the platter, surrounding it decoratively with the vegetables. Sprinkle the whole beautiful thing with chopped parsley. Serve with mustard sauce.

To Make Ahead: Although this meat should be cooked just before serving, leftovers can be wrapped in aluminum foil and simply reheated in the oven until warmed through. Any leftover sliced meat will make delicious sandwiches.

MUSTARD SAUCE

(2 CUPS)

1 cup mayonnaise
1 cup Mr. Mustard or other commercial hot mustard

¼ cup finely chopped onion
2 tablespoons minced parsley

Mix all ingredients in a serving bowl and refrigerate, covered with plastic wrap, until needed.

SOUR CREAM MUFFINS WITH BLUEBERRIES OR CURRANTS

(ABOUT 21 BLUEBERRY OR 18 CURRANT MUFFINS)

3 tablespoons butter or margarine
¾ cup sugar
¼ teaspoon salt
2 eggs
⅞ cup sour cream
1⅜ cups sifted all-purpose flour
½ teaspoon baking soda
¼ teaspoon ground nutmeg

Solid vegetable shortening (Crisco), to grease muffin tins
1 cup fresh or frozen blueberries, lightly floured, or ½ cup dried currants, lightly floured
2 tablespoons sugar, or cinnamon-sugar for the topping

Cream the butter, sugar and salt with your electric mixer at high speed. Beat for about 3 minutes until very smooth and creamy. Beat the eggs separately, then beat them into the sugar-butter mixture. Add the sour cream, blend well and set aside. These are the "wet" ingredients.

In another bowl, mix the dry ingredients with a fork—the flour, soda and nutmeg.

When ready to bake the muffins, preheat your oven to 425°. Grease 21 muffin pan sections very well with the solid shortening. Mix the wet and the dry ingredients together very gently, just until the dry are thoroughly moist, then stop! Fold in the floured blueberries or currants. Fill the muffin pans half full. Sprinkle each muffin with sugar or cinnamon-sugar topping and bake for 12 to 15 minutes, or until firm. Let cool for 2 minutes, then loosen the muffins from their pans and serve very hot.

To Make Ahead: These may be baked in the morning and reheated, but for best texture, it is advisable to bake them just before serving. Set out the wet and the dry ingredients in separate bowls in the morning if you wish, and combine them as directed just before baking. Leftover muffins freeze well. Reheat them wrapped in foil to prevent them from drying out.

BETTY LOU PORT'S HOT APPLE DUMPLINGS WITH CREAM
These are sublime!

(8 SERVINGS)

SAUCE:

1 ½ cups sugar
1 ½ cups water
¼ teaspoon cinnamon

¼ teaspoon nutmeg
10 drops red food coloring
3 tablespoons butter or margarine

PASTRY:

2 cups sifted all-purpose flour
2 teaspoons baking powder
1 teaspoon salt

⅔ cup solid vegetable shortening
  (Crisco), chilled
½ cup milk

TO ASSEMBLE:

8 medium-sized tart apples (we
  like Pippins)
4 teaspoons butter or margarine

Extra sugar, cinnamon, and
  nutmeg, to sprinkle
2 cups heavy cream, for serving

In a small saucepan, combine the sauce ingredients. Stir over medium heat until the sugar has dissolved and set aside.

Sift together the flour, baking powder and salt. Cut in the shortening with a pastry cutter or two knives, until the mixture resembles coarse crumbs. Add the milk all at once and stir just until the flour is moistened. Form the dough into a ball, then flatten it into a rectangular shape. Roll it out on a well-floured surface to form a 24 x 12-inch rectangle. Cut the rectangle into 8 six-inch squares.

Peel and core the apples and place one in the center of each square of dough. Place about ½ teaspoon butter or margarine in the center of each apple, then sprinkle each one generously with extra sugar, cinnamon and nutmeg. Moisten the edges of the dough with water and fold the corners of each square to the center. Pinch the edges of the dough together, enclosing each apple in a little package of dough (see illustration). Place the dumplings about an inch apart in an ungreased baking dish. Refrigerate, if desired, until ready to bake.

Just before baking, reheat the sauce ingredients and pour over the dumplings. Sprinkle the tops with a little extra sugar. Bake at 375° for 35 minutes. Serve warm with cream, plain or lightly whipped.

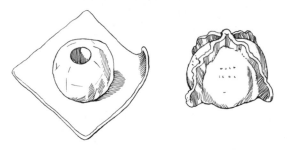

To Make Ahead: These dumplings are really at their best made ahead and reheated. They can be frozen, before baking, in their baking dish, but freeze the sauce in a separate container. Thaw before baking.

A Sophisticated New York Dinner for Six or Eight

Coquilles Saint Jacques

WHITE GRAVES

Roast Filet of Beef with Madeira Sauce

RED BORDEAUX

Paul's Pommes Diana

French-Style Baked Peas†

-or-

Stuffed Tomatoes à la Provençale†

Strawberry-and-Chocolate Meringue Cake

Irish Coffee

N E W Y O R K, noted for many of the world's finest restaurants, has provided the inspiration for this very sophisticated menu. Unfortunately, it is rather expensive, so serve it on very special occasions—when you want to "do the town" in the intimacy of your own home!

The table should be set with your best china and silver. Paul likes to put a fresh red rose on each lady's napkin. It gives the table a formal touch.

Our recipe for Coquilles Saint Jacques is the product of much time and consideration. We think we've reached a perfection of ease and elegance. Gourmet food stores and some supermarkets carry the inexpensive scallop shells used for serving this splendid first course. You can make the coquilles ahead of time and freeze it right in the shells. Serve with a chilled white Graves.

Included in the following menu is a sure recipe for "doctoring up" canned beef gravy so that it tastes like an authentic French brown sauce. This is a wonderful sauce to use any time, and it's even easier to make than our Basic Brown Sauce (page 106). For this occasion, it is flavored with Madeira and served over slices of Roast Filet of Beef, a rich and delicious combination. A red Bordeaux is our choice to accompany it.

Because there is a certain amount of last-minute effort required in the preparation of this dinner, we recommend serving our tasty French-Style Baked Peas from the New Orleans dinner (page 34). The little peas are perfect with this menu, and will ease your last-minute fuss. If you feel the need for an additional or alternative vegetable, use the Stuffed Tomatoes à la Provençale (page 149). They will look beautiful on the plate, and they, too, can be made perfectly ahead of time.

The most glamorous presentation of potatoes we know, Pommes Diana, is Paul's variation on Pommes Anna, an old French recipe. Served on a platter, they are gorgeous, all crispy, brown, and sprinkled with parsley. They are served cut into wedges like a cake.

One of the most elegant desserts in the world is made from layers of meringue filled with sweetened whipped cream, chocolate and fresh strawberries. It is our version of the Boccone Dolce (Sweet Mouthful) served at Sardi's famous restaurant, and it's a favorite among our friends and students. We serve it often when strawberries are in season.

Irish Coffee is not essential to this menu, but it has certainly proved to be a crowd-pleaser in our home. We always serve it to celebrate Saint Patrick's Day—and it adds a friendly, festive touch to many other menus.

Here is a splendid dinner, worthy of any of the elegant restaurants in New York City—and you're serving it in your own home. Compliments to the chef!

TIMETABLE: Weeks ahead, if you like, make the Coquilles Saint Jacques. To serve, simply thaw at room temperature for 2 hours, sprinkle with butter and grated cheese, then slide under the broiler until lightly browned and bubbly. Up to a week ahead, make the meringue layers for your dessert. Wrap them airtight in plastic wrap—they will wait perfectly.

All brown sauces improve with reheating. So, the day before your party, make the Madeira Sauce. Press plastic wrap into the surface to prevent a skin from forming and refrigerate until ready to reheat. Assemble the peas in their baking dish and place them in the freezer. Slide them directly from the freezer into the oven an hour before serving. If you have only one oven, substitute Stuffed Tomatoes à la Provençale for the peas. Those may be placed in the oven after you remove the meat. Assemble them a day ahead and refrigerate.

The morning of the party, cook the potatoes. To serve, simply reheat them on top of the stove before turning them out of the pan. We don't recommend making them more than 12 hours ahead, since potatoes will lose their flavor if they stand too long.

The Boccone Dolce must be assembled 2 to 6 hours before serving and refrigerated until dessert time.

Roast your filet 45 minutes before serving. It will take about 20 minutes. You may heat the Coquilles at the same time under the broiler unit, if your oven has two separate units. Otherwise you will have to wait until the roast is done. Simply place the roast on a hot tray or in a warm spot and cover loosely with foil to hold in the heat. The roast should "relax" for about 15 minutes before carving.

While the roast is "relaxing," serve the Coquilles—and enjoy the delight of your guests.

COQUILLES SAINT JACQUES
(6 TO 8 SERVINGS)

1 ¼ pounds sea or bay scallops, cut into ½-inch pieces
1 ½ cups dry white wine
1 teaspoon salt
1 bay leaf
½ pound mushrooms, sliced
2 tablespoons chopped shallots
3 tablespoons butter
4 tablespoons flour
¾ cup milk
2 egg yolks, lightly beaten

½ cup heavy cream
2 teaspoons fresh lemon juice
Salt to taste
A good dash of cayenne
1 tablespoon minced parsley
½ cup finely grated Swiss cheese
2 tablespoons grated Parmesan cheese
2 tablespoons butter, to dot the tops before broiling

Place the scallops in a large strainer or colander and rinse them very well under cold running water, as they can be very sandy. Set the strainer or colander into a bowl filled with cold water and let the scallops soak until you are ready for them. Most of their sand will sink to the bottom of the bowl.

In a saucepan, simmer the wine, salt and bay leaf for 5 minutes. Add the scallops, mushrooms and enough water to just cover them. Bring them to a boil. Turn down the heat, cover the pan, and simmer gently for 5 minutes. Remove the scallops and mushrooms with a slotted spoon and set aside. Strain the liquid through a clean dish towel into another saucepan. This process will remove the last of the sand. Add the shallots to the liquid, bring to a boil, and let boil rapidly for 5 to 10 minutes, or until the liquid is reduced to 1 cup of concentrated "stock."

In a stainless-steel or enameled skillet (iron or aluminum will discolor anything containing egg yolks), melt the 3 tablespoons of butter and stir in the flour. Let the mixture cook a minute to remove the raw floury taste, then stir in the boiling reduced stock and the milk. Bring back to a boil while stirring with a whisk and let the sauce cook for 1 minute. Mix the yolks with the cream and stir ½ cup of the boiling liquid into them, mixing rapidly with your whisk. Then pour the yolk mixture into your pan of sauce, reduce the heat to very low (high heat does drastic things to egg yolks), and stir quickly for about 2 minutes until the sauce is thickened. Remove from the heat; stir in the lemon juice, the salt, cayenne to taste and the minced parsley.

Remove about one-third of the sauce from the pan and set it aside to spoon over the tops of the coquilles when finished. Stir the scallops and mushrooms into the remaining sauce. Butter 6 or 8 scallop shells (see illustration) or individual ovenproof ramekins and fill them with the scallop mixture. Spoon the reserved sauce evenly over all. Freeze now if desired.

To serve, defrost the shells at room temperature for 2 hours, then sprinkle with the two kinds of cheese and dot with butter. Set the shells on a baking sheet containing rock salt to hold them steady (this is not absolutely essential, but nice). Broil them about 8 inches from the heat for 5 to 10 minutes or until browned.

To Make Ahead: Freeze as directed, or refrigerate for up to 24 hours before broiling.

ROAST FILET OF BEEF WITH MADEIRA SAUCE

(6 TO 8 SERVINGS)

1 three- to five-pound filet of beef
Salt and pepper
6 tablespoons (¾ stick) butter for
the filet

Chopped parsley to garnish

Madeira Sauce

2 tablespoons butter, or margarine,
or beef drippings
1 onion, chopped
2 carrots, coarsely chopped
1 stalk celery, coarsely chopped

1 clove garlic, minced
3 tablespoons cognac or brandy
1 ten-ounce can beef gravy
1 teaspoon tomato paste
½ cup Madeira

To make the sauce, melt the 2 tablespoons of butter or margarine, or beef drippings which you have saved from something else, in a heavy-bottomed saucepan. Add the onion, carrots, celery, and garlic and cook them over medium heat, stirring occasionally, until the onion is lightly browned. Stir in the cognac or brandy, then stir in the gravy, tomato paste and Madeira. (The rest of the can of tomato paste may be frozen for another purpose.) Bring the mixture to a boil and let it simmer for no less than 10 minutes. Do not taste it during this time—the wine flavor will be strong and unpleasant. After 10 minutes, taste the sauce and season it with salt and pepper. Remove from the heat and press plastic *strain out vegetables* wrap into the surface to prevent a skin from forming. Set aside or refrigerate until needed.

To roast the filet, heat the oven to 500°. Season the filet well with salt and pepper. In a small roasting pan, or ovenproof skillet, melt the 6 tablespoons butter. Roll the filet in the butter and roast it in the oven for about 20 to 25 minutes, turning it over halfway through. At the end of 20 minutes, insert a meat thermometer into the center of the roast—it should read about 125° to be served rare. Be sure to take it out before it reaches 140°—the meat will continue to cook after being removed from the oven, and you don't want it to be overdone. Remove the meat to a warm platter, and place it on a hot tray, if you have one. Cover loosely with a tent of foil to keep the heat in. The roast should "relax" for at least 15 minutes before it is sliced. Heat your dinner plates if possible—the meat will cool as it relaxes.

Reheat the sauce in a saucepan. Slice the filet into ½-inch slices, pour some sauce over the meat, and sprinkle with chopped parsley. Pass the rest of the sauce at the table.

To Make Ahead: Make the sauce the day before, or several days ahead if you like. The flavor improves with reheating. Roast the meat just before serving.

PAUL'S POMMES DIANA

(6 TO 8 SERVINGS)

3 large baking potatoes
½ pound (2 sticks) butter or
margarine
Salt and black pepper
1 tablespoon chopped chives

6 mushrooms, very thinly sliced
through the stems
6 ounces grated Parmesan cheese
Chopped parsley to garnish

To make this dish you will need a small skillet that can go into the oven.

Peel and slice the potatoes thin. If using the slicer side of a regular grater, hold the potato with a kitchen towel to protect your hand from the cutting edge.

Melt the butter or margarine in the skillet. Swirl it around to coat the sides, then pour the excess into another container and reserve. Make a single layer of the potatoes, creating an overlapping spiral starting from the center and working outward, and continuing up the side of the pan. Sprinkle the layer generously with salt, pepper and chives. Top with a few of the mushroom slices, placed well apart, followed by a blanket of Parmesan cheese. Drizzle the surface well with some of the reserved melted butter. Top with another layer of potatoes—this one need not be as neat because only the bottom one will show! Continue the same process until all the potatoes and cheese are used.

Heat the oven to 450°. Heat the pan on top of the stove until sizzling, then place it in the lower third of the oven for 30 minutes, or until the potatoes are well-browned and tender when tested with a fork.

To turn out, let it cool a minute, then work a spatula carefully around the edge. Loosen the bottom as much as possible without disturbing the shape. Place a serving dish over the pan. Holding the pan

63

over the sink, invert the whole thing onto the serving plate, pouring off the excess butter. Sprinkle the top with chopped parsley.

To serve, cut into wedges like a pie.

To Make Ahead: Pommes Diana may be made in the morning and reheated before turning out. It is usually best to cook potatoes the day of serving because they lose flavor on standing.

STRAWBERRY-AND-CHOCOLATE MERINGUE CAKE
Boccone Dolce or Sweet Mouthful

(8 SERVINGS)

MERINGUE:

4 egg whites, at room temperature
Pinch of salt
¼ teaspoon cream of tartar

½ teaspoon vanilla extract
1 cup sugar

FILLING AND FROSTING:

1 six-ounce package semisweet chocolate bits
3 tablespoons water
3 cups heavy cream

⅓ cup sugar
1 teaspoon vanilla extract
3 cups fresh strawberries

To make the meringue layers: Preheat the oven to 275°. Butter and flour three cookie or baking sheets. Draw an 8- or 9-inch circle on each one, using a plate or cake pan as a guide. Put the egg whites in the bowl of your electric mixer with the salt, cream of tartar and ½ teaspoon vanilla, and beat at high speed to soft peaks (the point at which the whites don't slide when the bowl is tipped). Add the 1 cup sugar gradually and continue beating until the whites are stiff—about 1 minute. Spread this meringue carefully and evenly over the circles to about ⅜-inch thickness (you may have some left over). Place each one on a separate level in the oven, or better yet, two ovens, and bake for 45 minutes. Without opening the oven door, turn off the heat and allow the meringues to rest in the oven for 45 minutes. They will be crisp and easily removed from the pan with a spatula. Let the meringues cool completely, then wrap them airtight in plastic wrap. If you break one, don't worry—no one will know once the cake is assembled. The meringue layers will keep nicely for up to a week at room temperature.

To assemble the cake (2 to 8 hours before serving), melt the chocolate in the 3 tablespoons of water in the top of a double boiler over boiling water. Whip the cream until it is stiff, then beat in the ⅓ cup sugar and 1 teaspoon vanilla. Slice all but 8 of the nicest strawberries.

Place a meringue layer on a serving plate and drizzle over it about one-quarter of the melted chocolate. Spread with a thick layer (¾ inch) of whipped cream and top this with a layer of sliced strawberries. Place another meringue layer on top, drizzle with more chocolate, spread with more whipped cream and the rest of the sliced strawberries. Top with the last layer of meringue. Frost the sides with almost all the remaining whipped cream. Drizzle the rest of the chocolate decoratively over the top of the cake. Put 8 dabs of whipped cream evenly inside the top edge of the cake and top each with a strawberry. Chill for at least 2 hours, but no longer than 6 hours, before serving.

To Make Ahead: The meringue layers will keep for a week if stored as directed. The Boccone Dolce has to be assembled 2 to 6 hours before serving—more than 6 hours will make it soggy, less than 2 doesn't give the meringues time to soften so that you can slice the cake easily. Keep the cake refrigerated until dessert time.

IRISH COFFEE

FOR EACH SERVING:

1 ½ teaspoons sugar
1 jigger Irish whiskey
6 ounces hot, black coffee

1 heaping tablespoon softly
whipped heavy cream

Early in the day, if you wish, put the sugar and the whiskey in Irish Coffee glasses or mugs. Lay a cookie sheet or something flat across the tops of the glasses to prevent evaporation. Whip the cream until it holds its shape and refrigerate until needed.

When ready to serve, prepare the coffee and pour it into the glasses. Top with the lightly whipped cream, spilling it over a spoon to form an even head on each serving. Serve immediately.

To Make Ahead: In the morning, fill the glasses with sugar and whiskey, as described. Whip the cream and refrigerate until needed. Make and add the coffee just before serving.

II

Menus for the Four Seasons

Springtime Sole

Steak Tartare

APÉRITIF WINE

Bourekakia

Filets of Sole à la Duglère

WHITE BURGUNDY

Spinach Strudel

-or-

Baked Petits Pois†

Madeline's Salad

Fried Camembert

Fresh Strawberry Tart

OUR FAVORITE springtime dinner is delicate, light enough for a luncheon, yet perfect for those gentle evenings when you don't wish to serve a heavy meal. Grace the table with a bowl of spring flowers and leaves.

We begin with Steak Tartare, which we enjoy only if the beef is very freshly ground and highly seasoned. It is most inviting when served premixed and in a molded shape (any cup or bowl will do). Surrounded by sprigs of parsley and crisp crackers or bread rounds, Tartare is irresistible. It is served with cocktails or an apéritif wine.

To enhance the Steak Tartare, we serve hot, tangy cheese puffs called Bourekakia. These are small triangles made with the traditional Greek *filo* (or *phyllo*) dough and folded around a filling of feta cheese and seasonings. The puffs are airy and delicious—they make delightful hors d'oeuvres at any time. If you live in a large city, you shouldn't have any difficulty finding the *filo* dough. All Greek delicatessens carry it, as well as some Italian delis. A 1-pound package of *filo* sheets will make at least 100 Bourekakia, or you can use half of that package to make one Spinach Strudel (page 76). Some specialty supermarkets now carry *filo* sheets, as well as narrow strips of strudel leaves of the same transparent consistency—just right for making the Bourekakia. When you locate a source for these products, why not buy some extra to keep on hand in your freezer? They stay fresh for a long time . . . til spring is just a memory.

70

The French excel in the preparation of fish, and among the many variations, Sole à la Duglère is one of the finest, well worth the last-minute effort. It is beautifully complimented by a chilled white Burgundy.

We like to serve Baked Petits Pois (page 131) with the fish; these buttery baby peas are the perfect accompaniment. As an alternate vegetable, we are including a recipe for Spinach Strudel. It is an elegant dish which uses the same *filo* required for the Bourekakia. If you serve the Strudel, omit the Bourekakia from the beginning of the menu. The flavors of the two recipes are similar, and would be repetitive. The Steak Tartare can stand on its own.

With this meal, we feel the delicate salad is most enjoyable when served in the European manner, after the main course. Garlic French Dressing, so simple to make, is the inspiration of Madeline Bigelow, retired owner of the once-renowned Madeline's Restaurant in Houston, Texas. It is best served with a very tender lettuce, such as Boston butter, Bibb, or Kentucky limestone when available. For a delightful taste contrast, serve wedges of breaded, freshly fried Camembert cheese with the salad.

For the final fresh delight of the evening, the Fresh Strawberry Tart, be sure to get the most beautiful, plump spring strawberries available. A tart shell is filled with pastry cream, then topped with whole strawberries, glazed with melted jelly and liqueur, and then garnished with fresh mint leaves. It is truly divine.

We know that this delightful springtime menu will be greeted with admiration. And it's so beautifully simple!

TIMETABLE: The Bourekakia may be made up to a month in advance of your occasion and frozen either before or after baking. The Spinach Strudel can be made at the same time. Freeze it after baking. You will probably want to have a supply of basic *roux* always on hand in the freezer; it is necessary for the filet of sole, as well as for other recipes in this book, and is indispensable for thickening sauces.

On the day before your party, make the pastry cream for the tart. Press plastic wrap into the surface to prevent a skin from forming, and refrigerate it until the next day. You can also prepare and bake your tart shell. Store it, covered, at room temperature (it would lose its crispness in the refrigerator). If you have chosen to serve the peas, assemble them with their seasonings in a baking dish and store in the freezer. Prepare the lettuce leaves as directed and store in the bottom of your refrigerator until you're ready to toss your salad. Finally, trim the outer white skin from the Camembert cheese, cut it into serving pieces, and coat with crumbs as described. Refrigerate until ready to fry.

The morning of your party, set your table and arrange the center-piece. Assemble the filets of sole and the poaching ingredients in a stainless-steel or ceramic skillet. Cover the pan and refrigerate it until you are ready to cook. Place the small mixing bowl you will be using to whip the cream in the freezer to chill. If serving the Spinach Strudel, set it out at room temperature to thaw. Wash and dry the strawberries quickly, but do not remove the hulls until just before assembling the tart. Sprinkle the berries lightly with liqueur to marinate, then place them in the refrigerator.

Buy your meat for the Steak Tartare no earlier than the morning of your party. Have it ground three times. Be sure to tell your butcher the purpose for which the meat is to be used so that he can be sure the grinder is free from traces of any other meats. Mix the beef with its seasonings and pack it into a mold no more than 2 hours before serving so it loses none of its fresh, red color.

The creation of the strawberry tart should take place no more than 3 to 4 hours before serving. Fill your pastry shell with the cold pastry cream, remove the hulls and leaves from the strawberries, and arrange them on top of the cream. Prepare and apply the glaze, then chill the tart until you are ready to serve it with the final garnish, the mint sprigs. Set out a small skillet and some oil for frying the Camembert. Make the salad dressing and leave it at room temperature. Chill the wine.

STEAK TARTARE

(4 TO 6 SERVINGS)

1 pound very fresh beef round, all fat removed and ground three times
1 small onion, chopped very fine
½ green bell pepper, chopped very fine
1 egg, beaten
2 teaspoons Dijon mustard
1 teaspoon capers, drained

1 tablespoon lemon juice
Salt to taste
Freshly ground black pepper, to taste
½ cup chopped parsley, or a sprig of parsley, for decoration
Rye bread rounds or crackers, for serving

No more than 2 hours before serving, combine all ingredients and mix thoroughly. Taste the mixture and correct the seasoning. Pack it into an oiled mold (any cup or bowl will do) and chill well.

To serve, turn the molded mixture out onto a cold plate and sprinkle with chopped parsley, or embed a parsley flower in the top of the molded shape before serving. Rounds of rye bread or crackers should be served on the side, along with butter knives or spreaders.

To Make Ahead: The meat should be purchased and ground no earlier than the morning of the day it will be served. In order for the meat to have a fresh, red appearance, mix the ingredients and pack into the mold not more than 2 hours before serving.

BOUREKAKIA
Puffed Cheese Triangles
(ABOUT 36 TRIANGLES)

You will have extra triangles, so freeze these for another occasion.

¼ pound feta (Greek white goat's
   milk cheese)
2 ounces cream cheese
1 egg, lightly beaten
Pinch ground nutmeg
Pinch ground white pepper

½ cup parsley, chopped fine
36 strips (about 8 x 4 inches) filo
   dough or strudel leaves
¼ pound (1 stick) melted butter
   or margarine

To make the filling, combine the feta, cream cheese, egg, nutmeg, white pepper and parsley.

Cut the *filo* or strudel leaves into strips approximately 8 inches by 4 inches. Prepare one strip at a time, covering the remaining strips with wax paper topped with a damp towel to keep them from drying out. Lay a strip on a damp cloth and brush it lightly with melted butter. Fold it in half lengthwise and brush it again with butter. Put 1 teaspoonful of the filling on a corner of the prepared strip, and fold the corner over to form a triangle (see illustration). Continue folding the pastry in triangles down the length of the strip, to form a multilayered triangle. Seal the ends with butter.

Bake on a lightly buttered baking sheet at 350° for 10 to 15 minutes, or until they are golden and puffed. Serve them hot with cocktails.

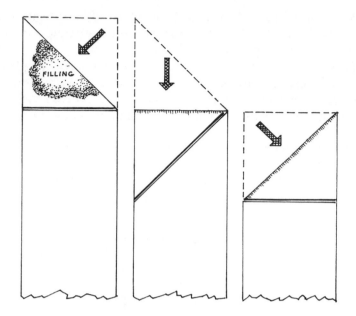

To Make Ahead: Triangles may be assembled in advance and refrigerated on their baking sheet, covered with foil, until ready to bake. Or bake them ahead and reheat them at 350° for about 5 minutes. They may also be frozen before or after baking. Thaw and reheat as described above.

FILETS OF SOLE À LA DUGLÈRE
(4 MAIN-COURSE SERVINGS, OR 8 SERVINGS AS A FIRST COURSE)

8 sole filets of equal size
1 one-pound can whole-pack
*   tomatoes, or 3 whole tomatoes,*
*   peeled,* seeded, and coarsely*
*   chopped*
8 medium mushrooms, washed and
*   quartered*
3 tablespoons chopped parsley
2 tablespoons chopped shallots

1 tablespoon lemon juice, or more
*   to taste*
1 teaspoon salt
Cayenne pepper, to taste
2 cups dry white wine
1 ½ cups heavy cream
3 tablespoons roux, *to thicken*
1 tablespoon chopped parsley to
*   garnish*

   * See note, page 25.

74

Fold the sole filets in half, silvery side in, and place them in a single layer in a buttered skillet. This may be done early in the day if your skillet is of stainless steel or is porcelainized—the use of other metals will spoil the flavor of the fish. If using the canned tomatoes, drain them well and chop them coarsely, reserving the liquid for another use. Cover the filets with all the ingredients except the cream and the *roux*. Cover the skillet with a circle of buttered wax paper with a small hole cut in the center. This process allows the liquid to reduce in cooking while allowing the fish to steam and remain moist. About 30 minutes before serving, bring the contents of the skillet to a boil, reduce the heat, and simmer gently for 5 minutes or so, until you can pierce the fish easily with a fork. Remove the filets carefully from the poaching liquid with a slotted spoon, letting as much liquid as possible drain back into the skillet. Place the filets on a platter or serving dish that can go under the broiler. Remove all of the tomatoes and mushrooms from the skillet with a slotted spoon and arrange them on top of the fish. Set the fish into a low (about 225°) oven with one end of the dish higher than the other (a piece of kitchen tableware placed under one end will accomplish this easily). The reason for this is so that the excess liquid will drain to one end where it can be easily spooned out to prevent it from thinning your finished sauce.

Turn the heat as high as possible under the skillet and reduce the poaching liquid to about one-third its original volume. Add only 1 cup of the cream and set the other half cup in the refrigerator in a small mixing bowl. Add about 3 tablespoons of *roux* to the liquid in the skillet, little by little, while beating with a wire whisk. Be very sure to let the liquid come to a boil after each addition of *roux*. Keep adding and stirring until the sauce is thick enough to coat a spoon rather heavily, then remove it from the heat. Taste the sauce for seasoning and add some more cayenne, lemon juice and salt if it needs it. The flavor should be quite tangy, because the final addition of cream will dull it a bit.

Whip the remaining ½ cup of cream until it holds its shape, then fold it carefully into the sauce. This process is called *glaçage*, or "glazing." The whipped cream makes the sauce brown and puff beautifully when placed under the broiler.

Just before coating the fish with the sauce, be sure you spoon or blot out any liquid that has drained to the end of the serving dish. Then pour the sauce over the fish and slide the whole thing under the broiler for just a few seconds, until lightly browned. Watch it very carefully so that it doesn't burn. Sprinkle 1 tablespoon of chopped parsley over the top and serve immediately.

To Make Ahead: This dish must be prepared just before serving. You may assemble all the necessary ingredients, placing the fish and its cooking liquid in a stainless or porcelainized skillet in the morning. Set it, covered, in the refrigerator until ready to cook.

SPINACH STRUDEL

(10 SERVINGS)

*2 ten-ounce packages frozen
  chopped spinach*
1 large onion, chopped fine
2 tablespoons butter or margarine
*8 ounces feta (Greek white goat's
  milk cheese)*
*6 ounces pot cheese or ricotta
  cheese*
3 eggs, lightly beaten
1 cup chopped scallions
¼ cup chopped parsley

*1 tablespoon chopped fresh dill, or
  1 teaspoon dried dill*
¼ teaspoon ground nutmeg
Salt and pepper to taste
½ pound filo *(or* phyllo) *pastry
  leaves**
*½ pound (2 sticks) melted butter
  or margarine*
*1 cup soft, fresh bread crumbs,
  made in the blender*

Thaw the frozen spinach completely. Sauté the chopped onion in the 2 tablespoons of butter or margarine until soft and transparent. Add the well-drained spinach and cook over low heat, stirring often, until all its moisture has evaporated. Remove the pan from the heat. Stir in the feta and the pot or ricotta cheeses, the eggs, scallions, parsley, dill and nutmeg. Season to taste with salt and pepper. Set the mixture aside to cool.

Open the package of *filo* dough and remove 1 sheet carefully. Cover the remaining sheets with wax paper topped with a damp towel to keep them from drying out. Place the single sheet of dough on a slightly damp towel. Brush it well with melted butter or margarine, then sprinkle it with some of the bread crumbs. Place another sheet of dough on top and brush that with butter and sprinkle with crumbs. Continue making layers in this manner until you have used 6 or 8 sheets, or half the 1-pound package.

Place the cooled spinach-cheese mixture along one long side of the

* The entire 1-pound package of *filo* should be used at once, so either double the strudel recipe and make 2 strudels, or make 1 strudel and many Bourekakia (see page 73).

prepared dough and roll up like a jelly roll. Lift the whole thing carefully, using pancake turners or spatulas, and place it, seam side down, on a cookie sheet. Bake the roll at 375° for 15 minutes, then remove it from the oven and cut 10 1-inch-deep slashes in each side of the roll, using scissors (see illustration). Return the strudel to the oven and continue baking for 15 to 20 minutes more, or until the pastry is golden. Serve the strudel immediately, cutting it into slices where the slashes were made.

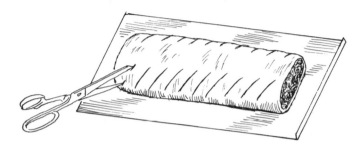

To Make Ahead: Bake the strudel as directed in the morning, or the day before, and simply reheat it at 375° for 15 minutes. Or make it in advance, let it cool, then wrap it tightly and freeze. Thaw and reheat as above, or, if you prefer, cut off the desired number of slices from the frozen strudel with a serrated knife, thaw, and reheat the slices on a baking sheet at 350° for about 10 minutes, or until hot through.

MADELINE'S SALAD

(4 SALADS)

3 heads Boston or Bibb lettuce, hearts only

Salt and freshly ground black pepper

DRESSING:

1 clove garlic
3 tablespoons vegetable oil

2 teaspoons apple cider vinegar

Wash the lettuce, discarding the tough outer leaves. Tear it into bite-sized pieces. Shake the lettuce pieces in a clean kitchen towel to remove most of the excess moisture. Wrap the lettuce in paper towels and store in a plastic bag in the refrigerator until ready to toss with the dressing. The small amount of moisture absorbed by the paper towels will keep the lettuce crisp and fresh for several days.

To make the dressing, slice the garlic clove thin. Place in a small glass with the oil and the vinegar and let stand at room temperature for an hour or more. When ready to use, lift out the garlic with a fork and stir the dressing lightly until it is bubbly but not completely emulsified.

Just before serving, place the lettuce in a salad bowl and sprinkle with salt and pepper. It is very important to use freshly ground black pepper for the flavor of this salad! Pour some of the dressing over the lettuce and toss until all pieces are lightly coated. If necessary, add more of the dressing, but be careful to underdress this salad or it will be soupy and limp!

To Make Ahead: Prepare the lettuce as described and store it in the refrigerator until needed. The dressing may be made in the morning and allowed to stand at room temperature. Do not toss the salad until just before serving.

FRIED CAMEMBERT

(8 SERVINGS)

8 ounces Camembert cheese	1 egg, beaten
Approximately ½ cup fine, dry bread crumbs, commercial or homemade	Oil for frying

Peel the cheese carefully and cut it into 8 equal pieces. Roll each piece in the bread crumbs, then in the beaten egg, then in bread crumbs again.

Heat oil ¼ inch deep in a small frying pan until it is quite hot. Fry the pieces a few at a time to brown on both sides. If you are not quick about this, the cheese will become runny. Serve hot with an icy-cold salad.

To Make Ahead: The cheese may be coated with egg and bread crumbs up to 24 hours ahead and refrigerated until ready to fry.

FRESH STRAWBERRY TART

(6 TO 8 SERVINGS)

2 boxes fresh, ripe strawberries

4½ teaspoons kirsch or cognac, plus extra for sprinkling straw-berries

Crust for a single-crust pie (page 147), or a commercial frozen pie crust*

2 cups hot milk

½ cup sugar

6 tablespoons cornstarch

5 egg yolks

1½ teaspoons vanilla extract

¾ cup red currant jelly

4½ teaspoons sugar

Sprigs of fresh mint, or fresh leaves for decoration

Wash, but do not hull, the strawberries. Place them in a small bowl and sprinkle lightly with a little kirsch or cognac. Chill and marinate for at least 1 hour, or until ready to use.

Roll out the pie dough and place it in an 8- or 9-inch tart or pie pan. If possible, freeze the crust in the pan for 15 minutes before baking, to prevent shrinkage. Prick the bottom of the crust all over with a fork and set the pan on a cookie sheet for easier handling. Bake at 450° for about 10 minutes, or until the crust is golden. Set the shell aside to cool, then remove it from the pan and set it on a flat serving dish.

To make the pastry cream or *crème pâtissière*, bring the milk just to a simmer in a small saucepan and set it aside. In another saucepan with a heavy bottom, combine the sugar and the cornstarch. Slowly add the hot milk while beating with a whisk. When the mixture is blended and smooth, place the pan over low heat and beat constantly until the custard comes to a boil and is thick. Remove from heat. Beat the egg yolks in a bowl and stir some of the hot custard into them. Then stir the yolks into the rest of the custard mixture and place over very low heat. Stir for 3 to 4 minutes, then remove from the heat and stir in the vanilla. If you can see any lumps, you should strain the mix-ture now. Press plastic wrap into the top of the custard to prevent a skin from forming, and set the pan in the refrigerator to chill.

To assemble the tart, spread the pastry cream in the baked pie shell. Hull the strawberries and arrange them decoratively over the top. This should be done not more than 4 hours before serving. In a small sauce-pan, boil the currant jelly, the 4½ teaspoons kirsch or cognac, and the sugar to 224° on a candy thermometer—you will have to tilt the pan

---

* To use a commercial frozen pie shell, remove the pie shell from its aluminum pan by running a dull knife around the edge just under the rim. It will lift out easily. Set it in the center of your baking pan and let it partially thaw—about 10 minutes. When it is just pliable, press it into the pan. Bake as you would a home-made shell.

to read the thermometer. Spoon this hot glaze over the strawberries in the pie shell. Chill until ready to serve, at which time you can decorate the tart with sprigs of mint of fresh leaves.

To Make Ahead: The shell and the pastry cream can both be made a day ahead. The strawberries may be washed, sprinkled with liqueur, and left to chill on the morning of your party. Fill and glaze the tart no longer than 3 to 4 hours before serving.

A Very Special Summertime Brunch

California Sunshine

Eggs Benedict

Pumpkin Spice Bread

Candied Bacon

Fresh Strawberries with a Dip

*R*EADY TO BREAK AWAY from the usual patterns of entertaining? Invite some of your favorite people to a summertime brunch! It's a delightful way to get together with your friends—and it's very easy on you! This menu is actually suitable for any time of the year. Simply substitute whatever attractive fruit is in season for the Fresh Strawberry Dip.

Begin the festivities with delicious California Sunshine. This gay and refreshing drink is made with equal amounts of freshly squeezed orange juice and pink champagne—hence the rosy-orange color. Pour it from a pitcher into your prettiest chilled goblets or stemmed wine glasses.

Eggs Benedict is always an elegant dish. The combination of poached eggs, ham, English muffins and hollandaise sauce is thoroughly satisfying without being too heavy. Happily, it is not really difficult to serve if you prepare all of the individual ingredients ahead of time. Besides our regular hollandaise recipe, we have included a simple Blender Hollandaise—both are excellent. Of course, the final assembly of the Eggs Benedict must be done at the last moment.

The recipe for our moist, spicy pumpkin bread was given to us by Betty Lou Port, a dear friend and a marvelous cook. Like most quick breads, this one is easy to make and freezes perfectly. Betty Lou serves the bread on a wooden board with a crock of whipped cream cheese to spread on the warm, fragrant slices. It truly melts in your mouth!

Candied bacon is heavily coated with brown sugar, baked flat in the oven, then served at room temperature. The sweet, smoky flavor is surprising.

Along with the eggs pass a platter of long-stemmed strawberries with their fluffy white dip after everyone has been served. They will cause a sensation!

Give some special meaning and memories to a midmorning occasion. With this combination of delights, you can't help but inspire a lovely day!

T I M E T A B L E : If you like, you can make the Pumpkin Spice Bread several weeks ahead and freeze it. We always make two loaves at a time in order to have an extra one on hand for another occasion.

The day before your party, cook the bacon as directed and store it, covered, at room temperature. Mix the dip for the strawberries and place it in its serving dish. Press plastic wrap into the surface to prevent a skin from forming, then keep it in the refrigerator until ready to serve. Poach the eggs in the usual manner, but undercook them slightly and store as directed. Chill the pink champagne and place your goblets or glasses for the California Sunshine in the freezer or refrigerator until serving time.

On the morning of your party, squeeze and chill the orange juice. Toast and lightly butter the English muffins as you fry the ham or Canadian bacon. Wrap both the muffins and the meat in foil packages to stay warm in a low oven. Up to 2 hours before your guests arrive, make the Hollandaise Sauce. And set it over warm (not hot!) water in your double boiler. Slice the olives or truffles and set them aside until needed. Wash and dry the strawberries quickly, then arrange them on their serving dish with the bowl of dip in the center.

Just after your guests arrive mix the pink champagne and orange juice in a pitcher. (The sound of the "pop" adds a festive touch.)

Fifteen to twenty minutes before serving, place the foil-wrapped loaf of Pumpkin Spice Bread into the oven to warm. Then begin assembling the Eggs Benedict. After everybody has been served eggs, bread, and bacon, pass the whole strawberries with their creamy dip.

There! Very little to do, and you and your friends are enjoying the best brunch ever!

CALIFORNIA SUNSHINE

(8 SINGLE SERVINGS)

1 bottle pink champagne, chilled
1 quart freshly squeezed orange
  juice, chilled

A few drops of Crème de Cassis
  (optional)

Mix all ingredients together in a pitcher. Serve in chilled goblets or wine glasses.

EGGS BENEDICT

(8 SERVINGS)

4 English muffins, split
8 thin slices ham or Canadian
  bacon

8 poached eggs
8 slices truffle, or black olive
Hollandaise sauce (page 85)

Eggs Benedict must be assembled at the last moment, but the individual ingredients may be prepared ahead of time. You may even poach the eggs the day before serving if you undercook them slightly and plunge them into ice water as soon as they are ready. Store them in the ice water in the refrigerator and reheat by transferring them with a slotted spoon to a pan of hot, not boiling, water. Leave them in the hot water just long enough to heat through.

Toast and butter the English muffins and keep them warm, wrapped in foil, in a low oven until you need them. Fry the ham or Canadian bacon slices quickly on both sides and keep them warm, wrapped in foil, in the same oven.

Just before serving, top each muffin half with a slice of ham or Canadian bacon and then with a well-drained poached egg. Pour warm hollandaise sauce over the egg and muffin, then top with a slice of truffle or black olive.

To Make Ahead: Prepare all of the individual ingredients ahead of time as described, and simply assemble them at the last minute.

PERFECT HOLLANDAISE SAUCE

(APPROXIMATELY 2 CUPS)

6 egg yolks
3 tablespoons white wine vinegar
½ teaspoon salt
A generous dash cayenne

6 tablespoons cream or milk
¾ pound (3 sticks) cold butter
½ teaspoon fresh lemon juice

In a glass double boiler, or in a stainless or ceramic pan, beat the egg yolks, vinegar, salt, cayenne, and cream or milk with a wire whisk or a slotted spoon. Set the pan into or over very hot, but not boiling, water. Keep stirring until the sauce begins to thicken. When it coats a spoon, start adding the cold butter about 1 tablespoon at a time. When a piece of butter has completely melted into the sauce, add another piece, and so on, until you have used all the butter. If the sauce seems too thick to you, thin it with a few drops of milk. Stir in the lemon juice, then taste and correct the seasoning.

To Make Ahead: The sauce will stay warm for up to 2 hours, if you leave it over the pan of hot water, off the heat, and cover the top of the container tightly with plastic wrap.

Note: If you expose a hollandaise or béarnaise sauce to too much heat, the yolks will cause the sauce to curdle. This problem is easily solved by beating the curdled sauce, a little at a time, into an extra egg yolk, using a wire whisk. Do not be dismayed if you must resort to this procedure—experts say that the extra yolk can only improve the sauce!

BLENDER HOLLANDAISE SAUCE

(APPROXIMATELY 2 ½ CUPS)

1 pound butter
4 egg yolks
3 tablespoons boiling water
2 tablespoons fresh lemon juice

Dash cayenne
¼ teaspoon white pepper
Salt to taste

Melt the butter over low heat. Place the egg yolks in the container of an electric blender. Cover and run on low speed for 1 minute, while slowly adding boiling water through the center cap. Leave the blender on low speed and add butter slowly through center cap. Then add the lemon juice, cayenne and white pepper until just mixed. Season to taste with salt.

To Make Ahead: This sauce should be made within 30 minutes of serving. Set out all the ingredients in advance. The sauce takes only a few minutes to make.

PUMPKIN SPICE BREAD
(2 EIGHT-INCH LOAVES OR 1 TEN-INCH TUBE)

2 cups granulated sugar
1 cup brown sugar, firmly packed
2 cups (1 one-pound can) pumpkin
1 cup vegetable oil
4 eggs
4 cups sifted all-purpose flour
2 teaspoons baking soda
1 teaspoon salt

1 ½ teaspoon ground nutmeg
1 ½ teaspoon ground cinnamon
¾ teaspoon ground ginger
2 cups raisins
1 cup chopped pecans or walnuts
⅔ cup water
2 teaspoons granulated sugar, to sprinkle over the top before baking

Combine the sugars, pumpkin, oil and eggs in a large mixing bowl and beat until well-blended. Sift together the flour, baking soda, salt and spices; add to the pumpkin mixture and mix well. Stir in the raisins, nuts and water. Spoon into two well-oiled 9 x 5 x 3-inch loaf pans or one 10-inch tube pan. Sprinkle the 2 teaspoons of sugar evenly over the top of the batter. Bake at 350° for 60 to 75 minutes or until firm in the center. Let cool in the pan for an hour and then turn out on racks to cool thoroughly. We like it best when served warm with whipped cream cheese.

To Make Ahead: The bread may be made 2 or 3 days ahead. When cool, wrap in foil and store at room temperature. For best flavor, warm before serving. It also freezes perfectly.

CANDIED BACON

(8 SERVINGS)

½ pound commercial bacon
2 cups light-brown sugar, loosely
packed

Nonstick coating spray, for pan

Let the bacon come to room temperature, then cut the pieces in half crosswise.

Spread the brown sugar over a strip of wax paper and press the bacon pieces into the sugar to coat both sides heavily. Keep turning and pressing until each piece is thickly coated. Lay the bacon, with space between slices, on the slotted rack of a broiler pan that has been heavily sprayed with nonstick coating. Bake at 350° for 20 minutes, or until the bacon is cooked and brown. Keep checking it during the final 10 minutes, as it can burn easily. Remove the bacon to a piece of aluminum foil and let cool to room temperature, turning occasionally to prevent sticking.

Serve on a platter, crisscrossed in lattice fashion.

To Make Ahead: Store at room temperature, covered for up to 24 hours.

FRESH STRAWBERRIES WITH A DIP

(8 SERVINGS)

About 24 very large, fresh straw-
berries, with stems
1 seven-ounce jar marshmallow
creme

½ cup mayonnaise
2 teaspoons lemon juice
1 tablespoon orange juice

Buy the best ripe, long-stemmed strawberries that you can find. Wash and arrange them in a serving dish, with a small bowl in the center or next to it for the dip.

Mix three parts marshmallow creme with one part mayonnaise. Thin with lemon juice and orange juice for flavor. Taste and correct the seasoning. Let your guests help themselves by holding a stem and dipping a strawberry into the cream mixture.

To Make Ahead: The dip may be stored in the refrigerator for several days. Cover it tightly with plastic wrap.

A Menu for When the Leaves Fall

French Onion Soup Gratinée

DRY FINO SHERRY

Duck à l'Orange with Sauce Bigarade

HEAVY, ELEGANT BURGUNDY

Wild Rice with Sherry and Duck Livers

Zucchini Doheny

La Salade

Rum Cream Pie

*H*ERE IS OUR FAVORITE menu for crisp autumn evenings, to be enjoyed by candlelight with a pine fire crackling
in the hearth. A centerpiece of fall leaves and gold chrysanthemums
adds a perfect touch to the evening.

Our dinner begins with bowls of steaming French Onion Soup
Gratinée. Ours is a delicious simplified version of the soup once served
in Les Halles, the old market district of Paris where merrymakers used
to gather after midnight for songs and onion soup. We substitute beef-
stock base, available in jars, for homemade beef broth. It's much easier
and the difference is not noticeable. The soup will be very special if
you serve it with a dry Fino sherry.

Duck à l'Orange is always spectacular. Serve these crispy, glazed
ducks on a large platter, sprinkled with shredded orange peel and surrounded by wild rice sautéed with butter, sherry and shallots.

Orange-flavored Sauce Bigarade quite defies description. For this
recipe we recommend that you take a short-cut by using canned beef
gravy as one of the ingredients. The sauce is slightly tart and well-
seasoned, so any canned flavor is undetectable. For the main course,
choose a full-bodied red wine. We enjoy a heavy, elegant Burgundy
with duck.

Zucchini Doheny is named after our friend, Carole Wells Doheny,
who gave us this original recipe. She is a stunningly beautiful woman
who enjoys creating recipes that are nutritious—and this is no exception.

The flavor of the zucchini improves immensely if baked a day ahead and reheated to serve.

La Salade is simple and delightful—fresh greens tossed with our easiest and favorite French dressing. It can accompany the entrée or follow it, as you prefer.

We finish in splendor with chocolate-crusted Rum Cream Pie. It is rich, though light and velvety in texture. There is no fuss to it if you make it the day before serving. It should be served chilled, and, if you wish to plan far ahead, can even be frozen.

What better way to savor the crisp beauty of fall than a richly satisfying fireside dinner with your friends?

T I M E T A B L E : For best flavor you should make the onion soup days ahead of your party and store it in the refrigerator or freezer.

Most of your preparations can be completed the day before the party. Make the Rum Cream Pie and keep it refrigerated, lightly covered with plastic wrap, until serving time. Assemble and bake the zucchini casserole—it tastes much better when reheated. Mix the salad dressing in a jar. For the best flavor, cover and leave it at room temperature. Wash and crisp the salad greens as directed. Cook the wild rice—it will reheat when you sauté it with the sherry, duck livers and shallots. Or, if you must eliminate all last-minute fuss, prepare the wild rice recipe completely, then reheat it in a covered casserole in the oven. The difference will be barely noticeable.

The morning of your party, set and decorate your dining table. Set out your largest platter and soup bowls. Cook the ducks and make the sauce. Both will reheat beautifully. Prepare the garnishes, orange slices and watercress. Toast the bread rounds and grate the cheese for the soup.

After your guests arrive, you need only to reheat the various dishes and toss the salad. It is truly remarkable that such convenience and elegance are combined in the same menu.

FRENCH ONION SOUP GRATINÉE

(4 TO 6 SERVINGS)

2 tablespoons butter or margarine
4 large onions, sliced thin
6 cups rich beef bouillon (canned, homemade, or from bouillon cubes)
¼ cup dry vermouth
2 teaspoons Worcestershire sauce, or more to taste

⅛ teaspoon Tabasco sauce
Brown gravy seasoning (Kitchen Bouquet) to taste, for color and flavor
¼ cup grated Parmesan cheese, or more to taste

TOPPING:

4 to 6 half-inch slices of French bread, buttered and toasted

About 8 ounces grated Swiss, Gruyère, or Monterey Jack cheese

Melt the butter in a large stock pot. Add the sliced onions and sauté over medium-high heat, stirring occasionally, until they are lightly and evenly browned. This will take 10 minutes or longer. Be very careful not to scorch the onions, as any burnt flavor will ruin the soup.

When the onions are lightly browned, add the rest of the soup ingredients, except for the grated Parmesan cheese. Simmer, uncovered, for 30 minutes. The flavor will improve greatly if you now allow the soup to cool, and refrigerate it overnight.

When ready to serve, reheat the soup. Sprinkle in the grated Parmesan cheese and ladle the hot soup into a large ovenproof tureen or individual ovenproof soup bowls. Float the toasted bread on top and spread the grated cheese evenly over the top. Slide the soup under the broiler until the cheese bubbles and is soft, but not browned.

To Make Ahead: Onion soup should be made at least 1 day ahead and and reheated to bring out its best flavor. It will freeze perfectly. Top with cheese and slide under the broiler just before serving.

DUCK À L'ORANGE WITH SAUCE BIGARADE

(4 TO 6 SERVINGS)

1 orange
2 four- to five-pound ducklings
2 small onions, cut in half

2 stalks of celery
Salt

SAUCE:

4 tablespoons drippings from the roasting pan
1 tablespoon red wine vinegar
1 cup orange juice
1 tablespoon sugar
1 tablespoon water
1 ten-ounce can beef gravy, or 1¼ cups of our Diana's Quick Basic Brown Sauce (page 106)
1 bay leaf

1½ tablespoons lemon juice
3 tablespoons red currant jelly
2 tablespoons orange marmalade
4 tablespoons cognac or brandy
2 tablespoons Grand Marnier
1½ teaspoons salt
Pepper
Roux (page 31), or cornstarch to thicken if necessary
A few drops red food coloring

GARNISH:

1 bunch watercress

1 orange, sliced

Remove the outermost peel (called the zest) from the orange with a vegetable peeler, then slice it thin. Or use a special implement called a zester (available in gourmet supply shops. See illustrations). Simmer it for 5 minutes in water to cover in a saucepan. Drain and reserve the peel. Cut off all of the white rind from the orange, remove the sections carefully, cutting between the membranes with a sharp paring knife, and set aside. The rind and orange sections will be used later as a garnish.

To roast the ducks, put 2 onion halves and a stalk of celery inside of each one, and place them on a rack in a roasting pan. Salt the ducks lightly and prick the skin all over with a dinner fork, taking care not to pierce into the meat. This will allow the excess fat to run out from under the skin during the roasting. Roast at 325° for 1½ hours, then increase the temperature to 450° and roast 30 minutes longer. Remove the ducklings to a platter and prepare the sauce. Do not cover the ducks or they will lose their crispness.

In a heavy-bottomed, medium-sized saucepan, put 4 tablespoons of the drippings from the roasting pan, along with some of the crusty brown bits scraped from the bottom. In a measuring cup, have the wine vinegar and orange juice ready. Stir the sugar and water into the drippings. Stir actively over high heat until the fat looks clear, then quickly pour in the juice and vinegar to prevent the sugar from burning—it will sizzle! Add the rest of the sauce ingredients, except for the *roux* and the food coloring, and simmer for 10 to 15 minutes. Thicken with *roux* or cornstarch dissolved in cold water if necessary, and stir in a few drops of red food coloring.

To serve, cut each duckling in half with poultry shears, removing the backbone. Discard the onions and celery. Arrange the ducks on a platter and surround them with watercress and twisted orange slices. Top with the orange sections and the prepared zest (orange rind). Spoon some of the sauce over the ducks and pass extra sauce in a gravy boat.

To Make Ahead: The ducks may be roasted in the morning. Keep them uncovered at room temperature. The sauce may also be prepared in the morning. Reheat the ducks at 300° for 30 minutes. Simply reheat the sauce in a saucepan. Any leftover sauce may be frozen—you may even want to double the recipe so that you will have extra to serve with other roast poultry. Freeze the extra giblets to enrich a stock, or to make duck soup, using the duck carcass.

WILD RICE WITH SHERRY AND DUCK LIVERS
(4 TO 6 SERVINGS)

8 ounces wild rice
1 or 2 duck livers
4 tablespoons (½ stick) butter
3 to 4 tablespoons chopped shallots

⅓ cup pale, dry sherry
Salt
Freshly ground black pepper

Place the wild rice in a kitchen strainer and wash it well by holding it under cold running water for several minutes. Then place it in a large saucepan and add water to cover by 2 inches. Boil for 30 minutes or until tender. Drain and set aside until needed.

Dice the duck liver fine. In a large, heavy skillet, melt the butter and then turn up the heat to high. Add the diced duck liver, the shallots and half the sherry. Cook, stirring, for 1 minute. Then stir in the cooked rice and the rest of the sherry and continue to stir constantly while it heats through. Season to taste with salt, pepper, and more sherry if needed.

To Make Ahead: The cooked wild rice will keep nicely in your refrigerator for several days. Or you may make this recipe completely ahead of time. Reheat it in a covered casserole, sprinkled lightly with water or broth to prevent it from becoming too dry, at 300° for 20 to 30 minutes. It may also be frozen successfully. Thaw and heat as above.

ZUCCHINI DOHENY

(4 TO 6 SERVINGS)

4 medium onions, chopped fine
1 tablespoon butter
2 tablespoons olive oil
¾ cup chopped parsley   ·
6 medium zucchini, sliced
Salt
Freshly ground black pepper

3 medium tomatoes, sliced into
¼-inch slices
About ⅔ cup freshly grated Parmesan cheese, or a combination of Parmesan and mozzarella or Monterey Jack cheese

Sauté the chopped onions in the butter and 1 tablespoon of the olive oil over medium heat until they are soft but not browned. Stir in the parsley and set aside.

Place the remaining 1 tablespoon olive oil in an earthenware or ceramic casserole with a lid. Arrange a layer of zucchini over the bottom and sprinkle it generously with salt and pepper. Top with some onions, then tomatoes, then cheese, sprinkling each layer with salt and pepper. Continue to build up layers in that order, ending with a layer of cheese. Cover and bake at 350° for 30 minutes. Remove lid and bake 10 minutes longer.

To Make Ahead: For the finest flavor this dish should be made a day or two ahead. Let cool and refrigerate, covered, for up to 48 hours. Reheat to serve.

LA SALADE

(4 TO 6 SMALL SERVINGS)

3 heads Bibb lettuce

DRESSING:

⅓ cup vegetable oil　　　　　　　　*Dash garlic salt*
4 teaspoons red wine vinegar　　　 *Salt and freshly ground black*
1 teaspoon Dijon mustard　　　　　　*pepper*
Several dashes Worcestershire
　sauce

Wash the salad greens well, discarding any tough outer leaves. Shake off the excess moisture in a kitchen towel. Wrap all the greens in paper towels and store them in a plastic bag in the bottom of your refrigerator until needed. The small amount of moisture that remains in the paper towels will keep your greens crisp for days. This is the way we prepare all of our salad greens as soon as we bring them home from the store.

Mix all the dressing ingredients together and store at room temperature for up to 24 hours. Any longer and the dressing should be refrigerated—but for the best flavor, do let it come back to room temperature before serving. Do not overdress your salads—it is usually best to use less dressing than you think you need. Then add more if necessary.

To Make Ahead: The dressing may be made well ahead and stored in the refrigerator. Let it come to room temperature before serving. Keep the greens cold, as described, until serving time.

RUM CREAM PIE

(10 SERVINGS)

2½ cups chocolate wafer crumbs*
6 tablespoons (¾ stick) melted
  butter or margarine
6 egg yolks
1 cup sugar

Grated sweet chocolate, to garnish
1 envelope (1 tablespoon)
  unflavored gelatin
2½ cups heavy cream
Scant ½ cup light rum

To make the crust, mix the chocolate crumbs with the butter and press the mixture firmly and evenly against the bottom and sides of an 8- or 9-inch spring-form pan. Bake at 350° for 10 minutes. Chill the crust until ready to fill.

For the filling, beat the egg yolks with the sugar, using a wire whisk or egg beater, until very thick and pale in color. Sprinkle the gelatin over ¼ cup cold water and set aside for 5 minutes to soften. Whip the cream until stiff and set it aside.

Stir the softened gelatin over hot water (the easiest way is just to set the measuring cup into some hot water) until completely dissolved. Add the melted gelatin to the yolk mixture and beat briskly. Now, using a rubber spatula, fold the whipped cream thoroughly into the yolk mixture. Fold in the rum.

Pour the filling into the prepared crust and chill for at least 4 hours. Before serving, remove the spring-form side of the pan and grate some sweet chocolate over the top for decoration.

To Make Ahead: This pie may be completely prepared the day before serving. Store in the refrigerator until serving time. It also freezes very well.

  * Crush the chocolate wafers with a rolling pin, or pulverize them in a blender.

A Winter Wellington

Kir

Paul's Terrine Maison

Beef Wellington

Sauce Périgueux

A CLASSIC RED BURGUNDY or A FINE BORDEAUX

Baked Petits Pois†

-or-

Glazed Baby Carrots

Salade Elegante

Crème Brûlée

SAUTERNE or BARZAC

*T*HIS MENU is a celebration! Go all out on wines, table setting, and flowers—the atmosphere should match the food! Begin your feast with Paul's lovely Terrine, accompanied by an icy Kir, a favorite apéritif. In France almost every restaurant has its Pâté or Terrine Maison. Ours is delicious, as well as convenient, since it will keep for a week in the refrigerator. Serve it in very cold slices on a bed of watercress or lettuce, with lots of warm, crusty French bread. It can be marvelous on a picnic, too . . . "a loaf of bread, a glass of wine, Paul's Terrine, and thou . . ."

The most impressive dish is the Beef Wellington, a roast filet spread with a mixture of mushroom *duxelle* and *pâté de foie*, and encrusted with pastry . . . the ultimate in haute cuisine. Although expensive, it is surprisingly uncomplicated to prepare. Save it for friends who appreciate good food and the love and effort that go into the preparation.

Brown sauce to accompany the beef is usually made by simmering browned veal bones for 12 hours with a long list of flavor ingredients. We were not surprised to discover that our students did not want to go to that trouble and asked for a simplified process. So we have devised a quick, easy recipe, using the same ingredients for flavor. We challenge anyone to taste the difference. Use it without apology any time a French brown sauce is required.

The word Périgueux implies the use of Madeira and finely chopped truffles. Canned truffles are exorbitantly expensive; moreover, we think they have very little flavor when used in such an aromatic sauce. They are overrated for our taste, not to mention our pocketbook. Take our advice and omit the truffles. You will then have a Sauce Madère.

The Cordon Bleu School of Cooking maintains that the filet should be wrapped in a *pâte brisée* (rich pastry dough) rather than the commonly specified puff pastry. This is very good news; puff pastry requires an expert touch, whereas *pâte brisée* is a guaranteed success every time—even in the hands of students inexperienced in the making of dough. The *brisée* also produces a more attractive dish because it doesn't fall apart from the steam while cooking. Serve a simple vegetable to complement this exciting entrée, such as our Baked Petits Pois (page 131), or Glazed Baby Carrots (page 107), or both. Either a classic red Burgundy or a good Bordeaux goes well here.

Our own creative energies have inspired the Salade Elegante. This combination of Belgian Endive, watercress and walnuts is a delightful surprise. We suggest that you serve it European style—after the main course.

Crème Brûlée is our finale. This cold, creamy vanilla custard with its crunchy caramel topping is a classic French dessert. Happily, there is no fuss involved in its preparation—yet it is always an exciting dessert to serve. At one famous restaurant in Paris the waiter cracks the sugar topping at your table, then pours flaming Grand Marnier liqueur along a knife into the crack. It's a real show-stopper—but don't try it yourself! Just crack the topping dramatically at the table. Serve it plain or over fresh fruit. A Sauterne or Barzac might be a splendid complement to the dessert.

This menu is thrilling, not only to eat, but to serve! The joy you will feel when you present your delighted guests with these creations is well worth the extra effort.

TIMETABLE: Basic brown sauce is called for in many French recipes, and you will want to use it to enrich various sauces and gravies so it's a good idea to keep a ready supply in your freezer. We freeze it in ice-cube trays, then transfer the frozen cubes to a plastic bag. When we need the sauce, we place a few cubes in a measuring cup to thaw. We also keep our Basic Creamy French Dressing on hand in the refrigerator—it keeps indefinitely.

The Terrine, the *duxelle* filling for the Beef Wellington, and the assembly of the Baked Petits Pois can all be done several days in advance, or, if you prefer, on the day before your party.

Also on the day before your party, make the dough for the

Wellington and refrigerate it. Brown the filet and refrigerate it as well; it must be cold when wrapped in the pastry. Use the pan in which you browned the roast to make your Sauce Périgueux or Sauce Madère. All you need do is reheat it over a low flame before serving.

Prepare the salad greens and chill the Chablis and the glasses for your apéritif.

Cook the carrots and make the Crème Brûlée on the morning of your party. If made earlier the sugar topping on the crème softens. Wrap the cold filet in the pastry according to directions, up to 2 hours before serving. The peas will cook in the same oven with the pastry-wrapped filet.

Everything is taken care of except the final touches! You should be able to spend all but 5 minutes or so enjoying your guests, knowing that you are about to thrill them with an elegant dining experience.

KIR
An aperitif

(8 SERVINGS)

1 fifth white Chablis   *Crème de Cassis*

Half fill wine glasses with well-chilled Chablis. Flavor to taste with a few drops of Crème de Cassis, a French liqueur made from black currants. Dry vermouth may be substituted for the Chablis, in which case the drink would be called a Vermouth Cassis.

PAUL'S TERRINE MAISON

(8 TO 10 SERVINGS)

1 ½ to 2 pounds fresh pork fat cut from the top of a pork loin and sliced by the butcher into ⅛-inch slices*

Have your butcher grind these all together, twice:

1 pound lean pork
1 pound calf's liver
¼ pound lean veal
⅔ pound fresh pork fat
4 tablespoons (½ stick) butter or margarine

⅓ cup finely minced shallots
1 small clove of garlic, pressed
¼ pound chicken livers
1 cup cognac or brandy
2 tablespoons heavy cream
2 teaspoons lemon juice
1 ½ tablespoons flour
1 egg, beaten
½ teaspoon allspice
2 tablespoons salt
1 teaspoon freshly ground black pepper

Line a 2- to 2 ½-quart terrine (see illustration), bread pan, *pâté* mold, or whatever pan seems appropriate, with the sheets of pork fat (or plain vegetable shortening). The strips may be arranged lengthwise or cross-wise, and they should overlap slightly and completely cover the bottom and sides of the mold. If they are long enough, let them hang over the sides of the mold, and later lap them back over the top of the filling; otherwise, save enough strips of fat to cover the top of the filling completely.

Put the ground meats in a mixing bowl. In a skillet, melt 2 table-spoons of the butter and sauté the chopped shallots and garlic over medium heat for 2 to 3 minutes, taking care that the shallots do not burn. Scrape all this into the bowl containing the meat. In the same skillet, melt the remainder of the butter or margarine and sauté the chicken livers for 2 to 3 minutes until stiffened but not really done inside. Remove them with a slotted spoon and set aside. Pour the cognac or brandy into the pan and bring it to a boil while scraping up any brown bits in the pan (in culinary terms, deglaze the pan). Pour

* A heavy coating of solid vegetable shortening or lard may be substituted, but will not be as authentic.

this over the ground meat. Add all the other ingredients except the livers, and mix together very well, until fluffy and well-blended. It is easiest to use your hands for this!

Pack half this mixture into the lined terrine, pressing it into the corners. Lay the sautéed chicken livers in a row down the length of the mixture. Pack the mold to the top with the rest of the ground meat mixture and cover the top with the remaining strips of fat (or dot with shortening) and seal the top of the mold with foil. Lay a cover or flat pan on top. Set the terrine into a larger pan filled with about an inch of boiling water and bake in a 350° oven for 2 hours or until you can see that any juices are clear and yellow, not pinkish and cloudy.

Remove from the oven and loosen the foil. Set a pan the same size as the one the meat is in on top of the *pâté* and set a heavy object, such as an iron frying pan or a brick, on top to weight it as it cools. This will make the *pâté* smooth and easy to slice. When cool, refrigerate it with the weight still in place until it is completely chilled. The weight may be removed once the *pâté* is cold.

Cut it into ½-inch slices. Serve cold on a plate garnished with watercress and perhaps tiny dill pickles—*cornichons*. Serve with warm, crusty French bread.

To Make Ahead: The terrine will keep nicely for up to a week if tightly sealed in plastic wrap. Do not freeze as this will change its texture entirely.

BEEF WELLINGTON

(8 SERVINGS)

1 whole tenderloin of beef*
1 tablespoon cognac or brandy
2 tablespoons (¼ stick) butter or margarine, melted

1 egg, to brush the crust
3 cups Sauce Périgueux (page 106)
Chopped parsley to garnish

* Order the whole loin tenderloin of beef in advance from your butcher. Ask him to remove the outside membrane and all fat. Have the tail, or small end, turned back and tied to the meat to make the filet an even thickness. Have the meat tied at 1½-inch intervals.

DUXELLE:

1 pound mushrooms
3 tablespoons minced shallots
2 tablespoons (¼ stick) butter or
margarine
1½ teaspoons flour
¼ cup heavy cream
1 teaspoon lemon juice

1 three-ounce can pâté de foie (we
use an inexpensive, truffled va-
riety)
3 egg yolks
2 tablespoons chopped parsley
2 tablespoons cognac or brandy
1½ teaspoons salt
Freshly ground black pepper to
taste

PÂTE BRISÉE (PASTRY CASE):

2 cups sifted all-purpose flour
½ cup sifted cake flour
½ teaspoon salt
1 teaspoon sugar
1½ sticks butter (not margarine),
cool but not too hard

1 egg, beaten
About ⅓ cup ice water
1 egg, beaten with 1 tablespoon
Water, to brush the crust

Sprinkle the beef with 1 tablespoon cognac or brandy and brush with melted butter. Roast at 475° for 15 minutes. Cool and refrigerate until needed. The meat must be cold when wrapped in the pastry.

To make the *duxelle:* Chop the mushrooms and shallots very fine. Melt the butter or margarine in a heavy, noniron skillet and add the shallots. Stir for a minute or two until they are soft, then add the mushrooms and stir to coat evenly with butter. Cook for about 10 minutes over medium heat, stirring now and then, until all the moisture that the mushrooms give off has evaporated. Sprinkle the flour over the mushrooms and shallots and stir well, then stir in the cream and all the other ingredients. Remove from the heat, let cool, and refrigerate until needed.

To make the dough for the pastry case: Sift together the flours, salt and sugar into a large mixing bowl. Add the butter and cut it into the flour with a pastry blender or two knives until the mixture resembles coarse meal. Using a fork, blend in the egg and just enough of the ice water to make a firm dough. Once the dough forms into one ball, *do not knead it.* Set it on a floured board, and with the heel of your hand push it away from you, little bits at a time. Do this twice, then form the dough into a ball, wrap it tightly in plastic wrap, and refrigerate for several hours or overnight.

Two hours before serving, place the dough on a floured board and roll it out into a long rectangular shape ⅛ inch thick. Trim off any excess dough and save it for the decorations. Spread two-thirds of the *duxelle* to the same size as the filet in the center of the rectangle, remove the string from the filet, and lay it on top. Fold the ends of the dough in first, cutting off and reserving any more than an extra inch. Place the rest of the *duxelle* on top of the filet. Then fold in the sides, stretching the dough slightly (it is very elastic) around the rest of the *duxelle* on the filet, overlapping no more than 1½ inches. This will be the bottom side. Set the wrapped filet right side up on a greased cookie sheet. Poke two holes in the top of the dough for vents. Make small rolls of aluminum foil (by wrapping small strips of aluminum foil around a pencil, then removing the pencil). Insert these rolls into the holes to form tiny chimneys which will keep the vents open and allow steam to escape during the cooking. Now cut the reserved dough into any kind of decoration you like. The classic decoration is a long, twisted stem with daisy-type flowers and several leaves. Beat an egg with 1 tablespoon of water and brush the pastry well all over, then decorate with the pastry cut-outs and brush over the decorations (see illustration). Insert a meat thermometer at an angle under one of the decorative leaves into the exact center of the roast.

Bake at about 375° for 30 minutes. It is done when the thermometer reads 135°. If the pastry is not brown enough, increase the heat to 450° for the last few minutes. Or, if the pastry is getting too dark, lower the heat to 350° for the last few minutes. Let the meat rest for 10 minutes before slicing.

To serve, slice at the table into 1½-inch slices. The dough will fall off the meat if the slices are too thin. Spoon over some Sauce Périgueux, or Sauce Madère, and sprinkle chopped parsley over each serving.

To Make Ahead: All the various parts of the Wellington may be prepared the day before and stored in the refrigerator. The filet may be wrapped in the pastry several hours before baking and refrigerated until needed.

SAUCE PÉRIGUEUX

(3 CUPS OR 8 SERVINGS)

½ cup Madeira
¼ cup dry white wine
2 tablespoons minced shallots
3 cups Diana's Quick Basic
  Brown Sauce (below)

1 tablespoon finely chopped
  truffles*
1 tablespoon cognac or fine brandy
2 teaspoons cold butter

In a small saucepan, over high heat, boil the Madeira, white wine and shallots until the liquid is reduced to ¼ cup (or one-third the original volume). Add the Basic Brown Sauce and chopped truffles. If the sauce is too thin, simmer it slowly for a few minutes; it will thicken as it reduces. Set aside.

Just before serving, bring the sauce to a boil. Then, off the heat, add the cognac and butter and stir until the butter has dissolved. This will give your sauce a lovely gloss.

To Make Ahead: This sauce may be made at least a day ahead and reheated to serve. Press plastic wrap into the surface to prevent a skin from forming. Stir in the cognac or brandy and the cold butter just before serving. Any leftover sauce will freeze beautifully.

DIANA'S QUICK BASIC BROWN SAUCE
Sauce Espagnole

(1 QUART)

¼ pound (1 stick) butter or margarine
1 large onion, chopped

2 carrots, chopped fine
¼ cup parsley (or parsley stems),
  chopped
¼ teaspoon dried thyme

* If the truffles are omitted, you have a Sauce Madère.

1 large clove garlic, cut in half and flattened
½ cup all-purpose flour
3 ten-ounce cans condensed beef broth or bouillon
3 cups water
1 cup mixed wine (we use ¼ cup sherry or Madeira, ⅓ cup dry white wine, and the rest a red Burgundy)

1 bay leaf
1 stalk celery, chopped
2 tablespoons tomato paste (freeze the rest for another use)
1 whole clove
1½ teaspoons Maggi seasoning, or Kitchen Bouquet
5 drops red food coloring
2 drops green food coloring
Black pepper to taste

Melt the butter in a 3- to 4-quart heavy-bottomed saucepan. Add the next five ingredients and cook, stirring often, until they start to brown. Stir in the flour and continue cooking, stirring often, until the mixture (or *roux*) turns a light brown color. Be careful not to scorch the flour or it will not thicken the sauce properly. When the flour is light brown, stir in all the remaining ingredients, except the Maggi or Kitchen Bouquet, the red and green food coloring, and the pepper. Bring to a boil, then lower the heat and simmer gently for 40 minutes, stirring occasionally. Strain the sauce and stir in the Maggi or Kitchen Bouquet and the red and green food coloring. Add pepper to taste.

To Make Ahead: It is very nice to have this brown sauce on hand in your freezer to use whenever a French Brown Sauce is called for. We freeze it in ice-cube trays and then transfer the frozen cubes to a plastic bag. The required amount can be thawed quickly. Use the cubes to enrich gravies.

GLAZED BABY CARROTS

(8 SERVINGS)

24 young, tender carrots
Water to cover
1 teaspoon salt
2 tablespoons sugar

¼ pound (1 stick) butter or margarine
1 tablespoon minced parsley to garnish

Peel the carrots. Leave them whole but trim the ends so they will be uniform in size.

Place the carrots in a heavy 4-quart saucepan with water just to cover them. Add the salt, sugar, and butter or margarine. Bring to a boil, then simmer for 10 to 15 minutes until all the water has evaporated and the carrots are glazed with a thick, buttery syrup. Toss the pan gently several times toward the end of the cooking to coat the carrots evenly with the glaze. Garnish with minced parsley.

To Make Ahead: The carrots may be cooked in the morning and refrigerated. Add 2 tablespoons of water to the pan and reheat while tossing gently over low heat.

SALADE ELEGANTE

(8 TO 10 SERVINGS)

4 heads French or Belgian endive
  (not *curly endive*)
1 bunch watercress, leaves only
4 heads Bibb lettuce

1 cup coarsely chopped walnuts
Basic Creamy French Dressing
  (*page 150*)

Set your salad plates in the freezer to chill. Cut the endive in half lengthwise and remove the core. Cut it again, crosswise through the middle, and soak in lukewarm water for 3 minutes or so. This will remove any bitter taste. Remove the leaves from the watercress and discard the stems. Wash the lettuce well and dry it thoroughly. Tear the lettuce into pieces and put it in a clean, damp dish towel along with the drained endive and the watercress leaves. Chill until ready to serve.

Toss all ingredients with the Basic Creamy French Dressing and serve on chilled salad plates.

To Make Ahead: The dressing keeps indefinitely in your refrigerator. The greens can be washed and kept crisp in a towel in the refrigerator for up to 2 days.

CRÈME BRÛLÉE

(8 SERVINGS)

2 cups half-and-half
2 cups heavy cream
8 egg yolks (freeze the whites for
  another use)

½ cup granulated sugar
2 teaspoons vanilla extract
1 cup dark brown sugar
Fresh fruit (optional)

You will need a 6-cup shallow glass dish, ceramic pan, or soufflé dish, and a larger pan filled with hot water to use as a water bath.

In a saucepan, heat the half-and-half and cream slowly, stirring, until hot—do not scald or boil—and set aside. Beat the egg yolks in the baking dish with a wire whisk, adding the granulated sugar gradually until the mixture is light-colored and creamy. Add a little of the hot cream to the yolks to warm them and stir quickly to blend. Add the rest of the hot cream and the vanilla, mixing well. Cover the dish with foil and set it into a pan of hot water. Bake at 350° for about 1 hour and 15 minutes, or until the custard is set—a knife inserted ½ inch from the center should come out clean. Remove from the oven and from the pan of water and chill thoroughly.

Using a large-mesh kitchen strainer, sprinkle the brown sugar evenly over the top of the chilled custard. If the sugar is freshly opened and has no lumps, it may not require this sifting. Set the dish in a bed of ice and place the custard under a *hot* broiler about 4 inches from the heat for 3 or 4 minutes, watching it carefully so that the sugar bubbles all over but doesn't burn. Serve immediately or refrigerate, uncovered, until serving time. Serve the custard as is, or spoon it over fresh fruit.

To Make Ahead: The custard may be made a day or two ahead and chilled. Do not glaze with brown sugar until the morning of serving day at the earliest, as the topping will become liquid if left any longer—still edible, of course, but more like a Crème Caramel.

III

Menus with a European Influence

A Formal French Dinner Party for Four

Chicken Liver Pâté Maison

CHAMPAGNE

Potage au Cresson

Chicken Breasts in Champagne

CHAMPAGNE

Baked Fresh Asparagus

Croissants

Crêpes Suzette

CHAMPAGNE

*T*HIS IS AN EPICUREAN dinner, delicate and pleasing to the eye. Because of its innate elegance, this menu has been a favorite with our students. The preparation involved is not difficult if you take advantage of your freezer, because almost every dish can be made ahead of time.

Buy the most beautiful fruits available for a sugar-frosted centerpiece. Fruits with nonporous skins—lemons, oranges, plums and grapes —will work best. To coat the fruits with sugar, lightly beat 2 egg whites, then brush the white mixture over one piece of fruit at a time. Pour granulated sugar over the fruit, using a bowl to catch the excess. After coating, set each piece of fruit on a rack (taken from your oven) at room temperature to dry for several hours. Then arrange the fruit decoratively in a silver or glass bowl and anchor it in place with toothpicks. For a final touch, add fresh leaves that have been washed and oiled.

We like to serve champagne throughout the evening, but you may serve cocktails with the *pâté* if you prefer. We won an award from *McCall's* Magazine for our recipe for Chicken Liver Pâté Maison. Its true beauty is not its exceedingly fine flavor, but the fact that, unlike most *pâtés*, it freezes without any sacrifice of flavor or texture. We like to pack it into inexpensive earthenware crocks to store in the freezer and use whenever an occasion arises. We admit it is a bit time-consuming and messy to prepare, but it's well worth it!

The dinner begins with a pale-green Potage au Cresson (Cream of Watercress Soup). Ours is subtle and elegant, yet easy to make. As with most soups and sauces, we believe that this actually improves with reheating.

Boned chicken breasts in an exquisite white champagne sauce are sure to please the most discriminating palate. For a lovely garnish, flute large mushroom caps (as illustrated), sauté them, and place one atop each piece of chicken at serving time as garnish. Asparagus, fresh, steaming and buttered, is the perfect complement, along with the flaky croissants available in the frozen-food section of your market.

Making crêpes is a bit tricky and takes some practice. The first attempt can be frustrating, but practicing can be fun, if you do it with a friend. All the practice crêpes may be stored in the freezer for future use. We suggest buying two or three crêpe pans. They are usually inexpensive and crêpes take some time to make, so once you get the knack of it, it's easier to cook two or three at the same time. The crêpes can then be frozen and stored indefinitely.

Crêpes Suzette compete for first place with Grand Marnier Soufflé as the most dramatic dessert of all. Be sure to dim the dining-room lights before you carry them in. Then, at the table, ladle flaming brandy over them. A sensational ending to a divine meal!

T I M E T A B L E : Make the *pâté* several weeks ahead. The recipe makes a larger quantity than you need for this dinner for four. Pack the excess into small crocks to store in the freezer. You will then have some on hand to enjoy whenever you want it. Thaw it overnight in the refrigerator or for several hours at room temperature, but be sure the pâté is well chilled at serving time, or it will become too soft.

We like to have frozen Watercress Soup on hand in 1-quart containers (which provide 4 servings each) so we can thaw it when needed. To serve, thaw, then heat in a heavy-bottomed saucepan, stirring often, over very low heat. Do not let it boil. The optional chopped watercress garnish should be prepared the day of the party.

Make the crêpes well ahead of time and freeze them according to directions. You will have more than you need, so you might want to experiment with other sauces and fillings for your family.

The chicken and its sauce taste best when freshly made, but if you don't want to spend so much time away from your guests, prepare it completely the day before serving. The difference is barely noticeable. When finished, place it in a shallow, ovenproof dish, let it cool, top with mushrooms, then cover with foil and refrigerate. Before serving, slide the foil-covered dish into a 350° oven for about 20 minutes.

On the morning of your party, glaze and arrange fruits for your centerpiece as described in the introduction to this chapter. Set the table with your finest china, silver and crystal. Chill the champagne.

It is not necessary to have a chafing dish or a warmer beside the dining table for the Crêpes Suzette. You can heat the crêpes in their sauce in an attractive pan on top of the stove, then take them to the dining room to flame them with the cognac. Whatever arrangement you use, set out the pan with the butter in advance and premeasure the sauce ingredients in a bowl. Near your place at the table, set the cognac, a ladle, and a small candle or votive light which you will use to heat the cognac before igniting. Review the whole procedure mentally several times so that you will be comfortable with it.

Place the asparagus in its baking dish with butter and seasonings in the morning so that all you need to do is set it in the oven at the proper time. Heat the frozen croissants according to directions.

When serving, it is easiest to arrange the chicken and asparagus on warm plates in the kitchen. Pass the hot croissants after everybody has been served.

CHICKEN LIVER PÂTÉ MAISON

(ABOUT 5 CUPS)

1 pound (4 sticks) butter
1½ pounds chicken livers
1 large onion, minced
½ cup peeled and chopped tart
 apple (about 1 small apple)
3 tablespoons minced shallots
⅜ cup cognac, apple wine, or
 applejack

3 tablespoons heavy cream
2½ teaspoons fresh lemon juice
¼ teaspoon Worcestershire sauce
2 teaspoons salt
⅜ teaspoon freshly ground black
 pepper

Place 2¼ sticks of the butter in the bowl of your electric mixer to soften to room temperature. Wash and dry the chicken livers (using paper towels) and cut them in half. Trim away and discard any greenish bile spots.

Melt ½ stick of butter in a large skillet. Add the chopped onion and cook slowly over medium heat until soft and very lightly browned. Add the chopped apple and the shallots. Cook a few minutes longer, taking care that the shallots do not burn. Using a rubber spatula, scrape this mixture into the container of an electric blender.

Add ½ stick more of butter to the same skillet and melt over medium-high heat. As soon as the foam from the butter begins to subside, add the chicken livers and stir them around for 3 or 4 minutes until they are brownish on the outside but still pink inside. Add the cognac, wine, or applejack and cook, stirring, for 2 to 3 minutes longer. Add this mixture to the ingredients in the blender. Add the cream and blend at the highest speed, forcing the mixture down into the blades with a rubber spatula. When you are sure that the mixture is as smooth as possible, pour it into a bowl and let cool completely to room temperature before proceeding or the texture of the finished *pâté* will be oily.

When the mixture has thoroughly cooled, beat the 2¼ sticks of butter in the electric mixer bowl until it is light and fluffy. Add the liver mixture to the butter gradually, beating well after each addition. Stir in the lemon juice, Worcestershire, salt and pepper.

Spoon the *pâté* into crocks or whatever containers you are using (3 1½-cup soufflé dishes are just the right size for this amount), smoothing the tops as evenly as you can with a rubber spatula or the back of a spoon.

Melt the remaining ¾ stick of butter in a saucepan over low heat, then let it rest for a minute or two off the heat. Skim any milk solids off the top with a ladle, then carefully pour the clear butter into another container, leaving the rest of the milk solids in the bottom of the pan. Pour the clarified butter over the top of the *pâté*. When it hardens it will form a lovely, edible seal.

Chill the *pâté* well before serving with toast rounds or with crusty French bread. If you are serving it in large quantities, set the container into a bed of ice to keep the *pâté* firm and of proper spreading consistency.

To Make Ahead: This *pâté* will keep well for up to 5 days in the refrigerator, and, unlike most other *pâtés*, this one freezes perfectly. Its lasting quality will not be quite as good after having been frozen, so do not keep it more than 2 to 3 days after thawing. Thaw it overnight in the refrigerator, or for several hours at room temperature, but be sure it is well chilled at serving time.

POTAGE AU CRESSON
Cream of Watercress Soup

(3 QUARTS, OR 8 TO 12 SERVINGS)

3 bunches watercress
1 large leek
2 tablespoons butter
2 ribs celery, chopped
1 large onion, chopped
¼ teaspoon salt

2 quarts strong chicken broth, or 8
  cups hot water with 1 three-
  ounce jar chicken stock base
1 pound medium baking potatoes,
  peeled and cut in half
1 cup (½ pint) heavy cream
White pepper to taste

Wash the watercress thoroughly and reserve the leaves from one-third bunch for the garnish. Chop the rest, stems and all. Cut off the green part of the leek and discard along with the tip of the root end. Cut the white part in half lengthwise and riffle each half as you would a deck of cards to see if the leek contains sand and dirt. If you see dirt between the layers, riffle each half several times under cold running water to rinse clean. This is the only way that you can be certain you will not have sand in your soup! When you are sure the leek is thoroughly clean, chop it coarsely.

Melt the butter in a large saucepan or soup pot and sauté the chopped watercress, leek, celery and onion for 4 or 5 minutes or until the onion is limp. Sprinkle with the salt, then cover and simmer for 10 minutes. Add the chicken broth, or water and chicken stock base, and the potatoes. Bring to a boil and simmer, partially covered, for 1 hour.

Ladle 3 cups or so of the soup at a time into a blender container. Blend on high speed until smooth. Pour the blended mixture into a heavy-bottomed saucepan. Add the cream and season to taste with a generous amount of white pepper and more salt if necessary. Bring this mixture just to a simmer, then remove it from the heat.

For an attractive garnish, chop the reserved watercress leaves fine and place them in a kitchen strainer. Hold them under hot running tap water for a minute to blanch them and to remove any bitter flavor. Refrigerate, if desired, until needed. Sprinkle the chopped watercress over each serving of soup.

To Make Ahead: Press plastic wrap into the surface of the soup to prevent a skin from forming. Store in the refrigerator for up to 3 days. Reheat, without boiling, in a heavy saucepan over medium heat, stirring often. We freeze this soup in 1-quart containers of 3 to 4 servings each.

Remove from the freezer on the morning of serving day to let thaw at room temperature.

CHICKEN BREASTS IN CHAMPAGNE

(4 SERVINGS)

This recipe is easily doubled or tripled.

4 small, whole breasts of chicken,
* split, boned and skinned**
¼ cup flour
1 teaspoon salt
½ teaspoon pepper
¼ pound (1 stick) butter

2 tablespoons oil
½ pound mushrooms
1 cup (½ pint) heavy cream
¼ cup champagne**
Salt and pepper, to taste

GARNISH:

8 large mushroom caps
1 tablespoon butter

Juice of ⅛ lemon
Chopped parsley

Place the boned and skinned breasts between two pieces of wax paper and flatten them slightly with the side of a mallet, the bottom of a skillet, a champagne bottle, or any other flat instrument. Place the flour, 1 teaspoon of salt and ½ teaspoon of pepper in a bag and shake the breasts in this mixture, shaking off the excess flour as you remove them from the bag.

In a large skillet with a lid, melt the butter with the oil over medium-high heat. Lightly brown the floured breasts on both sides. Wash the ½ pound of mushrooms quickly under cold running water, rubbing off any sand with your fingers. Dry them immediately so they do not absorb any water, and cut them into quarters through the stem. When the chicken breasts are lightly browned, add the mushrooms to the pan. Cover the pan, lower the heat, and cook slowly for 10 minutes (a little less if preparing this dish the day before serving, as the breasts

---

* It is best to skin and bone chicken breasts using only your fingers instead of a boning knife. Keep running and pushing your index finger along the ribs. The meat will separate from the bones easily.

** You may wish to save ¼ cup champagne from another occasion in the refrigerator for this purpose. It doesn't matter if it has gone flat—the bubbles are unnecessary.

will cook some more while reheating). Uncover the pan and remove most of the excess butter with a spoon. Add the cream and champagne and simmer slowly, uncovered, for 5 to 7 minutes more. Remove from heat.

While the chicken breasts are cooking, flute the mushroom caps with which they will be garnished. Remove the stems and decorate as desired (see illustration). A bar utensil that is used to make twists is a

handy gadget for this and its use requires no practice. Sauté the mushroom caps slowly in a small pan with 1 tablespoon butter and the lemon juice for 2 or 3 minutes. Mushrooms are always enhanced by the addition of lemon juice during the cooking.

To serve, remove the chicken breasts to a warm platter. Season the sauce with salt and pepper to taste. If it has become too thick, thin it with a little milk or cream. Pour the sauce over each breast and top with a mushroom cap. Sprinkle with a little chopped parsley just before serving.

To Make Ahead: The texture of the sauce is not quite so perfect when the dish is made ahead of time and reheated, but only you will notice the difference. It can be made up to 24 hours in advance and reheated in a baking dish, covered with foil, in a 350° oven for 10 to 20 minutes, depending on whether or not the dish has been refrigerated. We do not recommend freezing this.

BAKED FRESH ASPARAGUS

(4 SERVINGS)

About 20 fresh asparagus spears *Salt and pepper*
2 to 3 tablespoons butter *4 thin lemon slices to garnish*

Break off the ends of the asparagus stalks at the point where they snap easily when bent. Use a vegetable peeler to remove the outer skin from the bottom of the stalks only. Arrange the stalks in a single layer in a baking dish and dot them well with butter. Sprinkle with salt and pepper. Cover the dish tightly with a lid or with foil and bake at 325° or 350° for about 20 minutes, or until the asparagus are just tender—test them by piercing the bottoms of two or three stalks with a fork. Garnish each serving with a slice of lemon.

To Make Ahead: The asparagus may be assembled in the baking dish early in the day with butter, salt and pepper. Bake just before serving. The dish may be baked in the same oven with the Chicken Breasts in Champagne.

BASIC CRÊPES

(ABOUT 20 FIVE-INCH CRÊPES)

2 cups milk, or more if needed
4 egg yolks
1½ cups Wondra or other instant-blending flour
Pinch of salt

2 tablespoons vegetable oil
¼ pound (1 stick) butter, clarified*
Additional plain melted butter

It is best to use an iron French crêpe pan measuring 5 inches across the bottom when making the crêpes. These are available in stores that carry gourmet cookware, and are usually not expensive. Season the pan by scouring it with kitchen salt. Heat ¼ inch oil in the pan, and let it cool to room temperature. Wipe out the excess oil with a paper towel. Never wash the pan with detergent; wipe it after each use or rinse in plain water if necessary. Other pans may be used, even Teflon-coated ones, so if you don't wish to invest in the special one described, experiment with what you have on hand.

To make the batter, place the milk, egg yolks, flour, salt and vegetable oil in a mixing bowl and blend well with a wire whisk until smooth. The batter will keep in the refrigerator for several days.

* Melt the stick of butter in a saucepan over low heat, then let it rest for a minute or two off the heat. Skim any milk solids off the top with a ladle, then carefully pour the clear butter into another container, leaving the rest of the milk solids in the bottom of the pan. The clear butter you have obtained is called "clarified butter" and it has many uses. It will not spoil as does plain butter, and it can stand a much higher temperature without burning, so it is better for frying.

To cook the crêpes, place your empty crêpe pan over medium-high heat and allow it to heat until a drop of water will dance on the surface. Wipe some clarified butter inside the pan with a paper towel or pastry brush. Using a 2-ounce ladle, add just enough batter (a little more than 1 ounce), while twisting the pan in a circular motion, to cover the bottom of the pan. Ignore any small holes. It may be a bit difficult at first to get the feel of this, but you'll catch on!

Let the crêpe cook on one side for a minute or two until lightly browned—you should peek underneath using a spatula—then turn it over, using the same spatula, to brown the other side lightly. The first side to brown is the "good" side; the second will look a bit spotty. No matter how expert you become at making crêpes, the first one will usually not be perfect, as it is used to test the heat of the pan and the thickness of the batter. If it seems necessary, thin the batter with just a little milk. We have made the recipe a little thick on purpose, because it is easier to thin the batter than to thicken it.

After the crêpe is cooked on both sides, invert the pan, letting the crêpe fall onto a clean kitchen towel to cool. As the crêpes cool, stack them neatly, brushing plain melted butter (not clarified) between each one.

You will soon develop a rhythm and will find that you can have 2 or even 3 crêpes cooking at the same time. (*Note:* We recommend crêpe-making as a project if you want to quit smoking, because there simply isn't time to stop and light a cigarette—something like the proverbial one-armed paperhanger with the hives!)

When all the crêpes are cooled and stacked, wrap them in foil, 6 or 8 to a package, and store them in the refrigerator or the freezer.

Use your best-looking crêpes to wrap around the filling of your choice, and save the odd-looking ones for Crêpes Suzette—the flaws will not show when you fold them in quarters.

To Make Ahead: The foil-wrapped crêpes may be stored for several days in the refrigerator, or for months in the freezer. You must be sure that they are at room temperature before trying to separate them, or they will tear. If you're in a hurry, warm the package in the oven before separating.

Note: If you plan to use the crêpes for desserts only, feel free to add any seasonings you think are appropriate to the batter, such as 1 tablespoon brandy, 1 teaspoon vanilla, 1 teaspoon grated lemon rind, or 2 tablespoons sugar, etc.

CRÊPES SUZETTE

(4 SERVINGS; DOUBLE OR TRIPLE
THE RECIPE, AS DESIRED)

12 five-inch crêpes (3 per serving)
(see page 121)

2 tablespoons cognac or brandy to
flame the crêpes at the table

SAUCE:

6 tablespoons (¾ stick) butter
2 tablespoons sugar
2 tablespoons orange juice

2 tablespoons Grand Marnier
liqueur
1 teaspoon grated orange rind, or
"zest"*

Melt the butter for the sauce slowly in a chafing dish or any attractive skillet that you can bring to the table. Add the sugar, orange juice, Grand Marnier and orange rind and cook for 2 to 3 minutes until the sauce becomes syrupy. Lay each crêpe individually in the sauce, turning to coat both sides, and fold them neatly into quarters. Let simmer for 1 minute to heat through.

For a dramatic effect at the dining table, turn off the lights in the dining room, leaving only candlelight. In front of your guests, heat the cognac or brandy in a ladle, ignite, and pour it over the crêpes. Rotate the pan as it flames so that all the alcohol will burn off. Serve 3 crêpes to each guest, spooning some of the sauce over each serving.

To Make Ahead: Make and store the crêpes as described in the Basic Crêpes recipe (page 121). Set out all the ingredients and the pan for flaming the crêpes early in the day to save last-minute confusion. Pre-measure the sauce ingredients into a small bowl.

* The fine outer skin of an orange, called the "zest," can be removed in several ways: Use a very fine grater, taking care not to remove the white bitter rind with the peel, or a vegetable peeler to remove just the outermost skin, which must then be chopped; or, easiest of all, there is a a gadget called a zester which can be purchased at gourmet cookware shops.

An Imperial Russian Menu

Frozen Vodka

Caviar Pâté

Mushroom Soup with Cognac

Chicken Kiev

CHAMPAGNE or MEURSAULT

Fried Potato Nests with Baked Petits Pois

Frances Pelham's Paskha

*I*N RUSSIA, when the spring thaws clear the 250,000 miles of lakes, streams and rivers, the whole nation goes on a caviar binge. You can enjoy a binge of your own any time of the year by serving a smooth, fish-flavored *pâté* frosted with black caviar and red salmon roe. With it we like to serve fine Stolichnaya vodka, the bottle encased in a block of ice. The vodka itself doesn't freeze, but becomes thick and syrupy. We present the frozen bottle to our guests resting on a purple linen napkin. Straight vodka, syrupy or not, has the potency of white lightning, so we serve it in very small straight-sided glasses. *Na zdorovie!* (To your health!)

Chicken served in the manner of Kiev is a dramatic entrée. In its native form, however, filled with unseasoned butter, it is fairly bland. Diana's addition of aromatic herbs to the golden pool of butter held captive in a deep-fried chicken breast makes a remarkable taste treat. And since we already have the deep-fat fryer out for the chicken, we are going to innovate a bit on Russian Straw Potatoes, a favorite of the Russian court since Peter the Great. Freshly cut matchsticks of potato are put into a potato-basket deep fryer until golden and are thus transformed into edible bird's nests, which may be filled with hot, tiny peas. The final garnishes on the plate will be watercress, a twist of orange, and perhaps a delicately carved rose made from a steamed beet. Champagne would probably be served with this entrée in Russia. If you prefer a French wine, a chilled Meursault would be an excellent choice.

Russian friends have told us of their childhood winters, months of bleak, bitter-cold greyness during which they looked forward to spring and the Easter celebrations. During the last ten days of Lent, the focal point of every household is the kitchen, where busy hands are baking kulich and pressing paskha, the traditional Easter sweets. Children ask to be told again and again of the array of food that will appear on the table after Easter Mass. Always sure to be included, paskha is a sweet, cone-shaped cheesecake flavored with liqueur and candied fruit. This rather unorthodox version, introduced to us by a non-Russian friend, is so simple to make that we enjoy serving it not only at Easter, but all year long.

You have here an Imperial Russian menu, brought to ultimate simplicity in an American kitchen.

TIMETABLE: The Caviar Pâté will keep for up to 3 days in the refrigerator, but it also freezes beautifully, so make it any time. Thaw and frost with caviar on serving day. A bottle of vodka encased in ice can be used over and over again. When the vodka runs out, simply refill it from a fresh bottle.

Mushroom Soup freezes well or will keep for up to 5 days in the refrigerator.

Paskha is patient. Make it ahead, then remove it from the mold and store, wrapped carefully, in the freezer or refrigerator. It is served chilled.

Chicken Kiev may be prepared up to the cooking point a day in advance and then chilled until time to deep fry. It is even possible to freeze it uncooked, with only a slight sacrifice of texture.

You can place the tiny peas in the casserole with their baking ingredients the day before serving. Slide them directly from freezer to oven when needed.

Fried Potato Nests are tastiest prepared on serving day, and you may as well wait until then because you will be using deep fat to cook the chicken anyway. Fry them the morning of your party. Let cool and leave at room temperature until time to reheat. At the same time, prepare some garnishes for the plate and refrigerate until needed.

The only dish that requires last-minute attention is the Chicken Kiev. It must be deep-fried just before serving.

FROZEN VODKA

We use Stolichnaya, the only imported Russian vodka, for this purpose, to lend a true Russian flavor to the evening. Of course, any brand of vodka may be served in this manner.

Set a full bottle of vodka into an ice bucket or other container, such as a large tomato-juice can. Fill the container almost to the top with water and freeze until solid. Run hot water over the outside of the container to remove the solid block of ice containing the vodka bottle (see illustration). The vodka is now to be poured right from this block of ice —set it on a napkin in a silver bowl to catch the water as the ice melts. If you are careful not to keep it out of the freezer too long, the same ice-encased bottle may be used over and over again and refilled as necessary. It's a good idea to store extra bottles of vodka in the freezer so that when you refill the empty bottle, the vodka is already the proper texture.

CAVIAR PÂTÉ

(2 CUPS, OR AT LEAST 8 SERVINGS)

1 stick sweet butter or margarine
2 seven-ounce cans water-packed tuna, drained
1 tablespoon chives, chopped fine

1 six-ounce jar herring tidbits in wine, drained
¼ teaspoon garlic powder
½ teaspoon sugar
1 tablespoon water

To Decorate and Serve:

1 four-ounce jar black lumpfish	*Parsley*
caviar	*Rye, pumpernickel, or plain bread*
1 four-ounce jar red salmon roe	*rounds*

Melt the butter or margarine and pour it into the container of a blender. Drain the tuna and add it to the butter in about three stages, blending until it is completely smooth. It will be necessary to scrape down the sides of the blender often with a rubber spatula. Add the chives, drained herring, garlic powder, sugar and water and continue blending until there are no visible lumps.

Line a small bread pan (approximately 3 x 5½ inches) or any other plain 2-cup mold with plastic wrap. Spoon the mixture into the mold, then tap the bottom several times against the counter to settle the mixture into the pan and to prevent air holes. Refrigerate for 1 to 2 hours, or until firm.

Before serving, turn the *pâté* out onto a serving plate or board. Spread the sides of the loaf with the black caviar. Drain the jar of salmon roe for 5 minutes in a kitchen strainer to remove excess liquid. Spread the roe on top of the loaf. Surround the *pâté* decoratively with parsley and bread rounds of your choice.

To Make Ahead: The unfrosted *pâté* freezes beautifully or will keep for at least 3 days, tightly wrapped, in the refrigerator. If frozen, thaw it completely before frosting with caviar and roe as described. Frost no earlier than 3 hours before serving.

MUSHROOM SOUP WITH COGNAC

(8 servings)

¾ pound mushrooms	*2 tablespoons chicken stock base*
1 small onion	*(Spice Islands)*
1 stalk celery	*1½ cups (12 ounces) heavy cream*
4 tablespoons (½ stick) butter or	*Salt*
margarine	*White pepper*
¼ cup flour	*Cayenne (ground red pepper)*
4 cups hot water	*3 to 4 tablespoons cognac, to taste*

GARNISH (OPTIONAL):

¾ *cup heavy cream, whipped* ⅛ *to* ¼ *teaspoon paprika*
24 *very thin slices of raw* 2 *tablespoons chopped chives*
 mushroom

Chop the mushrooms, onion and celery together very fine, or put them through a meat grinder. Melt the butter or margarine in a large, heavy pot. Stir in the chopped or ground mushrooms, onion and celery and cook for 10 minutes over medium heat, stirring occasionally. Stir in the flour and cook 2 minutes longer. Remove the pan from the heat and stir in the hot water, chicken stock base and cream. Return the pan to the heat and bring the mixture to a boil, then simmer gently for 30 minutes. Season the soup to taste with salt, white pepper and cayenne. Remove the pan from the heat and add cognac to taste.

   This soup has exceptional flavor. Serve it as is, or top each portion with a dab of whipped cream followed by a few thin slices of raw mushroom. Add a light sprinkling of paprika and chives.

To Make Ahead: Mushroom soup freezes beautifully. It will also keep in the refrigerator for up to 3 days. To preserve the full flavor of the cognac, it is best to add it just before serving.

CHICKEN KIEV
(8 SERVINGS, ALLOWING 2 PIECES PER SERVING)

You should have either a deep-fat fryer or a deep saucepan and a frying thermometer.

8 *whole chicken breasts (small* *Salt*
 ones are best!), split, boned and *Oil or solid vegetable shortening*
 skinned *(Crisco), for deep frying*

SEASONED BUTTER:

½ *pound (2 sticks) butter or mar-* 1 *tablespoon minced shallots, or* 1
 garine *teaspoon minced garlic*
1 ½ *teaspoons fresh lemon juice* 1 *teaspoon dried tarragon*
  4 *teaspoons finely minced parsley*

COATING:

6 egg yolks*   ¾ cup flour
3 tablespoons vegetable oil   1 ½ cups fine, dry bread crumbs

Skinning and boning chicken breasts is not difficult, but does require practice. We find it easiest to do most of the work with our fingers because we are less likely to pierce the chicken meat than when using a boning knife. Most markets carry boned chicken breasts these days, so you needn't bother with this if you don't want to.

Pound the boned and skinned breasts, one at a time, between pieces of wax paper, to ⅛-inch thickness. They may be stacked between layers of wax paper to wait in the refrigerator for up to 24 hours before coating them.

To make the butter filling, mash the butter or margarine well with a large spoon to soften it, then slowly mix in the lemon juice, a few drops at a time. Add the other seasonings and mix well. Place the butter on a piece of aluminum foil and form it into a crude brick or roll and put it in the freezer to harden for at least an hour, or until needed.

When you are ready to assemble the breasts, peel off the top layer of wax paper. Have the wide end of the breast toward you. Sprinkle the meat with a little salt, then place about a tablespoonful of the chilled butter on the wide end. Roll the breast away from you, tucking in all the ends with your fingers. You should end up with a crudely formed roll—don't worry about the shape of it at this point.

Break the 6 egg yolks into a small bowl and beat in the 3 tablespoons of oil. Place the flour on one plate and the bread crumbs on another. Dip each rolled chicken breast into the flour, then pat the flour all over the surface and into any cracks. Shape the rolls gently with your hands so that they are slightly pointed at each end and symmetrical in shape. Using a soft pastry brush, carefully paint the surface of each roll with the egg yolk–oil mixture, taking care to cover all surfaces. Now, set the rolls in the bread crumbs and use a spoon to sprinkle the crumbs over them, coating them completely.

Thirty minutes before serving, heat the oven to 250°. Heat oil or shortening, 3 inches or more deep, to 370° in a very deep saucepan or special deep-fat fryer. Cook no more than 4 of the chicken rolls at a time, lowering them into the fat slowly with a slotted spoon or a deep-fry basket. Fry 4 to 5 minutes until they are well-browned.

The cooked breasts can be kept warm on paper towels in the oven

* Freeze the whites to use for another purpose.

for no more than 10 minutes. Open the oven door slightly and leave it ajar after 10 minutes to keep them 5 minutes longer.

To Make Ahead: The crumb-coated rolls may be stored for up to 18 hours in the refrigerator before frying. They may also be frozen, in which case they should be thawed in the refrigerator for at least 8 hours before frying.

BAKED PETITS POIS

(8 SERVINGS)

3 ten-ounce packages frozen tiny peas (petits pois)
1½ teaspoons salt
1 tablespoon sugar
⅛ teaspoon ground black pepper
4 tablespoons butter or margarine, in a chunk

Place the frozen peas in a heavy 2- to 3-quart casserole with a tight-fitting lid. Top with all the remaining ingredients. Cover with a layer of heavy aluminum foil *and* the lid of the casserole and bake at 350° for 50 minutes. Your oven temperature really should be accurate for this, so it is a good idea to use an oven thermometer and check it periodically. Stir the peas before serving.

To Make Ahead: Assemble all ingredients in their baking dish up to 3 days in advance and store in the freezer. Remove from the freezer an hour before baking.

FRIED POTATO NESTS WITH BAKED PETITS POIS

(8 TO 10 BASKETS)

6 large baking potatoes
1 to 2 quarts vegetable oil or shortening, for frying
Salt

You will need a special wire gadget, available at shops that carry gourmet cookware, designed for frying potato nests (see illustration). It consists of two concentric baskets with handles that clamp together. Before using, season the utensil by setting it into a pot of oil. Heat the oil to 450° to 475°, then turn off the heat and let the basket cool in the oil. Never wash with soap or detergent. It may be rinsed with water if necessary.

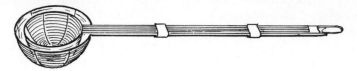

To make potato baskets, shred a potato into matchstick-sized pieces using a shredder, a Mouli saladmaker or a medium grater. Place the potatoes in a mixing bowl and toss them with some vegetable oil to coat them completely. This will prevent the potatoes from turning dark on exposure to air.

Heat some oil to 375° in a deep kettle or deep-fat fryer of at least 3-quart capacity. The pot should be half full to allow room for spattering. Immerse both baskets of the potato fryer in the oil to preheat. Remove the large basket from the oil and hold it over paper towels. Immediately spoon in about a cupful of the shredded potatoes and smooth them lightly to an even thickness with the back of a spoon. Remove the smaller basket from the hot oil and clamp it into the potato-lined basket. Slowly immerse the fryer in the hot oil. Check for doneness in 4 or 5 minutes, or when the oil stops bubbling. When the basket is golden brown and appears fully cooked, remove the utensil from the oil and hit it sharply against the sink several times around the outside edges of the basket. Gently pry out the inner basket. If the potato nest doesn't fall out easily when you turn over the large basket, hit the basket sharply on the top to loosen it. Set the nest on paper towels and salt it generously. Allow it to drain and cool to room temperature while you make another.

Before serving, reheat the nests if necessary and fill with Baked Petits Pois (page 131), or with any creamed mixture, cooked vegetable, or poached or scrambled eggs.

To Make Ahead: Store the cooked baskets at room temperature for up to 12 hours, or wrap them individually and refrigerate for up to 24 hours. You may freeze them, carefully wrapped, for longer storage. To reheat, have the baskets at room temperature on a cookie sheet. Place in a preheated 350° oven for 5 to 10 minutes.

FRANCES PELHAM'S PASKHA

(APPROXIMATELY 16 SERVINGS)

4 eight-ounce packages cream cheese, at room temperature
½ pound (2 sticks) butter (not margarine!), at room temperature
2 cups confectioner's sugar, pressed through a strainer
3 egg yolks
2 teaspoons Grand Marnier, Cointreau, or Triple Sec

¾ teaspoon vanilla extract
1 cup mixed candied fruit (including orange peel, lemon peel, citron, red and green candied cherries), chopped
5 ounces toasted slivered almonds
Grated rind (zest, see note, page 123) of 1 lemon
Fresh berries or other decorations, as desired

Place the cream cheese in the bowl of an electric mixer and beat at low speed until it is completely smooth. Add the butter and continue beating until well combined. Add the confectioner's sugar gradually while beating, followed by the egg yolks, one at a time. Finally, beat in the orange liqueur and the vanilla extract.

Mix together the chopped candied fruit, nuts and lemon rind. Using a large rubber spatula, fold them carefully into the cheese mixture.

You may use an 8-cup charlotte pan, an imported paskha mold, or a medium-size (2-quart) flower pot as a mold for paskha. Line the mold with several layers of wet cheesecloth. Spoon in the mixture and smooth the surface evenly. Tap the mold gently against the counter several times to settle the paskha and to prevent air holes. Refrigerate for at least 4 hours until the mixture is quite firm.

Before serving, unmold onto a serving plate. Carefully remove the cheesecloth. Garnish as desired with fresh berries or candied fruit (see illustration).

To Make Ahead: This dessert will keep beautifully for at least a week in the refrigerator, tightly wrapped in plastic wrap. Freeze if desired.

An Italian Dinner
for a Couple or a Crowd

Low-Calorie Antipasto Vegetables

-or-

Classic Antipasto Tray with Caponata

SOAVE or VERDICCHIO

Veal Parmigiana

VALPOLICELLA or BARDOLINO

Fenwick's Fettucine

Stuffed Mushrooms Florentine

Almond Tortoni

*H*ere's a menu we love. It can be an intimate dinner for a few friends or a magnificent buffet for a large gathering. The table can be set as formally or as casually as the occasion demands. A centerpiece of fruit would be inviting, or a floral arrangement in red, green and white—the colors of the Italian flag. We might take an example from the Italians and provide candlelight and a leisurely pace. They have taught us to dine slowly while enjoying relaxed conversation.

We have included two recipes for antipasto. One is a low-calorie version, simple to make and wonderful to have on hand any time you are dieting. It is a tasty and satisfying snack which keeps beautifully in the refrigerator for a week. More spectacular is a traditional antipasto tray, on which an assortment of Italian salamis and salads surrounds a center of homemade Caponata, an eggplant relish. Cherry tomatoes, scallions, provolone or Gorgonzola cheeses, marinated mushrooms and artichoke hearts complete the picture. As an accompaniment, serve *grissini* or other breadsticks. If you wish to serve wine with the antipasto, we recommend a chilled Soave or Verdicchio—both are easily available and moderately priced. This array of food looks, smells, tastes, and is delightfully Italian—and it's only the beginning!

Our entrée is Veal Parmigiana: tender veal cutlets, breaded and sautéed, then topped with mozzarella cheese and tangy tomato sauce. The meat may be sautéed in the morning and set into a baking-serving dish. All you need to do at the last minute is apply the toppings and place the pan in the oven to heat the veal and melt the cheese. The Italian wines, Valpolicella and Bardolino, both provide a perfect complement to the veal.

Probably the most versatile recipe in this book is our Basic Italian Tomato Sauce. It is slow-simmered and very tangy. We keep a supply of it in the freezer to use for Veal Parmigiana, spaghetti, fried mozzarella, Eggplant Parmigiana, or as a meatless tomato sauce any time.

Fenwick's Fettucine is delicious and easy. It is the original recipe of David Fenwick, one of our favorite pupils. David is a dapper gentleman who teaches his own favorite recipes to our class on the spur of the moment. This creamy noodle dish is splendid served in a chafing dish for a buffet.

Stuffed Mushrooms Florentine are a delightful addition to this and almost any other meal. They are fun and easy to make and can be frozen, then baked without thawing.

Such a hearty dinner is complemented by a light finishing touch. Almond Tortoni is an Italian favorite. Sherry, macaroon crumbs, almond extract and maraschino cherries are folded into sweetened whipped cream and beaten egg whites. The mixture is then spooned into frilled paper cups and stored in the freezer until serving time.

This menu, with its assortment of colors and textures, illustrates the wide variety of Italian cuisine. *Che benissima!*

TIMETABLE: Most of this meal may be prepared in advance and stored in the freezer. We like to double the recipe for the tomato sauce so that we have extra on hand for other uses. Frozen tortoni will keep nicely in the freezer for weeks—it is served directly from the freezer like an ice cream. The Stuffed Mushrooms Florentine can be prepared and frozen, then baked, without thawing, in the same oven as the Veal Parmigiana. Low-Calorie Antipasto Vegetables will keep a week or more in the refrigerator.

On the morning of your party, bread and sauté the veal. Arrange it in an attractive baking dish that can double as a serving dish, then top it with the mozzarella cheese. Set the whole thing aside at room temperature until ready to bake. *Do not cover the meat with the tomato sauce until just before baking or the breading on the veal will become soggy.* Several hours before serving, place the butter, cream, and seasonings for the fettucine in a chafing or serving dish at room temperature. You can arrange the antipasto tray at this time, but do not top the Caponata with parsley until an hour or so before serving, so it will look fresh.

Thirty minutes before serving the main course, slide the frozen Stuffed Mushrooms Florentine into a 375° oven. Follow them 15 minutes later with the Veal Parmigiana and its sauce. Have a large pot of salted water boiling for the noodles. Time their cooking according to directions on the package. When the noodles are done, drain them well (do not rinse) and turn them immediately into the chafing dish or skillet containing the butter, cream and seasonings. Toss them gently, as you would a salad. The heat from the noodles will melt and blend all of the ingredients.

Remove the veal and the mushrooms from the oven. Surround the veal with the stuffed mushrooms and sprigs of parsley. Light the candles, and the scene is set for an Italian feast!

LOW-CALORIE ANTIPASTO VEGETABLES
(8 SERVINGS)

1 head cauliflower, broken into flowerettes
2 stalks celery, cut diagonally into 1-inch pieces
2 large carrots, peeled and cut lengthwise into 2-inch strips
2 green bell peppers, or 1 red and 1 green, cut into 1-inch pieces
1 four-ounce can pitted black olives
1 bunch scallions, white part only, cut into 1-inch pieces

¼ pound fresh green beans, cut in half crosswise
¾ cup red wine vinegar
¾ cup water
3 tablespoons vegetable oil
1 tablespoon olive oil
1 tablespoon sugar
1 to 2 cloves garlic, minced or pressed
1 teaspoon dried oregano leaves
Pinch of sweet basil
Chopped parsley, to garnish
Salt and pepper, to taste

In a large skillet with a lid, combine all the ingredients and bring to a boil. Simmer covered for 5 minutes. Cool, and refrigerate in a large jar or glass bowl for at least 24 hours before serving. Stir the mixture once a day, or whenever you think of it. Serve on salad plates or as part of an antipasto tray. We love to nibble on the vegetables while dieting, or any time, for that matter!

To Make Ahead: These vegetables must be prepared at least 24 hours before serving. They will keep for a week or more in the refrigerator.

CAPONATA

(8 OR MORE SERVINGS)

1 large eggplant, or the equivalent
⅔ cup olive oil
2 medium onions, diced fine
1 cup diced celery
1 one-pound can solid-pack
  tomatoes
⅓ cup wine vinegar
1 tablespoon sugar
2 teaspoons salt

¼ teaspoon pepper
Several dashes of cayenne
1 teaspoon Italian herb seasoning
  (Spice Islands)
1 four-ounce can sliced or diced
  black olives
2 tablespoons capers and some of
  their juice
2 tablespoons pine nuts

Cut the eggplant into ½-inch cubes. Heat ⅓ cup of olive oil in a large, preferably stainless-steel skillet and sauté the eggplant for five minutes, stirring often. It will absorb the oil and change color somewhat during this process. Remove the eggplant to another container.

Add the remaining oil to the same skillet and sauté the onions until they are transparent. Add the diced celery and the tomatoes with their liquid. Cook over medium-high heat for about 15 minutes, stirring often, until the sauce has reduced and is thickened. Stir in the vinegar, sugar, seasonings, and the sautéed eggplant and cook, covered, for 10 minutes. Add the olives, capers and pine nuts and cook uncovered 10 minutes longer. Taste for seasoning and add more vinegar if a sharper flavor is desired. Chill well before serving.

Serve the Caponata as an antipasto, garnished with chopped parsley as a side dish with meat or fowl, or as a deliciously different sandwich filling.

To Make Ahead: Caponata must be made ahead of time to attain its full flavor. It keeps nicely in the refrigerator for 2 weeks and freezes perfectly.

CLASSIC ANTIPASTO TRAY WITH CAPONATA

Arrange any or all of the following ingredients on a large, round tray with the Caponata (page 138) in the center. Serve with *grissini* or other breadsticks and a chilled Soave or Verdicchio.

sliced salami
salads (from an Italian
   delicatessen)
marinated mushrooms
marinated artichoke hearts
cherry tomatoes
black and green olives
squares of provolone or
   Gorgonzola cheese

fresh scallions
fresh radishes with sweet butter
   and salt
smoked oysters or clams
well-drained sardines
carrot or celery sticks
Italian pickled peppers

BASIC ITALIAN TOMATO SAUCE
(8 SERVINGS)

For Veal Parmigiana the sauce should be quite thick (simmer 4 hours). A medium thickness (simmer about 3 hours) would be right to use as a spaghetti sauce.

½ *stick butter or margarine*
¼ *cup olive oil*
1½ *large onions, chopped very*
   fine
2 *to 3 cloves garlic, minced or*
   pressed
1 *six-ounce can tomato paste*
2 *one-pound fourteen-ounce cans*
   whole, peeled Italian tomatoes

2 *bay leaves*
½ *cup parsley, chopped fine*
½ *teaspoon dried oregano leaves*
1 *medium strip lemon peel*
1 *cup dry white wine*
2 *tablespoons Worcestershire*
   sauce
Salt and pepper, if needed

Melt the butter with the olive oil in a large heavy skillet. Sauté the onions and garlic for about 10 minutes, until the onions are very soft but not browned. Stir in all the other ingredients and bring the mixture to a boil. Simmer very slowly over low heat for 3 to 4 hours, stirring occasionally, until the sauce reaches the desired thickness. Remove the pan from the heat and take out the bay leaves and lemon strip. Let cool.

If a completely smooth sauce is required, strain it through a coarse strainer or put it through a food mill. Do not put it in a blender—that would destroy the consistency of the sauce. We almost never strain the sauce; we like the slightly chunky texture the way it is.

To Make Ahead: The sauce will keep in the refrigerator for a week. It freezes perfectly.

VEAL PARMIGIANA

(8 SERVINGS)

8 veal cutlets of equal size, ¼ inch thick
Salt and pepper
4 eggs, beaten
2 cups dry bread crumbs, plain or seasoned
½ cup grated Parmesan cheese

½ to ¾ cup olive oil, or a mixture of olive oil and vegetable oil
1 pound mozzarella cheese, cut into ¼-inch slices
Basic Italian Tomato Sauce (page 139)
Parsley sprigs to garnish

Pound and flatten the veal to ⅛-inch thickness between sheets of wax paper (or have your butcher do this for you). Season lightly with salt and pepper. In a dish, beat the eggs lightly and, in another dish, mix the bread crumbs with the Parmesan cheese. Dip both sides of the veal cutlets into the egg and then into the crumb mixture. Let them stand for 10 minutes before cooking. Heat ½ cup olive oil in a large skillet and sauté the veal until just cooked—no more than 1 or 2 minutes on a side or the veal may get tough. Add more oil if needed. Continue until all the veal has been sautéed.

Place the veal pieces in a shallow, buttered baking dish, preferably an attractive one that can go on the table. Place a slice of mozzarella cheese on top of each piece—the slices of the cheese should be smaller than the pieces of veal, or it will run off the top during the heating. Spoon thick Basic Italian Tomato Sauce over each piece to cover completely and bake at 350° until the pieces are heated through, and the cheese has melted—about 15 minutes if the veal and cheese were at room temperature, a little longer if refrigerated. Garnish with parsley sprigs and serve.

To Make Ahead: The sauce should be made ahead. Sauté the veal pieces and top them with the cheese the morning of your dinner party. Do not spoon on the tomato sauce until ready to bake, or the breading on the meat will get soggy.

FENWICK'S FETTUCINE
(TO SERVE 8 AS A SIDE DISH, OR 4 AS A MAIN COURSE)

¼ *pound (1 stick) butter or margarine*
4 ounces grated Parmesan cheese
1 cup (½ pint) heavy cream
¼ teaspoon Beau Monde seasoning, or other seasoned salt

⅛ *teaspoon ground nutmeg*
⅛ *teaspoon ground white pepper*
½ *pound medium-wide egg noodles (fettucine)*

Several hours before serving, place all ingredients except the noodles into a chafing dish or serving dish to come to room temperature. You may set the pan on top of the pilot light of your range, or over very low heat, so that the butter will melt slightly. When melted, set it aside at room temperature.

Just before serving, cook the noodles according to package directions in lots of boiling salted water with a little oil added to keep the water from boiling over. When the noodles are just tender, drain them in a colander and turn immediately into the sauce ingredients. Toss gently, as you would a salad. Serve immediately, or keep warm in a chafing dish with a water jacket, or on a hot tray.

To Make Ahead: Set out the sauce ingredients several hours ahead to come to room temperature. Cook the noodles and toss with the sauce ingredients within 15 minutes of serving.

STUFFED MUSHROOMS FLORENTINE

(16 MUSHROOMS, OR 8 SERVINGS)

*1 ten-ounce package frozen
  spinach, or 1½ pounds fresh
  spinach, thoroughly washed
16 large fresh mushrooms
10 tablespoons (1¼ sticks) butter
  or margarine
1 large clove garlic, minced
1 large onion, chopped very fine*

*¼ cup fine bread crumbs
1¼ teaspoons salt
⅛ teaspoon pepper
¼ teaspoon dry mustard
¼ teaspoon nutmeg
About 2 tablespoons grated
  Parmesan or Romano cheese*

Cook the spinach until tender in a small amount of unsalted water. Drain it thoroughly, pressing out all the water with the back of a spoon. Purée the spinach in a blender, or chop it very fine with a knife. Set aside until needed.

Rinse the mushrooms quickly under running water, holding them stem side down. Dry with paper towels and remove the stems. Chop the stems fine and set aside.

Melt the butter or margarine in a large skillet, add the garlic and cook for 1 minute, then remove the pan from the heat. Dip the mushroom caps into the garlic butter, turning to coat them well. Place the mushrooms, caps down, on a cookie sheet or in a baking dish. Reheat the remaining butter or margarine in the skillet. Sauté the chopped onion and mushroom stems for 5 to 10 minutes, or until they are very soft but not browned. Add the spinach and all the rest of the ingredients except the cheese, and mix well. Fill the mushrooms with this mixture, mounding it high, and sprinkle with grated cheese. Bake at 375° for 15 minutes.

To Make Ahead: The stuffed but *unbaked* mushrooms may be cooled to room temperature and frozen on the cookie sheet. When they are solidly frozen, pack them into freezer containers. Bake without thawing at 375° for 20 to 25 minutes. They will also keep in the refrigerator for up to 24 hours.

ALMOND TORTONI

(6 TO 8 SERVINGS)

Almond macaroons may be difficult to find in markets, except during Jewish holidays, when they are traditional. If you can't find them, either make some yourself or use other cookie crumbs—the almond extract and ground almonds will provide enough almond flavor.

1 egg white
4 tablespoons confectioner's sugar,
  pressed through a sieve
1 cup (½ pint) heavy cream
1 tablespoon dry sherry or Marsala
1 teaspoon almond extract
½ cup almond macaroon crumbs,
  or other cookie crumbs

6 each red and green maraschino
  cherries, chopped
¼ cup toasted slivered almonds,
  ground in the blender
4 additional maraschino cherries,
  halved, for decoration

Beat the egg white until it forms a soft peak when the beater is lifted, then gradually beat in the sugar and continue beating until the white is thick and glossy. Whip the cream and fold in the sherry or Marsala, almond extract, macaroon crumbs and chopped red and green cherries. Finally, fold in the beaten egg white.

Spoon the mixture into individual paper baking cups—foil ones are nice because they hold their shape. Sprinkle the almonds over the top and place in the freezer for at least 3 hours. Top each tortoni with half a maraschino cherry before serving.

To Make Ahead: Tortoni will keep beautifully in the freezer for weeks. Store the cups in a box in a single layer to prevent them from getting crushed.

A French Country Menu for Six

Quiche Lorraine

WHITE BURGUNDY or BEAUJOLAIS

Stuffed Tomatoes à la Provençale

Marinated Asparagus Salad

Chocolate Mousse Served in Flowerpots

Homemade Coffee-flavored Liqueur

HE CASUAL CHARM of this menu is ideal for most informal occasions. It is equally suitable for a brunch, a luncheon, or a late supper. With advance planning it can be served easily to an after-theater group—your guests will wonder how you did it so easily!

Use natural, loosely woven fabrics for your table linens, and fresh daisies or garden flowers in an earthenware container for a centerpiece. If you have large dinner plates, or "chop plates" as they are sometimes called, use them for the main course; the quiche, marinated asparagus, and stuffed tomato look beautiful together on one plate. A white Burgundy, well chilled, or even a Beaujolais, will make a lovely accompaniment.

Quiche Lorraine (cheese and bacon custard pie) can be served at any time of day. Our own rather unorthodox version, topped with crisp bacon, Parmesan cheese and chopped parsley, is smooth in texture and tangy in flavor. If you lack the confidence to prepare a homemade crust, a frozen pie shell, available at the market, is acceptable, but we do think that our recipe for pie and tart crust (page 147) is foolproof, and we urge you to try it. All good cooks should learn to make crust sometime—few things are more versatile or more economical.

Stuffed Tomatoes à la Provençale is one of the most appetizing vegetables imaginable. It is easily made the day before serving and is a popular complement to almost any meal.

Use our Basic Creamy French Dressing to marinate asparagus—fresh, frozen or canned will do. Or, for a more exotic touch, marinate canned hearts of palm instead. We usually cover our leftover vegetables in this dressing, place them in the refrigerator, and use them the next day as a salad or relish. The dressing is easy to make, and it keeps for a long time in the refrigerator.

Making coffee-flavored liqueur is fun, inexpensive and easy. One year we gave it as Christmas presents in beautiful antique bottles. Naturally, you may use a commercial liqueur if you don't have the time or patience to wait a month for your "private label" to age properly.

Chocolate Mousse adds the final touch of elegance to this meal. We like to serve it in tiny flowerpots topped with green-tinted coconut grass. A perfect daisy is inserted into the center of each one just before serving. The mousse takes only minutes to make and can be stored in your freezer for any occasion, from picnics to ladies' luncheons.

TIMETABLE: The coffee-flavored liqueur must be made, set aside, and allowed to age for at least a month before serving. If you are not planning so far in advance, simply use a commercial liqueur to make the Chocolate Mousse.

Prepare the Chocolate Mousse and fill the tiny flowerpots several days, or even weeks ahead, if you have freezer space to store them. Tint the coconut and press it into the top of each service, then wrap them individually in foil to store. Also prepare and roll out the pie crust well ahead of time and freeze it in the pan to save last-minute hassle. We think it improves with freezing and should always be baked in a frozen state to prevent shrinkage. Basic Creamy French Dressing will keep for weeks, so make it whenever it comes to mind and keep it on hand in the refrigerator for this menu and many other uses.

The day before or the morning of your party, thoroughly drain the canned or freshly cooked asparagus or canned hearts of palm. Place them in a glass or ceramic dish and pour a generous amount of the dressing over them. Set the dish in the refrigerator to allow the vegetables to marinate. The dressing may then be used again for another purpose. Also at this time prepare the Stuffed Tomatoes à la Provençale, but do not bake them until just before serving.

Sometime on the day of the party, partially bake your pie shell according to directions and set it aside at room temperature until ready to fill. Cook the pieces of bacon until crisp and set them aside on paper towels at room temperature. Mix all the quiche filling ingredients, except for the bacon, in a small mixing bowl and refrigerate until needed. If serving a white wine, set it in the refrigerator to chill.

About 45 minutes before serving, preheat the oven, beat the quiche mixture with a whisk to blend it, add half the cooked bacon and pour the mixture into the partially baked pie shell. Set this in the oven to bake for 25 minutes. The tomatoes can go into the same oven about 10 minutes later, so that both will emerge at the same time. Immediately upon removing the quiche from the oven, decorate the top as described, and let both the quiche and the tomatoes cool for 10 minutes before serving. During that time, arrange the marinated vegetables on the dinner plates and sprinkle with parsley. *Bon appétit!*

CLASSIC PIE OR TART CRUST
(1 10-INCH TART SHELL, 2 SINGLE-CRUST PIE SHELLS, OR 1 2-CRUST PIE)

3 tablespoons ice water (or more, depending on the humidity)
2 cups sifted all-purpose flour
¾ teaspoon salt
1 tablespoon sugar (optional, for a sweet pastry)

½ cup solid vegetable shortening (Crisco), or lard
4 tablespoons (½ stick) butter or margarine
1 egg, slightly beaten
4 teaspoons fresh lemon juice

Set out the cold water with an ice cube in it. Sift the flour and salt (and the sugar, if you're making a sweet crust) together into a large mixing bowl. Using a pastry cutter or two knives, cut the shortening and the butter or margarine into the flour until the pieces are the size of small peas. Beat the egg with the lemon juice and ice water. Sprinkle it evenly over the flour mixture while lifting the flour with a knife to distribute the liquid evenly. Then cut the liquid into the flour, using only one knife, until all the flour is moistened. If necessary, sprinkle on a little more ice water. When all the flour is moistened, press the mixture firmly, forming one or two patties of dough. Either roll it immediately or refrigerate it, tightly wrapped, for up to 3 days.

To roll the dough, we find it is easiest to use a pastry cloth and a stockinette cover for our rolling pin. They are sold together in hardware stores. Lacking these, use any floured surface. Sprinkle the surface generously with flour and place the dough on top. Sprinkle the dough often with extra flour as you roll it out from the center. Turn the dough over occasionally while rolling and sprinkle it with more flour. Always roll from the center and stop before you reach the edge of the dough. For flans or tarts which will be removed from their baking dishes before serving, the crust should be rather thick, almost ¼ inch. For pie crusts, it should be thinner. When you are finished with the rolling out, wrap the circle of dough around the rolling pin and lift it over the top of the baking dish. Ease the dough into the pan carefully, taking care not to stretch it. This is very important, because if the dough is stretched it will shrink away from the sides of the pan during the cooking.

Trim away all but ½ inch of the excess dough from around the rim for a pie shell; ¼ inch for a tart. If you are making a pie shell, make a decorative edge by building up an even rim of dough and fluting it with your fingers. Hook it over the sides of the pan to hold it in place during the cooking. The rim of a tart can be folded over and built up just a bit higher than the edge of the pan. Prick the bottom of the shell all over with a fork. If possible, place the pan of dough in the freezer for at least 30 minutes before baking. We have found that the shell will not shrink as much during the cooking if it is frozen at the time it goes into the oven. If you must bake it immediately, line the shell with a piece of aluminum foil and fill it with rice or beans. Bake as directed for half the stated time, then remove the foil and rice or beans and finish the baking. The beans or rice may be saved in a jar to be used again and again for the same purpose.

Preheat the oven to 425°. For a fully baked shell, bake it for 15 to 20 minutes until the shell is a deep golden brown. Peek in the oven after 10 minutes or so. If the edges are browning too quickly, lower the heat to finish the baking. Cool the shell and keep it at room temperature until needed.

To Make Ahead: The dough will keep nicely, if tightly wrapped, for up to 3 days in the refrigerator, or for months in the freezer. It is best not to refrigerate a baked shell, or any pie for that matter, because the crust will lose its flaky quality.

QUICHE LORRAINE
Cheese and Bacon Custard Pie

(6 SERVINGS AS A MAIN COURSE, OR 8 TO 10 SERVINGS AS A FIRST COURSE)

*1 partially baked single-crust pie shell (page 147)**

1 pound thick-sliced bacon
2 whole eggs, plus 2 egg yolks

* To partially bake a pie shell, place it on a cookie sheet for easier handling. Line it with a single layer of aluminum foil, and fill it with beans or rice (which may be used again for the same purpose). Bake at 425° for 10 minutes. Remove the foil and beans, prick the bottom all over with a fork, and continue baking for 5 more minutes. Let the shell cool on the cookie sheet to room temperature.

1 cup (½ pint) heavy cream	*1 teaspoon salt*
½ cup milk	*¼ teaspoon black pepper*
½ cup (8 tablespoons) grated	*1 teaspoon dry mustard*
Parmesan cheese	*1 tablespoon chopped parsley*

Preheat the oven to 375°. Cut the bacon crosswise into ½-inch strips and fry until crisp. Drain well on paper towels and set aside.

Beat the whole eggs and egg yolks together lightly. Add the cream, milk, 6 tablespoons of the Parmesan cheese, salt, pepper, dry mustard and half the cooked bacon. Pour this mixture into the partially baked crust. Bake at 375° for 25 minutes until the custard is almost set—the center should move slightly when you shake the pan gently.

Remove the quiche from the oven and sprinkle the top with the remaining bacon, followed by the 2 remaining tablespoons of Parmesan cheese and the chopped parsley. Let the quiche cool for 10 to 15 minutes before serving.

To Make Ahead: The pie crust may be baked as directed in the morning and left at room temperature. Fry the bacon and leave it at room temperature as well. Mix the filling ingredients and refrigerate them in the mixing bowl until ready to add the bacon and pour into the shell. If you prefer, the quiche may be baked ahead of time, though the texture will not be quite as perfect when reheated. Set the baked quiche aside at room temperature. (Do not refrigerate!) Reheat at 350° for 10 to 15 minutes.

STUFFED TOMATOES À LA PROVENÇALE
(6 LARGE HALVES)

3 large, firm tomatoes	*1 teaspoon dried sweet basil*
Salt	*½ teaspoon dried oregano*
¾ cup dry bread crumbs	*¾ teaspoon salt*
1 medium clove garlic, minced or	*¼ teaspoon freshly ground black*
pressed	*pepper*
½ cup parsley, chopped fine	*¼ cup olive oil*

Cut the tomatoes in half crosswise. Carefully squeeze out and discard the seeds, leaving the sectional walls of the tomatoes intact. Sprinkle the insides of the tomatoes with salt and turn them upside down on paper towels to drain for 5 minutes. This will draw the excess water out of the tomatoes and keep them from becoming soggy during the cooking.

In a small bowl, combine all the other ingredients. Fill each tomato half with the mixture, mounding it slightly. Arrange the tomatoes, sides touching, in an oiled baking dish just large enough to hold them without crowding. Bake at 375° for 15 to 20 minutes, or until the filling is slightly browned. Remove them from the oven and let cool at room temperature for 10 minutes before serving.

To Make Ahead: Stuff the tomatoes up to 24 hours ahead of time. Refrigerate, covered with plastic wrap, until ready to bake. Do not freeze.

BASIC CREAMY FRENCH DRESSING
(1 ½ CUPS, OR 6 SERVINGS)

¼ cup tarragon vinegar
1 teaspoon fresh lemon juice
1 egg, lightly beaten
½ cup heavy cream
⅛ cup olive oil
½ cup vegetable oil
1 clove garlic, peeled and flattened
  with a knife

1 teaspoon Dijon mustard
¾ teaspoon Worcestershire sauce
½ teaspoon sugar
1 teaspoon salt
¼ teaspoon ground white pepper
¼ teaspoon freshly ground black
  pepper

Place all ingredients into a 1-quart, screw-top jar, cap tightly, and shake until well-blended. Or blend the dressing in an electric blender, using a smaller clove of garlic. Chill thoroughly and shake well before using. Be sure you don't serve the garlic clove to an unsuspecting guest!

To Make Ahead: We use this dressing over any combination of salad greens, or to marinate canned or fresh asparagus, hearts of palm, cooked artichokes or any leftover cooked vegetables. It will keep indefinitely in the refrigerator, and is great to have on hand. Do not freeze it.

MARINATED ASPARAGUS SALAD

(6 SERVINGS)

30 to 36 spears well-drained,   *1 ½ cups Basic Creamy French*
  cooked asparagus   *Dressing (page 150), to cover*

Place the asparagus in a glass dish in a single layer. Cover with generous amount of dressing and refrigerate until serving time.

To Make Ahead: This salad may be assembled and refrigerated up to 36 hours before serving. Cover the dish tightly with plastic wrap.

———————

CHOCOLATE MOUSSE SERVED IN FLOWERPOTS

(ABOUT 4 SERVINGS, DEPENDING ON THE SIZE OF YOUR CONTAINERS) *

Small-size red clay flowerpots   *Fresh or artificial flowers*
⅓ cup flaked coconut   *Plastic straws, if using fresh*
3 to 5 drops green food coloring   *flowers*

MOUSSE:

1 six-ounce package semisweet   *2 whole eggs, plus 2 egg yolks*
  chocolate bits   *1 teaspoon vanilla extract*
2 ½ tablespoons Homemade   *¼ cup sugar*
  Coffee-Flavored Liqueur (see   *1 cup (½ pint) heavy cream*
  page 152) or any liqueur of
  *your choice***

Melt the chocolate in the liqueur over very low heat and set it aside. Combine the whole eggs, extra yolks, vanilla and sugar in the container of an electric blender and blend for 2 minutes. Add the cream and blend 1 minute longer. Add the chocolate mixture and blend until smooth.

   If you prefer to serve the mousse in a bowl instead of in flowerpots,

---

* Do not double this recipe, as only the above amounts will fit into the blender at one time. If you require more than the given amount, make the recipe several times—it is not necessary to wash the blender each time and the recipe takes only minutes to make.

   ** If using a strongly flavored liqueur, such as Grand Marnier, use part liqueur and part water to make the 2 ½ tablespoons liquid required for the recipe.

pour it now into the container you will be using. Some people like to serve it in *pots de crème;* however, it has been our experience that men often do not enjoy eating out of dainty little *pots de crème,* so they are best served only to the women.

To serve the mousse in flowerpots, use the smallest red clay ones that you can find. Cover the holes in the bottoms with small pieces of plastic wrap on the inside. Fill the pots with the mousse to within ¼ inch of the top and chill thoroughly. Shake the coconut in a large screw-top jar with a few drops of green food coloring until the coconut is evenly tinted.

Press the tinted coconut into the top of each mousse to give the appearance of grass, and, just before serving, decorate with fresh or artificial flowers. If you are using real flowers to decorate, insert a plastic drinking straw into the center of each mousse and trim it even with the top so it doesn't show. Put the stem of the flower into the straw for support. Artificial flowers can be pressed directly into the surface of the mousse.

To Make Ahead: The mousse must be made at least 3 hours before serving and chilled thoroughly. It will keep for several days in the refrigerator, or for months in the freezer. If frozen, thaw in the refrigerator 2 to 3 hours before serving. We like to take the flowerpots to a picnic directly from the freezer, wrapped in foil to prevent them from becoming too soft en route.

HOMEMADE COFFEE-FLAVORED LIQUEUR
(ABOUT 2 QUARTS)

4 cups sugar
4 cups water
1 two-ounce jar good-quality instant coffee (not coffee crystals)

1 bottle (a fifth) inexpensive vodka
1 whole vanilla bean

Bring the sugar and 3 cups of the water to a boil. Stir to dissolve the sugar. Heat the other cup of water and stir the instant coffee into that. Mix the two liquids together and add the vodka.

Pour the mixture into a very large bottle, or divide it evenly among two or three bottles. Split the vanilla bean lengthwise. Divide it evenly between the bottles and cap tightly. Let stand at least a month before using. Strain the liqueur into an attractive bottle to serve.

To Make Ahead: The mixture should be assembled and allowed to age at least a month before using, so that the flavor can develop fully. As any liqueur, it will keep indefinitely.

A Spanish Paella Party

Sangría

Pepitas

Gazpacho

Paella

POUILLY-FUMÉ, GEWURZTRAMINER or SANGRÍA

Flan

*A*T A SPANISH-STYLE party the table decor can be bold and bright. We enjoy arrangements of vivid paper flowers or real sunflowers in earthenware pots. The Paella itself, with its variety of colorful ingredients, is always the centerpiece—it steals the show!

In Spain the methods for making Paella are infinite. Each region uses different meats, sausages and seafood, depending on what is locally available and in season. All too often Paella is served bland and dry. After much experimentation we have developed a formula that satisfies our American students; it is spicier and has more liquid than most Paellas we've tasted. We love this zesty one-dish meal. Easy to prepare and fairly inexpensive, it is the perfect entrée for a festive casual party. Paella takes its name from the pan in which it is cooked and served. The pans are available in gourmet shops and restaurant-supply houses, and cost from three to twenty dollars. They resemble "forty-niner" gold pans, with the addition of small handles on either side. If you have a large Paella pan, the recipe is easily doubled or tripled for a large crowd.

At many of our parties we serve Sangría in a giant brandy snifter we found at a florist supply shop, but a punch bowl is equally suitable. Just before serving we like to stir in frozen bing cherries and sliced frozen peaches, in addition to the traditional slices of lemon and orange. The Sangría can be served during the cocktail hour or throughout the entire meal. (*Note:* Our wine authority disagrees. He recommends a Pouilly-Fumé or Gewurztraminer—though not Spanish—as they can stand up to the spiciness of Paella.) Roasted pumpkin seeds or Pepitas, available at most markets, can be set out for your guests to nibble on as they sip their Sangría.

Gazpacho is an icy-cold soup which has the flavor and crispness of salad. We love its fresh flavor and usually have it on hand as a summer refresher. In Spain's fine restaurants, bowls of chopped vegetables and croutons are passed as condiments.

One of the most popular desserts in Spain, and in most Latin countries, is Flan, a caramel-coated custard. Its cold and creamy texture is a delightful conclusion to a heavily seasoned meal. It is not really necessary to flame the custard with rum or brandy before serving, but we enjoy the dramatic effect.

If you wish to transport this entire menu to a beach party or cookout, simply substitute fresh fruit and cheese for the Flan, which requires gentle handling. While you are doing the final cooking of the Paella over a campfire, your guests will enjoy the iced Sangría and Gazpacho. We know from experience that this menu, combined with a warm fire, stars and the soft roll of surf, will inspire beautiful memories.

TIMETABLE: Do prepare everything at least a day or two before your party, so you can really enjoy yourself. The Sangría will taste much better if it is allowed to stand for at least 24 hours. Add the chilled club soda and frozen fruit when you are ready to serve.

Mix and refrigerate the Gazpacho, and chill the bowls in which it is to be served. Make the croutons. Purists insist that the chopped vegetables should be added at the last minute, but we think that the flavor is improved if the vegetables are included beforehand and allowed to stand overnight in the refrigerator.

You can prepare the chicken for the Paella in its spicy broth up to 3 days in advance and store it in the refrigerator. Or it can be frozen for a month or more.

The Flan must be made at least 6 hours prior to the time it is served. It will keep well for 2 days if covered with plastic wrap and refrigerated.

The morning of your party, decorate and set the table, assemble the garnishes for the Paella, and set the pumpkin seeds in serving dishes. Just before your guests arrive, put on a flamenco record, slip a rose between your teeth and practice shouting "Olé!"

SANGRÍA

(8 OR MORE SERVINGS)

2 fifths red Burgundy
½ cup Cointreau or Triple Sec
¾ cup cognac or brandy
Juice of 6 oranges
Juice of 2 lemons
1 cup sugar

2 oranges and 1 lemon, sliced
1 ten-ounce package frozen sliced peaches
1 ten-ounce package frozen bing cherries
Chilled club soda to taste

In a large refrigerator container, combine the Burgundy, Cointreau or Triple Sec, cognac or brandy, orange juice, lemon juice and sugar. Chill for several hours—or even better, for several days.

To serve, pour the mixture into a punch bowl or other large serving container. Add the fruit slices, frozen fruit and chilled club soda to taste.

To Make Ahead: Mix is directed and store in the refrigerator for up to 4 days. Add the fruits and club soda just before serving.

GAZPACHO

(8 TO 10 SERVINGS)

1 one-pound fourteen-ounce can whole tomatoes, diced, and their liquid
1 forty-six-ounce can tomato juice
1 cup red wine vinegar
¼ cup olive oil
3 tablespoons Worcestershire sauce
1 teaspoon oregano leaves, crushed
1 clove garlic, pressed

2 green bell peppers, chopped fine
1 medium cucumber, peeled and chopped fine
2 stalks celery, chopped fine
Salt to taste
Tabasco sauce to taste
1 avocado, peeled and sliced thin (optional)
½ bunch scallions, sliced fine
*Homemade croutons**

* To make the croutons, dice 3 to 4 slices of bread. Heat some olive oil in a heavy skillet until it begins to smoke. Add some of the bread cubes, taking care not to crowd them. Stir quickly until they are browned on all sides. Remove them with a slotted spoon and drain on paper towels. Repeat until all bread cubes have been browned.

Combine the first 10 ingredients. Mix well and season to taste with salt and Tabasco sauce. Chill for several hours in the refrigerator.

Serve in chilled soup bowls garnished with slices of avocado (optional). Pass the scallions and croutons at the table for guests to help themselves.

To Make Ahead: Gazpacho, with the vegetables mixed in, keeps well in the refrigerator for 3 days. If stored longer, the chopped vegetables will lose their crisp, fresh quality. The soup may, however, be stored longer and the vegetables mixed in before serving.

The croutons may be made several days ahead and stored in an airtight container at room temperature.

PAELLA

(8 TO 10 SERVINGS)

2 tablespoons olive oil
1 large onion, sliced
2 medium green or red bell
   peppers, sliced

8 to 10 chicken thighs, or other
   chicken parts
½ cup vegetable oil
2 cups raw "converted, parboiled"
   rice (we prefer Uncle Ben's)

SAUCE BASE:

1 cup dry white wine
1 tablespoon red wine vinegar
2 cups chicken broth
2 cups canned beef broth or
   bouillon, diluted according to
   instructions on the label
¼ teaspoon saffron threads*
1 teaspoon paprika

¼ teaspoon ground coriander, or
   crushed coriander seeds
2 bay leaves
⅛ teaspoon cayenne
½ teaspoon dried oregano
½ teaspoon dried thyme
2 cloves garlic, minced or pressed
Salt and pepper to taste

* Ask the manager of your market for saffron. It is usually stored in the dark because it loses strength when exposed to light.

GARNISHES:

Pitted black olives
1 ten-ounce package frozen peas
1 ten-ounce package frozen artichoke hearts, partially thawed
1 large tomato, peeled,* seeded
  and chopped, or 12 halved
  cherry tomatoes
½ pound cooked pork roast or
  ham, cut into 1-inch cubes
½ pound cooked pork sausages of
  your choice

1 pound cooked large shrimp
24 clams or mussels, soaked in cold
  water and scrubbed clean
½ cup toasted slivered almonds
  (optional)
Pimiento-stuffed olives (optional)
1 tablespoon capers, drained (optional)
2 lemons, cut into sixths
¼ cup chopped parsley

You will need a large paella pan or attractive skillet for the final assembly and serving of this entrée.

Heat the olive oil in a small saucepan. Add the sliced onion and bell
peppers and sauté, covered, for 10 minutes. Set aside.

Meanwhile, dry the chicken pieces very well. Heat the vegetable
oil in a large skillet. Brown the thighs lightly on all sides. Pour out all
the fat, then add the sautéed onion and bell peppers to the skillet with
the chicken. Stir in all the sauce-base ingredients and bring to a boil
over high heat. Lower the heat, cover the skillet, and simmer slowly for
15 minutes. You may, if you like, cool this mixture to room temperature,
then cover and refrigerate it until needed, or even freeze it. This is the
complete base for your paella. The rest of the preparation is simply a
matter of assembly.

When you are ready for the final cooking, be sure to have all the
garnishes within arm's reach. About 20 minutes before serving, pour
the chicken and its sauce into a 6-quart or larger paella pan or skillet
and bring to a rapid boil. Sprinkle in the rice and mix it down into the
liquid with the back of a spoon. Let boil rapidly for 5 to 6 minutes. Do
not cover the pan or stir the rice!

Sprinkle on the black olives, frozen peas, artichoke hearts and
tomato. Arrange the ham or pork and the sausages over the top. Press
all these things down into the rice with a spoon, but do not stir the mixture or the rice will become gummy. Reduce the heat and simmer for
10 minutes, or until the rice is tender and most of the liquid is absorbed.
Top with the cooked shrimp and reduce the heat to very low.

* See note, page 25.

Meanwhile, simmer the mussels or clams in ¼ inch of water in a covered saucepan just until they open, for 5 to 10 minutes. (Any clams that do not open after 10 minutes of steaming should be discarded.) Place the open clams on top of the Paella, hinged and open side down. Finish the Paella by topping with any of the optional garnishes and the lemon slices and parsley. Serve immediately with hot French bread.

To Make Ahead: The chicken and its seasoned cooking liquid may be prepared ahead of time at your convenience and either frozen or refrigerated for up to 3 days. Set out all the garnishing ingredients several hours ahead. Do not start the final cooking of the Paella until near serving time. If necessary, you may keep the finished Paella warm in a 200° oven for up to half an hour.

FLAN

(8 SERVINGS)

1 ¾ cups sugar
4 whole eggs, plus 4 egg yolks
2 thirteen-ounce cans evaporated milk

2 ½ teaspoons vanilla extract
¼ cup brandy or rum (to flame the custard at the table)

To cook the flan, you will need a 6- or 8-cup soufflé dish, or charlotte mold, or a 3-quart ovenproof saucepan, and a larger pan containing an inch or more of hot water (water bath) in which to place the custard dish during the cooking. The finished dessert requires a serving plate with a rim which will catch the overflow of caramel when the custard is turned out of its mold.

First, you must caramelize part of the sugar. Use a heavy-bottomed saucepan for this, and if the mold you will be using is ceramic, be sure to preheat it in the oven so that it won't crack when you pour the hot, caramelized sugar into it. Heat 1 cup of the sugar in the saucepan over medium-high heat, stirring constantly, until the sugar melts completely and turns a golden brown. Be careful not to touch the caramel with your hands—it is very hot! Pour the caramel into the mold, then rotate the mold to coat the sides. Set it aside to cool while making the custard. The caramel will harden inside the mold, but will become liquid again during the cooking.

To make the custard, beat the eggs and extra yolks together in a blender or a large mixing bowl. Add the milk, the remaining ¾ cup of sugar, and the vanilla and blend or stir for 20 to 30 seconds. Pour this mixture into the caramel-coated mold, cover, and set it in a larger pan containing an inch or more of hot water. Bake the custard in its water bath at 350° for 1 hour and 15 minutes or longer, until a knife inserted into the center comes out clean. You may refrigerate it until ready to turn it out, or let it cool for 10 to 15 minutes, then invert it carefully onto a serving plate with a rim. Chill for several hours.

At serving time, heat the brandy or rum in a ladle, ignite it, and pour over the Flan. When the flame has died, cut the Flan into wedges.

To Make Ahead: Flan must be made at least 6 hours before serving so that it has enough time to chill thoroughly. It may be prepared up to 2 days in advance and stored in the refrigerator, loosely covered with plastic wrap. Do not freeze.

A German Party
for Eight or More

Sauerbraten

GERMAN BEER

Potato Pancakes

Sweet-and-Sour Red Cabbage

Homemade Applesauce

Homemade Sweet Butter

German Rye Bread†

Vanilla Bavarian Cream
with Fruit and Kirsch

THE HEARTY MEAT-AND-POTATO cuisine of Germany appeals very much to the American palate. The main dishes of this typical German menu are Sauerbraten (*braten* meaning "roast") and Sweet-and-Sour Red Cabbage. Their zesty sweet-and-sour flavors are surprising. Crisp Potato Pancakes and Homemade Applesauce round out the menu.

Although these recipes are designed to feed eight hungry people, they can easily be increased to serve a large gathering because there is no last-minute fussing required. The menu would be especially suitable for serving on a crisp fall evening to an after-the-game crowd.

For decoration we like to fill antique German beer steins with blue, white and yellow field flowers. They liven up our table and add a casual Bavarian atmosphere.

You will want to use your largest dinner plates because there is such a variety of food, and hearty appetites are inevitable.

To serve Sauerbraten it is necessary to plan ahead. The pot roast requires up to 5 days of soaking in a pungent marinade. So buy the meat 5 days before your party and place it in the marinating liquid. Every time you open the refrigerator and see it there, your enthusiasm will be renewed.

Potato Pancakes are delicious with almost any German meal. Our recipe allows you to make the pancakes in advance and store them in the freezer. It's not necessary to thaw them—just reheat them in the oven until crisp.

Reheating plays a large role in this meal. It improves the flavor of the Sweet-and-Sour Cabbage as well as that of the Homemade Applesauce.

Buy a fresh, moist German rye bread to serve with a crock of sweet homemade butter. Making the butter is easy. You don't need a churn, just a blender!

Do serve beer with this meal. For authenticity, you might wish to use one of the many fine imported "lager" or "export" beers from Germany. They are available in most liquor stores.

As a finale, serve a delicate Vanilla Bavarian Cream. This is a delicious molded custard, served with a sauce of fresh fruit marinated in kirsch, a cherry-flavored liqueur.

You have here a menu from a country whose people love to eat. This dinner is robust and guaranteed to fill your guests with *gemütlichkeit.*

TIMETABLE: Five days before you plan to serve your meal, place the meat for the Sauerbraten into the marinade, cover with plastic wrap, and store in the refrigerator. Forget about it until the day of the party. The applesauce will last a long time in the refrigerator, so make it at your convenience.

The red cabbage may also be cooked several days in advance. It will keep in the refrigerator and can even be frozen. At the same time, you can make a large batch of potato pancakes, serve some for dinner, then freeze the rest for your party. It isn't necessary to thaw the pancakes before reheating. Simply spread them on a cookie sheet and place in the oven until they are crisp.

Homemade butter will not keep as well as the commercially packaged brands, so make it within 3 days of serving.

On the day before your party, prepare the Bavarian Cream, and refrigerate it until you are ready to turn the mold out onto a serving plate. This can be done several hours before dessert, but it must be kept chilled until serving time. Spoon the fruit sauce over it just before serving.

Set the table on the morning of your party. Start to simmer the meat 4 hours before serving. At the same time, prepare the fruit sauce for the dessert. Almost everything else on the menu needs only reheating. After that, you're free to enjoy your guests—and your food!

SAUERBRATEN

(8 SERVINGS)

*1 four- to five-pound beef pot
  roast
1 tablespoon salt
½ teaspoon black pepper
2 tablespoons vegetable oil
6 tablespoons (¾ stick) butter or
  margarine*

*3 tablespoons flour
1 tablespoon sugar
2 beef bouillon cubes
8 gingersnaps, crushed or
  pulverized in the blender
Chopped parsley*

MARINADE:

*2 onions, sliced
1 carrot, sliced
1 rib celery, chopped
4 whole cloves*

*4 black peppercorns
1 cup red wine vinegar
2 bay leaves
3½ to 4 cups cold water*

Five days before serving, sprinkle the meat with salt and pepper. Place it in a glass or ceramic bowl—a 3-quart Pyrex casserole is the right size. Cover the meat with all the marinade ingredients. Seal the bowl tightly with plastic wrap and place it in the refrigerator. Now forget about it until serving day.

Remove the meat from the refrigerator 4 hours before serving. Lift it out of the marinade and pat it dry with paper towels. Strain and reserve the marinade. Heat the vegetable oil and 1 tablespoon of the butter in a large skillet, add the meat, and brown it on all sides. When the meat is browned, add the marinade and bring to a boil. Lower the heat and cover the pan. Let simmer slowly for 2 to 3 hours, or until tender when pierced with a fork.

Melt the remaining butter in a small pan. Stir in the flour and sugar and cook, stirring, until this *roux* becomes a good medium brown—the color of coffee with light cream. Add it to the skillet with the meat. Stir in the bouillon cubes. Cover the pan and simmer 15 minutes to an hour longer, until the meat is very tender.

Remove the meat to a serving platter, covering it loosely with a tent of foil to hold in the heat. Skim all the excess fat from the top of the pot juices and discard it—there will be a lot! Bring the juices to a boil over medium-high heat. Stir in the crushed gingersnaps. Use a wire whisk to stir the gravy until it comes to a boil and thickens. Season the sauce to taste, then strain most of it into a sauceboat.

Slice the meat across the grain and arrange on a warm platter.

Strain the remaining gravy over the meat and sprinkle with chopped parsley. Surround the platter with hot Potato Pancakes.

To Make Ahead: Sauerbraten should be cooked just before serving, but any leftovers will reheat beautifully. Heat the leftover gravy to simmering. Add slices of meat and cook very slowly until the meat is just heated through.

POTATO PANCAKES
(ABOUT 16 THREE-INCH PANCAKES)

Vegetable oil for frying   *Bacon grease for flavor*

PANCAKES:

2 cups grated raw potatoes (about   *2 eggs, beaten*
   4 potatoes)   *1 tablespoon flour*
1 small onion, grated   *2 tablespoons chopped parsley*
1 teaspoon salt   *⅛ teaspoon ground nutmeg*
¼ teaspoon black pepper

Mix all the pancake ingredients together. Heat ¼ inch of vegetable oil combined with bacon grease, in a proportion of 5 or 6 parts oil to 1 part grease for flavor, in a heavy frying pan—an iron skillet is especially good for this purpose. Drop rounded tablespoonsful of the potato mixture into the hot oil to form pancakes, and brown them well over medium-high heat. Turn to brown the other side. Drain well on paper towels.

To Make Ahead: The pancakes may be stored in the refrigerator for up to 2 days, or in the freezer between layers of plastic wrap. Reheat them on a cookie sheet in a 375° oven until very hot and crisp. It is not necessary to thaw the pancakes before reheating.

SWEET-AND-SOUR RED CABBAGE

(8 SERVINGS)

1 2½- to 3-pound red cabbage
6 tablespoons (¾ stick) butter or
  margarine
½ cup fresh lemon juice
½ cup dry red wine

3 tablespoons honey, or 4½
  teaspoons sugar
1½ teaspoons salt
½ cup red currant jelly
1 large, tart apple, peeled, cored,
  and grated fine

Wash the cabbage and discard the tough outer leaves. Cut the cabbage lengthwise through the core into quarters. Slice each section crosswise as thinly as possible. Cut the butter into small pieces.

Combine the lemon juice, red wine, pieces of butter, honey or sugar, and salt in a 5- to 6-quart flameproof casserole with a tight lid. Bring the mixture to a boil on top of the stove. Add the cabbage and toss it in the liquid until it is completely coated. Bring the mixture to a boil once more, then cover it tightly and place it in the middle of a 325° oven to bake for 2 hours. You should check the cabbage once or twice during the cooking time and, if necessary, add 1 or 2 tablespoons of water. This will not be required if the lid is really tight.

Add the jelly and grated apple and allow the cabbage to cook, covered, 15 minutes longer.

To Make Ahead: This cabbage tastes much better if made ahead of time and reheated to serve. It stores well in the refrigerator for up to 4 days or in the freezer. When we freeze it, we like to store it in boilable freezer bags, so we don't need to thaw it before reheating.

HOMEMADE APPLESAUCE

(8 TO 10 SERVINGS)

4 pounds cooking apples
¾ cup water
1 teaspoon lemon juice

Sugar to taste
¼ to ½ teaspoon cinnamon

Peel and core the apples, then cut them into eighths. Place them in a heavy saucepan with the water and lemon juice. Cover the pan and cook over medium heat for about 30 minutes, or until the apples are tender. Stir the mixture every 10 minutes, or whenever you think of it.

Add sugar, a little at a time. Apples vary in sugar content, so we cannot tell you exactly how much you will need. Add cinnamon to taste. Serve the applesauce warm or cold.

To Make Ahead: Applesauce will keep very well in the refrigerator for a week or more. It may be reheated before serving if desired.

HOMEMADE SWEET BUTTER
(⅓ CUP OR ABOUT 4 SERVINGS) *

1 cup heavy cream	*3 ice cubes*
¼ cup cold water	

Pour the cream into the container of an electric blender and blend until whipped. Add the water and ice cubes and blend for about 5 minutes, at which time the butter particles will separate from the whey. Pour the contents of the blender through your finest-meshed strainer and knead the butter with the back of a wooden spoon until all the excess liquid has drained off. Press into a crock or serving dish.

To Make Ahead: Homemade butter does not keep as well as the commercial kind, so make it only 2 to 3 days before serving. Let it come to room temperature before serving so it will spread easily.

VANILLA BAVARIAN CREAM WITH
FRUIT AND KIRSCH
(8 TO 10 SERVINGS)

1½ tablespoons (1½ envelopes)	*¼ teaspoon salt*
unflavored gelatin	*1½ cups milk*
⅓ cup cold water	*2 teaspoons vanilla extract*
*6 egg yolks****	*1½ cups heavy cream*
¾ cup sugar	

    * Do not double this recipe. Make it twice to serve eight.
    ** When using only the yolks of eggs, freeze the whites for another use. Some of their qualities are actually improved with freezing.

168

SAUCE:

2 cups strawberries, raspberries, or   *2 teaspoons kirsch*
  sliced peaches   *1 teaspoon sugar*

For this dessert you will need a 6-cup charlotte mold, soufflé dish, or other mold.

Sprinkle the gelatin over the surface of the cold water. Set it aside to soften for 5 minutes while you make the custard.

Using a wire whisk, beat the egg yolks in the top of a double boiler (glass is best, aluminum will not do) until they are light in color. Beat in the ¾ cup sugar and the salt. Bring the milk just to a boil in a saucepan, then beat it gradually into the yolks. Place the mixture over boiling water and cook it for 5 minutes, stirring often. It will not thicken during this time, but the yolks will lose any raw flavor.

Remove from the heat and stir in the softened gelatin and the vanilla. Then chill, stirring once in a while, until it just begins to set. Whip the cream just until it holds a shape, and fold it into the chilled custard mixture. Pour this into a cold, wet mold. Chill at least 3 hours or overnight.

To make the fruit sauce, wash the fruit thoroughly and sprinkle with kirsch and 1 teaspoon sugar at least 3 hours before serving.

To unmold the Bavarian Cream, dip the bottom of the mold briefly into hot water, then break the suction by inserting a knife along the inside edge of the mold as you turn the cream onto a plate. Any imperfections may be smoothed over with a knife. Chill until serving time.

To serve, spoon some of the fruit and its sauce over the top of the cream. Pass the rest of the sauce at the table.

To Make Ahead: Bavarian cream must be made at least 3 hours before serving and allowed to chill. It will keep well in the refrigerator for up to 48 hours. Do not freeze. The fruit can marinate for up to 6 hours.

I V

Menus from South of the Border

A Mexican Fiesta
for Ten or More

Mimi's Margaritas

Frances Pelham's Chile con Queso

Puerco Picante

Rice Casserole with Sour Cream, Cheese and Chilies

Tomato Slices Topped with Guacamole and Bacon Bits

Fresh Fruit Platter with Melon Roses

Lemon Snow Pudding

with Custard Sauce and Raspberries

*M*EXICO IS OUR SECOND HOME. We have lived there, from time to time, in the beautiful mountain town of San Miguel de Allende. This picturesque town, three hours by car from Mexico City, is an artists' colony filled with interesting colonial history. Cooking is considered as much an art as the painting, writing, and crafts taught at the Instituto Allende. Most of the Americans who live there are terrific cooks; in fact, we think there are more fine cooks living there than in any other town of its size anywhere! The fact that people living in Mexico have more leisure time and household help than in the United States probably accounts for their culinary expertise (and, indeed, for this book!). *Comida*, the main meal of the day, is served between one and three o'clock in the afternoon. It is a gigantic, multi-course feast with the emphasis on good food and conversation.

This menu, as brassy and full of fun as a mariachi band, is typical of the town, but it lends itself to the use of American supermarket ingredients. You will find no exotic chilies in these recipes.

Mimi, Diana's mother, makes the best Margaritas on either side of the border. We make them from scratch in San Miguel, since frozen Margarita mix is not available. They taste just as good, but are more difficult to make than the recipe included here. Mimi's secret for making a great Margarita is to add an egg white before whirring the mixture in the blender. The result is airy, smooth-tasting and delicious. Making Margaritas for more than eight people is tedious unless you have someone to help you. For a larger crowd, beer would be the best choice. If serving outside, you would be smart to fill a large tub or wheelbarrow with ice to keep the bottles of beer chilled. Guests can help themselves. *Salud!*

Our dear *amiga*'s recipe for Chile con Queso is the best chafing-dish dip ever. Serve it any time with cocktails—you don't have to save it for a Mexican meal. If you have any left over, use it for a great omelette filling.

The main course is best served buffet style. Decorate the table with gay paper flowers and brightly colored napkins. If you have pottery, now is the time to use it—your fine china will be too formal for such a lively and casual party.

Puerco Picante is a true Mexican "chile," different from anything your guests have tasted before. It really should be made a day or two before serving (a blessing to the hostess). We like to complement it with a casserole of rice, cheese and green chilies, along with a salad of tomato slices topped with guacamole and bacon. A fruit salad using papaya, pineapple and coconut is authentically Mexican and will soothe fiery palates.

And Lemon Snow Pudding supplies the cool, refreshing taste one craves after a spicy meal. It is an old-fashioned dessert given a new personality when topped with fresh berries. It is made up to 48 hours ahead, then spooned ice cold and shimmery onto serving plates, topped with a vanilla custard sauce and surrounded by berries.

These unique and exciting recipes combine perfectly for a sensational party menu. No surprise—our Mexican neighbors have always celebrated their many holidays (thirty or more per year!) with all kinds of festive company food. *Qué bueno!*

TIMETABLE: You can make the Chile con Queso 2 days before your party and refrigerate it. Before serving, reheat it in a double boiler and pour it into a chafing dish with a water jacket. If you are serving margaritas, salt the rims of the glasses as directed and place them in the freezer or refrigerator until needed.

Make the Puerco Picante 1 to 3 days before the party. It will reheat easily and the flavor will improve greatly. Also make the rice casserole and reheat it in the same oven.

The day before or on the morning of your party, prepare the Lemon Snow Pudding and its Custard Sauce. Cover the pudding loosely with plastic wrap and leave it in the refrigerator. Press some plastic wrap into the surface of the sauce to prevent a skin from forming. Cook the bacon pieces for the tomatoes and set them aside at room temperature.

The guacamole should be made no more than 2 hours before serving. Slice and top the tomatoes with the guacamole and arrange them on a parsley-lined platter. Cover them with plastic wrap and refrigerate until ready to place on your buffet table. The fruit platter should also be arranged no more than 2 hours before serving. Everything is in order—enjoy a fiesta in your own home!

MIMI'S MARGARITAS
(3 GENEROUS DRINKS)

The addition of the egg white is Mimi's secret! It cuts the acidity of the lime juice, making the frothiest and smoothest-tasting Margarita north of the border! Only 3 can be made at one time, so it will be necessary to make 4 or more batches of these.

1 cut lime and coarse salt (kosher salt) for the glasses
1 six-ounce can frozen Margarita mix
6 ounces (¾ cup) tequila

½ ounce (1 tablespoon) Cointreau or Triple Sec (or Blue Curaçao for a turquoise-colored drink)
1 egg white
4 ice cubes

Rub the rims of large wine glasses with the cut lime and dip them in coarse salt to coat the rims decoratively. Keep the glasses in the freezer or refrigerator until you are ready for them.

Just before serving, blend all the other ingredients in an electric blender until smooth.

FRANCES PELHAM'S CHILE CON QUESO
A Chafing Dish Dip

(12 OR MORE SERVINGS)

This also makes a terrific omelette filling.

*1 green bell pepper, chopped very
    fine*
1 tablespoon butter
*1 can cream of mushroom soup,
    undiluted*
*½ pound fresh mushrooms, sliced
    and sautéed in 2 tablespoons
    butter*
*¾ pound sharp Cheddar cheese,
    cubed*

*¼ pound Velveeta cheese, cubed,
    for smoothness (or use Mon-
    terey Jack, or all Cheddar)*
*1 pound bay shrimp, fresh or
    canned (optional)*
*½ of a 4-ounce can diced green
    chilies (or more to taste), or
    1 fresh or canned jalapeño chile,
    seeded and chopped*
¼ teaspoon or more garlic flakes
Salt and white pepper, to taste

Sauté the chopped green pepper in the butter in the top part of a double
boiler over direct heat. Add all the other ingredients, then place over
boiling water and cook, stirring occasionally, until the cheeses are completely melted. Transfer the mixture to a chafing dish with a water
jacket or to a cheese fondue pot. Serve with tortilla chips or potato
chips for dipping.

To Make Ahead: This can be made 3 or 4 days ahead and refrigerated.
Reheat to serve in a double boiler.

PUERCO PICANTE

(12 SERVINGS)

*7 to 9 pounds lean pork shoulder
    roast*
1 teaspoon salt
*2 tablespoons commercial mixed
    pickling spices*
*1 tablespoon whole cumin seeds
    (comino), or ground cumin*

*1 teaspoon whole black pepper-
    corns*
1 teaspoon oregano leaves
5 cloves garlic, pressed
*2 tablespoons dark-red chile
    powder*
*½ of a three-ounce jar Mexican
    chile powder (Gebhardt's)*

3 eight-ounce cans tomato sauce
2 tablespoons (¼ stick) butter or
　margarine

1 large onion, chopped fine
2 cups canned chicken broth (or
　more)

Trim all fat from the pork and cut the meat into 1-inch cubes. Using an electric blender, grind together the salt, pickling spices, cumin, peppercorns and oregano. Place these spices in a mixing bowl with the garlic, chile powders and tomato sauce. Cover the bowl and set the mixture aside while you brown the meat.

　　Melt the butter or margarine in a large pot. Add the meat and brown very slowly, stirring it occasionally, until most of the liquid the meat gives off has evaporated—this will take about an hour. Add the chopped onion and sauté until transparent. Stir in the sauce mixture and chicken broth and simmer for about 2 hours until the meat is tender. If the sauce becomes too thick, add a little more chicken broth. Serve with rice or buttered noodles.

To Make Ahead: The flavor will improve greatly if the pork is made ahead and either refrigerated or frozen, then reheated to serve. Reheat, covered, at 350° for about 30 minutes or until thoroughly heated.

RICE CASSEROLE WITH SOUR CREAM, CHEESE AND CHILIES
(AT LEAST 10 SERVINGS)

6 cups cooked rice (white or
　brown)
3 cups sour cream
Salt and pepper
1 four-ounce can diced green
　chilies*

1 pound Monterey Jack cheese,
　coarsely grated
8 scallions, chopped with part of
　the green included
1½ cups grated Cheddar cheese,
　for the topping

Place one-third of the cooked rice in a well-greased, ovenproof serving dish of 4-quart capacity. Spread 1 cup of the sour cream over the rice and sprinkle generously with salt and pepper. Sprinkle with half the chiles, the Monterey Jack cheese and chopped scallions. Repeat the

---

* Canned chilies can vary in hotness. You may wish to taste them before using and add more if you love the flavor of chilies.

layers in the same order. Finish with the last third of the rice and the sour cream. Sprinkle with salt and pepper and top with grated Cheddar cheese.

Bake at 350° for about 20 minutes, or until the cheese is melted and the rice heated all the way through.

To Make Ahead: The casserole may be stored, baked or unbaked, in the refrigerator for 3 days.

TOMATO SLICES TOPPED WITH GUACAMOLE AND BACON BITS

(10 SERVINGS)

6 strips thin bacon, diced and
  cooked until crisp

5 large tomatoes

GUACAMOLE:

3 ripe avocados, seeded
  and diced
2 tomatoes, peeled,* seeded and
  diced
¼ medium onion, chopped fine

1 tablespoon fresh lemon or lime
  juice
1 small, hot chile, minced, or
  Tabasco sauce, to taste
Salt and pepper to taste

Cook the bacon and set it aside at room temperature.

No more than 2 hours before serving, gently combine all the guacamole ingredients. Remove the tops and bottoms from the whole tomatoes, then cut each one into two thick slices. Top each slice with the guacamole mixture, mounding it slightly. Arrange the tomato slices on a parsley-lined platter and refrigerate until needed.

Just before serving, warm the bacon pieces and sprinkle over the top of the guacamole.

To Make Ahead: The guacamole should be mixed not more than 2 hours before serving because it tends to darken on standing. The bacon and the tomato slices may be prepared in the morning.

* See note, page 25.

FRESH FRUIT PLATTER WITH MELON ROSES

(10 TO 12 SERVINGS)

5 or 6 bananas
1 cup mayonnaise
2 tablespoons fresh lemon juice
¾ cup grated coconut
2 fresh pineapples cored and cut
    into 12 spears each

4 fresh papayas, peeled and sliced
2 baskets fresh strawberries,
    washed
3 fresh oranges, peeled and sliced
2 ripe cantaloupes, to make melon
    roses (as illustrated below)

Cut the bananas in half lengthwise, then cut each half into 2 pieces crosswise. Thin some mayonnaise with a little fresh lemon juice. Dip the pieces of banana into the mixture. The lemon juice will keep the bananas from discoloring on standing. Roll the bananas in the grated coconut to coat them completely.

Prepare and arrange all the remaining fruit decoratively on a large platter.

To Make Ahead: The fruit should be prepared and arranged on the platter not more than an hour before your guests arrive. Refrigerate until serving time.

LEMON SNOW PUDDING WITH CUSTARD SAUCE AND RASPBERRIES

(10 TO 12 SERVINGS)

This dessert is beautiful served in a crystal bowl, then spooned into champagne glasses and topped with sauce and berries.

PUDDING:

3 tablespoons (3 envelopes) plus 1   *¾ cup fresh lemon juice*
  teaspoon unflavored gelatin   *2 tablespoons lime juice*
¾ cup cold water   *9 egg whites*
3 cups hot water   *Dash lemon juice or cream of*
2 cups sugar   *tartar*

CUSTARD SAUCE:

½ cup (1 stick) butter or   *9 egg yolks, lightly beaten*
  margarine   *1 cup boiling water*
¾ cup sugar   *2 teaspoons vanilla extract*

GARNISH:

1 thin slice lime   *1 pint fresh or frozen (thawed)*
Grated rind (zest, see note page 123)   *raspberries, or other berries*
  from 1 lemon, to sprinkle on top

Sprinkle the gelatin evenly over the ¾ cup cold water and allow to soften for 5 minutes. Stir the softened gelatin into 3 cups hot water along with the sugar, lemon and lime juice. Stir until the gelatin and the sugar are completely dissolved. Place the mixture in the refrigerator to chill until it is almost set, or, if you are in a hurry, place the bowl in a pan of ice and water. Stir the mixture often if using ice water, only occasionally if using the refrigerator.

Meanwhile, separate the eggs and place the whites in the clean, grease-free bowl of your electric mixer. Let stand until at room temperature. Add a few drops of lemon juice or a couple of dashes of cream of tartar to give them more volume when they are beaten.

When the gelatin mixture is almost completely set, beat the whites just to stiff peaks. Beat the gelatin mixture with a whisk until it is frothy. Thoroughly fold in half the beaten egg whites. Then fold in the other half thoroughly. Pour the mixture into a glass serving bowl (or a 2½-

quart mold if you prefer) and chill in the refrigerator until firm—at least 1 hour.

Serve with the following sauce: Melt the butter in the top of a double boiler over direct heat. Remove the pan from the heat and beat in the sugar. Beat in the egg yolks, then add the boiling water gradually while beating with a whisk. Place the mixture over boiling water and cook, stirring almost constantly, until thickened to a sauce consistency (about 5 minutes). Stir in the vanilla and immediately pour the sauce into a serving dish to stop the cooking. If it seems too thick, thin it with a little milk. Before storing the sauce in the refrigerator, press some plastic wrap into the surface to prevent a skin from forming.

Just before serving, garnish the top of the pudding with a thin slice of lime and some lemon zest. To serve, spoon the pudding into tall champagne glasses. Top with sauce and fresh or frozen raspberries.

To Make Ahead: Both the pudding and the sauce may be made 2 days in advance. Cover the Snow Pudding loosely with plastic wrap and store in the refrigerator. Press plastic wrap into the surface of the sauce to prevent a skin from forming and store it in the refrigerator. For best flavor, serve the sauce at room temperature. Prepare or thaw the berries just before serving.

A Merry Mexican
Brunch for Six

Fresh-Fruit Daiquiris

Huevos Diablos

Mexican Black Beans

Toasted Rolls and Corn Tortillas

*O*N LAZY WEEKENDS we enjoy entertaining friends and houseguests with this carefree menu. If we happen to have the sauce for the eggs and the beans in the freezer, there is no work involved at all.

Everybody loves the Fresh Fruit Daiquiris, so easy to make that you can turn the blender over to your guests and let them experiment with different fruits. Bananas, peaches, strawberries, apples, pineapples—singly or in combination—all yield a drink so luscious and refreshing that it's even great without the rum!

Huevos Diablos is a delectable dish of eggs baked in a spicy tomato and Parmesan cheese sauce. We discovered it on the menu of our favorite of all hotels, the Villa Santa Monica in San Miguel de Allende, Guanajuato. Whenever we serve it we are reminded of the inn's charming owner, Betty Kempe, and her daughter, Kiki Johnson, and of our early morning walks through the unbelievably lush, beautiful French Park that separated our house from the inn.

There the eggs are served with hot tortillas and Mexican bolillos, which are very similar to French rolls but heavier. We substitute French rolls, which are split lengthwise, buttered, and toasted. These are used to mop up the marvelous sauce, which should be relished down to the last drop.

Black beans, cooked in the Mexican style, make a tasty side dish, and, garnished with small rings of red onion or red and green bell pepper, they are a feast for the eye. We enjoy them either plain or spooned into a hot tortilla with some shredded lettuce for a do-it-yourself taco.

Here you have a *muy macho* menu that could easily become the weekend specialty of the man of the house.

TIMETABLE: The black beans are at their best when reheated, so make them at your convenience. They freeze beautifully.

The sauce for the Huevos Diablos may be made in large quantities and stockpiled in the freezer to be used whenever you want it.

The rest of the menu is last-minute but easy. About 30 minutes before serving, place the beans in a 350° oven to reheat. Add the eggs in their sauce to the same oven about 10 minutes later. Split, butter, and brown the rolls quickly under the broiler. Heat the tortillas, wrapped airtight in aluminum foil, in the same oven with the eggs and beans. Set out the fruits and other ingredients for the daiquiris and there you are! *Fantástico!*

FRESH-FRUIT DAIQUIRIS

(2 OR 3 SERVINGS)

Let your guests use their imaginations for fresh-fruit combinations. Our own favorite is one banana and half a fresh peach. Leave the peach skin on—it gives the drink a rosy hue. Omit the rum for party-poopers! You will have to make 3 or more batches of these as needed.

3 ounces light rum
3 ounces "sweet-and-sour mix" (a lemon-flavored liquid available at liquor stores)

2 ripe bananas, or 1 large, ripe peach (pit removed), or 2 cups fresh strawberries, or other fruit combinations
Approximately 8 ice cubes

Place all the ingredients in the container of an electric blender. Blend until smooth and slushy. Serve immediately.

HUEVOS DIABLOS

(6 SERVINGS)

2 tablespoons (⅛ cup) olive oil
1 large onion, minced
1 forty-six-ounce can tomato
   juice, or vegetable juice cocktail
1 teaspoon Worcestershire sauce
¼ teaspoon garlic salt

A good dash of cayenne
1 cup packaged grated Parmesan
   cheese (do not grate fresh
   Parmesan for this purpose)
6 large eggs
1 tablespoon butter
Paprika

To Serve:

6 or more French rolls, split,
   buttered, and toasted, or 12 hot
   corn tortillas

It is best to use individual casseroles or ovenproof soup bowls of about 2-cup capacity for baking and serving these eggs. A shallow 2-quart casserole may be used instead—in which case, regular soup bowls may be used for serving.

Heat the olive oil in a heavy saucepan over medium-high heat. Sauté the onions until they are transparent and just beginning to brown. Stir in the juice, Worcestershire, garlic salt and cayenne. Bring the mixture to a boil, lower the heat, and simmer, uncovered, for 30 minutes.

Just before baking the eggs, stir all but 1 tablespoon of the Parmesan into the hot sauce and pour the mixture into the baking dish(es). Break the eggs gently into the sauce. Dot each egg with butter and sprinkle the tops with the remaining Parmesan and a bit of paprika for color. Bake, uncovered, at 350° for 10 to 20 minutes, depending on the size of the containers, just until the egg whites are set.

Serve with toasted French rolls or tortillas for mopping up the sauce.

To Make Ahead: We keep this sauce on hand in the freezer at all times —so handy for weekend mornings, for quick suppers, and for houseguests.

MEXICAN BLACK BEANS

(ABOUT 2 QUARTS, OR 6 TO 8 SERVINGS)

1 one-pound package black beans
1 teaspoon baking soda
¼ cup olive oil
2 large onions, chopped
1 large garlic clove, pressed
1 green bell pepper, chopped fine
1 red bell pepper, chopped fine
1 bay leaf

¼ teaspoon each black pepper,
cumin, leaf oregano, and dark
chile powder
1 one-pound can whole tomatoes,
broken up into pieces
1½ teaspoons salt
Black pepper or cayenne to taste

TO GARNISH:

Thin rings of purple onion, and/
or thinly sliced rings of red and
green bell pepper

Wash and carefully pick over the beans. Place them in a heavy-bottomed saucepan with enough cold water to cover them by 1 inch and let soak overnight or for at least 8 hours. The beans will absorb some of the water.

Replenish with more water to a depth of 1 inch. Add the baking soda—do not add salt at this point as it will toughen the beans. Bring the beans to a boil over medium heat, skimming away any foam that rises to the top. When the foam has stopped rising, simmer the beans for about 35 minutes or until they are tender.

Meanwhile, heat the olive oil in a large, heavy skillet. Sauté the chopped onions until they have browned slightly. Add the garlic, green and red bell peppers, bay leaf and spices and sauté for 3 or 4 minutes. Set aside.

When the beans are tender, the water should be almost but not completely absorbed. Stir in the onion-pepper mixture and the tomatoes and simmer for about 30 minutes. Then stir in the salt, taste for seasoning, and add more black pepper or some cayenne if you want a spicier taste. Do not worry if the mixture seems a bit watery—it will thicken considerably on reheating.

Place the beans in an ovenproof serving dish. Cool and refrigerate or freeze.

Reheat the casserole of beans, thawed if it has been frozen, at 350°

for about 30 minutes or until the beans are hot. Longer heating will not harm them. Garnish with onion and/or pepper rings just before serving.

To Make Ahead: For finest flavor these beans should be cooked at least 1 day before serving. They may be either refrigerated or frozen. If frozen, thaw overnight in the refrigerator.

A California-Style Mexican Buffet for Twelve

Mexican Sangría

Nachos

King Crab Enchiladas

Fresh Corn Tamales

Chilies en Nogada

Brandied Papaya Fruit Salad

Helado y Nieve

(Ice and Snow)

$\mathcal{W}$E LOVE MEXICAN FOOD and serve it often when we entertain casually. Our friends enjoy the relaxed, friendly atmosphere such a menu provides. It can be great fun to experiment with Mexican dishes because there are no rigid rules to follow as in the cuisines of other countries. Ingredients are usually easily obtained throughout the United States.

We present in this chapter a sparkling and colorful menu that can be adapted to the season of the year and to your mood. Eliminate the Fresh Corn Tamales if fresh corn is out of season, or one of the other main-course dishes if the menu is too elaborate for your needs.

The mellow Sangría of Mexico is not nearly as potent as that of Spain because no brandy or cognac is added. Instead, the pitcher is lavishly garnished with large, green sprigs of fresh mint and the combination of wine, fruit and flavorings is allowed to blend for several hours. The addition of the mint makes the drink especially smooth and refreshing. Be sure to make enough Sangría to serve throughout the meal.

The inspiration for the Nachos and the King Crab Enchiladas came from dishes we discovered on the menu of an elegant Mexican restaurant overlooking the busy yacht harbor in Newport Beach, California. After working out the recipes and adding a few flourishes of our own, we were particularly pleased with the results—imaginative variations on typical Mexican food.

Nachos are fried tortilla wedges, or *tostaditas*, topped with two kinds of cheese and dabs of well-seasoned refried beans, sprinkled with minced hot chilies and baked. The whole dish is quickly assembled and provides an exciting hors d'oeuvre for any casual party.

The enchilada recipe is surprisingly easy. Other meats, and even cheese, may be substituted for the crabmeat in the filling because the sauce is really the key to success. We hope you will have as much fun as we do inventing combinations for fillings and garnishes to use with this tasty sauce.

Chilies en Nogada is a distinguished dish which originated in Puebla, where it is traditionally served on St. Augustine's Day (August 28) and the Mexican "Fourth of July" (September 15). The colors of the component parts—green chilies, white sauce and red pomegranate seeds—are those of the Mexican flag. The appearance and exceptional flavor of the meat-stuffed chilies will delight your guests. The extraordinary version included here was taught to us by a vivacious and witty San Miguel hostess, Maggie García. We have warm memories of the cooking classes that were conducted in San Miguel de Allende, Mexico, in 1971, for the benefit of the local orphanage.

There is no satisfactory substitute for fresh corn on the cob in making Fresh Corn Tamales, so if you develop a great liking for them be sure to make plenty when fresh corn is in season to store in your freezer.

We learned after one hilarious experience that the corn of Mexico is enormously different from the variety grown in the United States, so we have adapted this recipe to use the tender, plump kernels of American corn.

Tamales are time-consuming to make, so seat yourself comfortably with a friend or in front of the television and go to work. Admiring your accumulated handiwork, you will feel justifiably proud of the effort. Do save some tamales in the freezer to serve with holiday dinners, as is traditional in Mexico. They are delicious with either turkey or ham.

A Brandied Papaya Fruit Salad looks as beautiful as it sounds. It could be served as a dessert but is even more spectacular served as a salad on the same plate with a spicy entrée.

Helado y Nieve is our own invention for a busy day. Party-givers appreciate this glamorous dessert because it can either be made in advance or prepared simply in front of guests. Softened vanilla ice cream and pineapple sherbet are whipped together with different orange-flavored liqueurs and grated orange and lemon rinds. The luscious mixture is then presented mounded high in champagne glasses.

So here you have a unique Mexican-style feast that you and your guests will long savor.

Timetable: Preparations for this party should begin three days in advance. There is much to be done and you will enjoy the work more if it is spread out over several days.

If possible, make the corn tamales at the height of the corn season, when corn is inexpensive and at its peak. Freeze the tamales to use throughout the year. They thaw quickly and are an adventurous addition to many a menu. The preparation of this dinner will be simplified considerably if these are already on hand.

Three days before the party, fry the tortilla chips, cool and store them in an airtight container at room temperature. Discard the oil in the skillet and use the same pan for making the meat filling for Chilies en Nogada. Then cool and refrigerate the meat.

Two days ahead, make the enchilada sauce and the refried bean mixture for the Nachos. Store both in the refrigerator.

If you will be serving dessert directly from the freezer, prepare it now and freeze in serving dishes.

Buy the cooked crabmeat and make the filling for the enchiladas on the day before the party. Roll them and refrigerate as directed in the recipe. Prepare the oranges and pineapple for the salad and allow them to marinate in the refrigerator. Peel the chilies—if using fresh ones—for the Chilies en Nogada and refrigerate them. Set the buffet table, get out all serving dishes and glassware, and ready your home for the festivities.

In the morning, prepare the papaya boats and refrigerate them in a plastic bag. Make the sauce for the Chilies en Nogada and leave it at room temperature; seed the pomegranate and refrigerate the seeds for last-minute garnishing. Chop the jalapeños for the Nachos and cube the two cheeses. Prepare the Sangría. Thaw the tamales. The afternoon should be free for your own activities and some rest.

About 2 hours before guests arrive, allow the bean mixture, the enchiladas and the chilies for the Chilies en Nogada to come to room temperature. Chop the scallions and set out the sour cream for the enchilada garnish. Stir the Sangría, add the mint, and—if you like it chilled—refrigerate until serving. Set out all the ingredients needed for the final assembly of each dish and mentally rehearse the finishing touches. Heat the meat filling for the Chilies en Nogada in a small skillet, cover, and set aside. The filling will stay warm enough for serving Finish preparing the Papaya Fruit Salad, arrange attractively on a serving plate, and refrigerate.

After your guests arrive, assemble the Nachos and preheat the oven. The Nachos need only 10 minutes in the oven.

About 20 minutes before serving, reheat the reserved enchilada sauce, pour it over the enchiladas, and slide them into the oven. Steam the tamales. Finish assembling the Chilies en Nogada. All the dishes should now be ready to serve at the same moment.

One last thing before you join your guests. If you plan to prepare the dessert in front of them, allow the ice cream and sherbet to soften during the meal.

MEXICAN SANGRÍA

(2 GALLONS)

8 oranges	*2 cups confectioner's sugar*
2 lemons	*2 gallons red Burgundy*
8 whole cloves	*5 or 6 large sprigs of fresh mint*

Wash and thinly slice the oranges and the lemons. Place them in several large glass pitchers or a punch bowl, along with the whole cloves and the confectioner's sugar. Cover with the Burgundy and set aside at room temperature for at least 6 hours. Two hours before serving, stir the mixture well and add the sprigs of mint. Chill at this point, if desired.

Serve Mexican Sangría plain or over ice. You may wish to garnish each serving with a small sprig of fresh mint.

To Make Ahead: The ingredients should be combined and allowed to mellow for at least 6 hours. Insert the fresh mint not more than 2 hours before serving or the wine will discolor it.

NACHOS

(12 SERVINGS)

8 corn tortillas	*5 ounces sharp Cheddar cheese,*
About 2 cups vegetable oil or lard,	*cut into ½-inch cubes*
for frying	

5 ounces Monterey Jack cheese, cut into ½-inch cubes

2 to 3 canned jalapeño peppers, or more to taste, rinsed, seeded and minced

REFRIED BEAN MIXTURE:

¼ pound sharp Cheddar cheese, coarsely grated or chopped
2 tablespoons butter or margarine
1 one-pound can refried beans

1 bunch scallions, sliced, including some of the green tops
1 four-ounce can diced green chilies
Dash of garlic powder (optional)

Cut the tortillas into eighths and allow them to dry for several hours at room temperature or in a 200° oven for at least 20 minutes. Heat about ¼ inch oil or lard in a large skillet. Fry the tortilla pieces, a few at a time, until they are crisp and golden, turning them with kitchen tongs. Drain well on paper towels. These fried chips are called *tostaditas*.

To make the refried bean mixture, melt the ¼ pound Cheddar cheese with the butter in a heavy-bottomed saucepan over very low heat. Stir constantly to prevent burning. When the mixture is smooth and completely melted, stir in the beans, scallions and chilies. Taste and season with a bit of garlic powder. Let cool.

You will need an ovenproof baking dish, such as a ceramic quiche dish, for heating and serving the Nachos. Make a layer of *tostaditas* on the bottom of the dish. Cover with some of the cheese cubes, a sprinkling of chopped jalapeños, and small (¾-inch) dabs of the bean mixture. Top with more *tostaditas*, cheese, jalapeños, beans, etc., until all the ingredients have been used, finishing with a layer of cheese.

Bake at 350° for about 10 minutes, or until the cheeses have melted. Let cool for a minute or two before serving. Allow guests to help themselves with their fingers, and provide plenty of napkins.

Any leftover bean mixture you might have will make a delicious dip if heated and thinned with canned or bottled taco sauce. Reheat it in a double boiler.

To Make Ahead: The tortilla pieces may be fried in advance and stored in an airtight container at room temperature for several days. The bean mixture will keep well for a week in the refrigerator or for months in the freezer. Cube the cheese a day or two in advance and store it in a plastic bag. Assemble and bake the nachos just before serving.

KING CRAB ENCHILADAS

(12 ENCHILADAS)

1 pound Alaska king crabmeat
1 pound Monterey Jack cheese,
coarsely grated
2 bunches scallions, sliced, includ-
ing some of the green tops (1
bunch for the filling and 1
bunch to garnish the top)

Vegetable oil
12 corn tortillas
1 sixteen-ounce container sour
cream

BASIC ENCHILADA SAUCE:

½ cup (1 stick) butter or mar-
garine
½ cup flour
4 ten-ounce cans red chile
enchilada sauce (not labeled
"hot")

3 cups chicken broth (homemade
or canned)
¼ teaspoon oregano
¼ teaspoon ground cumin
2 teaspoons chicken stock base
(Spice Islands)

First make the enchilada sauce. Melt the butter in a heavy-bottomed skillet. Stir in the flour and cook, stirring, over very low heat for 3 to 4 minutes. This cooking for the *roux* prevents the sauce from having a raw, floury taste. Do not allow the flour to burn, though it is all right if it colors slightly. Remove the pan from the heat and let cool for a minute or so. Stir in the enchilada sauce and the chicken broth.

Return the pan to the heat and bring the sauce to a simmer while stirring with a wire whisk. Add the herbs and chicken stock base and let simmer over very low heat for 10 minutes, stirring often. If the sauce seems thin, continue simmering a few minutes longer. Set aside, covered.

Make the filling by shredding the crabmeat with your fingers, then combining it in a mixing bowl with the grated Monterey Jack cheese and half the scallions. Mix well to blend.

Heat ¼ inch of oil in a small skillet. Dip one tortilla at a time into the hot oil for a few seconds to soften it, then dip it into the enchilada sauce. Stack the tortillas on a plate as you finish dipping.

Place some of the filling mixture in the center of each tortilla and roll it up securely. Place the rolls, seam side down, in an ovenproof baking and serving dish, taking care that they are at least ¾ of an inch apart.

Just before baking, reheat the remaining enchilada sauce and pour it evenly over the top of the enchiladas. Bake at 350° for 15 to 20 minutes, or until the cheese is melted and the sauce is sizzling around the edges of the pan. Before serving, top each enchilada with a large dab of sour cream and a sprinkling of the remaining sliced scallions.

To Make Ahead: The sauce may be made days or even weeks in advance and either refrigerated or frozen. The tortillas may be rolled around the filling up to 24 hours ahead, covered, and refrigerated. Remove them from the refrigerator an hour before baking. Reheat the sauce and pour over the enchiladas just before baking. Enchiladas do not freeze successfully.

FRESH CORN TAMALES

(ABOUT 36 SMALL TAMALES)

4 large ears of fresh corn, with husks intact
1 seven-ounce can diced green chilies

8 ounces sharp Cheddar cheese, cut into small fingers

BASIC TAMALE DOUGH (MASA):

¾ cup lard (or 5½ ounces, if you prefer to weigh it), at room temperature
¾ cup quick grits
2 cups masa harina (corn flour made by Quaker)

2 teaspoons salt
1 teaspoon sugar
⅛ teaspoon white pepper, or a dash of cayenne
1½ cups lukewarm chicken broth
½ teaspoon baking powder

First make the dough. Beat the lard in an electric mixer for at least 5 minutes or until it is very fluffy. Meanwhile, grind the grits to a fine meal in an electric blender. Place the grits in a small mixing bowl with the *masa harina*, the salt, sugar and white pepper or cayenne. Stir the warm chicken broth into the flour-grit mixture and blend well, then gradually beat this, a spoonful at a time, into the lard, using the electric mixer. After all has been added, continue to beat the mixture for 5 minutes longer, then beat in the baking powder thoroughly. If you are making this mixture ahead of time, cover it tightly and keep it in a cool place (not in the refrigerator) until ready to use.

Cut away the bottom (stem) end from the ears of corn to release the husks, but leave any long points at the top of the husks. Carefully peel the husks off the cob, taking care not to split them, and reserve. Remove and discard the cornsilk. Using a sharp knife, cut the kernels off the cob and add them to the dough mixture in the mixing bowl. Scrape the cob itself with the back of a table knife to release any milk substance left on the cob and add that to the dough mixture as well. Discard the cobs. Beat the dough to blend the corn evenly.

To form the tamales, take a large husk or overlap two smaller ones to create a large one. Spread 1 to 2 tablespoons of the masa dough over the lower third of the husk to the edges. Place a teaspoonful of chilies in the center of the dough, and top with a finger of cheese. Fold in the sides of the husks to completely enclose the cheese—there should be some overlap. Carefully fold the filled section up over the rest of the husk. Tear a thin, lengthwise strip from an extra husk to use as a string to tie the tamale in a neat package around the center (see illustration).

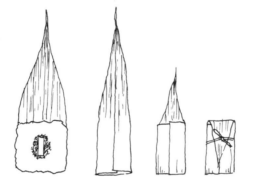

Stand the tamales, open end up, in the top section of a steamer, so that they are comfortably supporting each other in an upright position. Cover the pan and steam the tamales over boiling water for 1 hour, checking periodically to see that the water in the bottom doesn't boil away. Serve the tamales warm.

To Make Ahead: These tamales must be made when fresh corn is in season, so cook and freeze a lot of them when corn is at its peak. Thaw, then reheat them by steaming again for 15 minutes or until hot through. Their flavor is enhanced with reheating.

CHILIES EN NOGADA

(12 SERVINGS)

To be truly authentic, this dish should be made only when fresh pomegranates are in season (from late September to November). It is possible to substitute chopped pimiento for the pomegranate seeds but the flavor is not as delectable.

12 fresh mild green chilies
　(poblano chilies), or 12 canned
　whole green chilies

1 tablespoon vegetable oil
1 teaspoon vinegar
2 teaspoons grated onion

MEAT FILLING (PICCADILLO):

2 pounds coarsely ground pork, or
　beef
2 medium onions, chopped fine
2 cloves garlic, pressed
1 one-pound twelve-ounce can
　tomatoes, drained and chopped

1 cup raisins, soaked in ⅓ cup pale
　dry sherry for at least 20 min-
　utes
¾ cup chopped toasted almonds
A pinch each ground cinnamon
　and ground cloves
Salt and pepper to taste

SAUCE:

16 ounces cream cheese
1 to 1¼ cups whole milk

⅛ teaspoon garlic salt
1 cup fresh shelled pecans

THE FINAL DECORATION:

½ cup fresh pomegranate seeds
　(substitute diced pimiento if
　pomegranates are not available)

Several sprigs of flat Italian
　parsley, or fresh coriander (also
　known as Chinese parsley or
　fresh cilantro)

If using fresh chilies, place them on a foil-covered cookie sheet or oven rack and broil them about 5 inches from the heat for about 5 minutes. Keep turning them until all the sides are blistered and brown. (We advise wearing gloves when handling chilies because they can be irritating to eyes and skin.) When the chilies are done, remove them from the broiler and place them in a tightly sealed plastic bag to steam for 10 minutes or so. Then peel off the skin.

In preparing either fresh or canned chilies, make a slit down one side. Rinse away the seeds and veins under cold running water. Drain and dry. Place the chilies in a glass dish, sprinkle lightly with oil, vinegar and grated onion, and set aside at room temperature.

To make the meat filling, heat the ground pork or beef in a large skillet with the chopped onion and pressed garlic. When the meat has lost its pink color and is crumbly, stir in the chopped tomatoes, raisins, almonds, cinnamon and cloves. Bring to a simmer and cook gently for 5 minutes. Season with salt and pepper to taste and set aside.

Blend all the sauce ingredients, using half of each at a time for easier handling, in an electric blender. If the sauce is too thick, thin it very gradually with more milk. The sauce is served at room temperature.

To serve, open the chilies where they were slit. Place the meat filling in the center and fold the chile over the meat to enclose it completely. The filling should be slightly warm, though not hot. Spoon the white sauce over the center of the filled chilies and sprinkle pomegranate seeds over the top. Garnish the platter decoratively with leaves of Italian parsley or fresh coriander.

To Make Ahead: The meat stuffing may be made ahead and refrigerated or frozen. Reheat it before stuffing the chilies. The sauce will keep very nicely in the refrigerator for several days. Do not freeze. Allow it to come to room temperature before spooning it over the stuffed chilies. Do not try to freeze pomegranates.

BRANDIED PAPAYA FRUIT SALAD

(12 SERVINGS)

1 fresh pineapple, diced	2 large, ripe bananas
4 oranges, peeled and diced	1 cup fresh or frozen blueberries,
¼ cup brandy	or fresh strawberries
6 papayas, ripe but firm	1 cup grated coconut

Place the diced pineapple and oranges in a glass or stainless mixing bowl and sprinkle lightly with brandy. Refrigerate and allow to marinate for at least 2 hours.

Shortly before serving, remove the skin from the papayas with a sharp knife and cut them in half lengthwise. Scoop out the seeds. Trim away a small slice from the bottom of each half so that the papaya halves become "boats" which will stand firmly on the plates.

Slice the bananas into the pineapple-orange mixture. Fold in the blueberries (if frozen, it is not necessary to thaw them) or fresh strawberries. Spoon the fruit salad into the papaya halves and top each serving with a sprinkling of grated coconut.

To Make Ahead: The diced pineapple and oranges may marinate for up to 2 days. The other fruits should be added just before serving to preserve their fresh color. Prepare the papaya boats in the morning and refrigerate in a plastic bag until ready to assemble the salad near serving time.

HELADO Y NIEVE
Ice and Snow

(12 SERVINGS)

1 quart vanilla ice cream	2 teaspoons grated orange rind
1 quart pineapple sherbet	(zest, see note, page 123)
3 tablespoons Cointreau or Triple Sec	2 teaspoons grated lemon rind (zest)
3 tablespoons Grand Marnier	

Combine all the ingredients in the large bowl of an electric mixer and beat just until smooth. If you wish to do this in front of your guests, use an attractive bowl with a handle and let the ice cream soften for a few minutes before you begin.

When the mixture is smooth, spoon it into large stemmed wine or champagne glasses and serve immediately. The mixture will be soft like old-fashioned ice cream.

To Make Ahead: For convenience, store this dessert in the freezer right in the serving glasses until serving time. The liqueurs will keep it slightly soft, but it will be much firmer than when freshly made. If serving frozen, you may wish to sprinkle ground cookie crumbs or grated chocolate over the top for decoration before storing.

V

Eclectic Menus

An Easy, Man-Pleasing Menu for Six or Eight

Ceviche

Steak au Poivre à la Crème

SAINT EMILION

Tangy Tomatoes

Roquefort Salad à la Romanoff

Profiteroles au Chocolat

*W*E LOVE TO SERVE this meal at any time of year, for a casual evening or more formal dinner party, for guests or just for us. Our students are especially enthusiastic about it because preparations flow easily, with little last-minute fussing.

The first course, Ceviche, is a Mexican or South American seafood cocktail, a mouth-watering dish which is especially enjoyable in the summertime. We serve it often for luncheon, not only because we love the taste, but because it is very low in calories and carbohydrates. (We have to watch our weight constantly, loving to eat the way we do. To be honest, we've been on and off reducing diets for eleven years!) Ceviche consists of cubes of raw white fish, such as halibut, red snapper, cod or turbot, marinated in lime juice and combined with minced onions, chopped fresh tomato and oregano for seasoning. The lime juice actually "cooks" the fish without heat, making it firm and white and totally unlike raw fish. We serve it in glass dishes embedded in crushed ice, in abalone shells, or simply in curled lettuce leaves. It is a dish we urge you to try—we are sure you'll love it as we do.

The main course is Steak au Poivre à la Crème, an impressive dish that will unexpectedly stretch your meat budget. A thick sirloin or New York steak is broiled or pan-fried just before serving, then sliced diagonally into serving pieces which are arranged overlapping on a platter. Its quick, rich sauce is made of cream, Dijon mustard and cognac, and cooked right in the same pan as the steak. Spoon the sauce decoratively over the meat, along with a sprinkle or two of chopped parsley, and presto! Instant Gourmet!

A vegetable that always wows the men, especially with steak, is a casserole of Tangy Tomatoes, slow-simmered until very thick. The dish will become even more delicious if it is made a day or two ahead of time and reheated to serve. The recipe was given to us by a friend from Baltimore, who says that there one often encounters tomatoes prepared with brown sugar, a very happy combination, we think. Of course, if you don't plan far enough in advance to cook the tomatoes, any simple vegetable will complement the steak.

The salad for this menu does very well served either with the main course, or afterward in the European manner. If your guests are wine connoisseurs, you would be wise to serve a salad after the main course—vinegar in a dressing will interfere with the appreciation of a wine's "bouquet." This very special Roquefort Salad is made using the techniques Diana observed at the great Romanoff's Restaurant in Beverly Hills, California.

A dessert of Profiteroles is spectacular, but so easy if made in advance. First we make a basic choux paste, a very simple dough even for beginners, and extraordinarily versatile. It can be used for éclairs, cream puffs, *beignets* (fritters), or Profiteroles au Chocolat, tiny cream puffs baked, then split and filled with sweetened whipped cream or ice cream, and topped with a warm chocolate sauce. There is nothing more delicious! While you are at it, you may wish to double or triple the dough recipe and make lots of extra puffs to store in your freezer for another occasion when you are celebrating something important (such as voting, or having the dog groomed!).

If we had to choose our favorite menus in the book, this would certainly be one of them. It has style!

T I M E T A B L E : The first dish to prepare should be the Tangy Tomatoes, which may be made days or even weeks ahead of time. Their flavor improves greatly on reheating, and freezing doesn't affect them at all.

The tiny puffs for Profiteroles may be baked any time you wish and popped into a plastic bag in the freezer. Reheat them briefly in the oven before filling and they will be good as new.

Ceviche will last 5 days in the refrigerator but must marinate at least 6 hours before serving, so time this part of the dinner to your own convenience.

The morning of your party, prepare the salad bowl and place the crumbled Roquefort in the bottom. Your washed and torn greens go in the refrigerator, wrapped in paper towels, until needed. Make the dressing, cover, and leave it at room temperature.

At the same time, set out all your serving dishes and chop some parsley to sprinkle over the Ceviche and the steak slices. Keep the parsley in a glass, covered with a moist paper towel. Thaw the tomatoes if necessary. Coat the steak with pepper and leave at room temperature.

An hour (or longer) before serving, place the Ceviche in serving dishes and keep refrigerated. Set out all the sauce ingredients for the Steak au Poivre, and place the tomatoes in a low oven to reheat—they really can't be overdone.

Now, relax! The rest of the preparation is simplicity itself. This is a foolproof menu which can only further your reputation as a Chef Extraordinaire!

CEVICHE
Mexican Seafood Cocktail
(6 TO 8 APPETIZER SERVINGS)

Ceviche is served as a first course at the table or as a dip with fried wedges or tortilla. It is very low in calories *and* carbohydrates! Best of all, it will keep for up to 5 days in the refrigerator.

1 ½ pounds mild white fish filets (such as red snapper, cod, turbot, halibut, etc.)
⅓ cup lime juice
1 medium onion, minced
3 tomatoes, peeled* and chopped

¾ teaspoon dried oregano, or more to taste, rubbed between your palms
2 tablespoons minced parsley
1 ½ tablespoons olive oil
Salt and pepper, to taste
Cayenne or bottled hot sauce, to taste

Cut the fish into ½-inch squares. Place in a bowl and cover with lime juice. Refrigerate and allow to marinate for at least 1 hour, then add the other ingredients. You may wish to add more of certain things to your

* See note, page 25.

taste. Chill. The lime juice "cooks" the fish and causes it to become white and firm.

STEAK AU POIVRE À LA CRÈME
(6 TO 8 SERVINGS)

2 to 3 two-inch thick sirloin or
New York–cut steaks, about
1 ¼ pounds each, or 1 thick filet
mignon per person
3 tablespoons whole black pepper-
corns, or cracked black pepper
About ½ cup vegetable oil
4 tablespoons (½ stick) butter or
margarine

3 tablespoons minced shallots
⅓ cup cognac or brandy
2 beef bouillon cubes
2 cups heavy cream
1 tablespoon Dijon mustard or
more to taste
Chopped parsley to garnish

Trim the steaks of all fat. Wrap the peppercorns in an old kitchen towel, place on a chopping board, and pound with a heavy pan until crushed. (If this process does not appeal to you, simply use cracked black pepper that comes in a jar.) Press the pepper evenly into the surface of the steaks.

Place a heavy skillet (an iron one is a good choice) over medium-high heat. Add a little vegetable oil to the pan. When the oil is very hot, add the steaks and cook until brown on one side. This should take 4 or 5 minutes. Turn them to brown the other side. When the steaks are well browned, check for doneness. If necessary, lower the heat and continue cooking to the desired degree of doneness. Filet mignons will take only a few minutes, but larger steaks may require 15 to 20 minutes in all.

When the steaks are done, remove them to a warm platter and cover with foil to keep them from cooling while you make the sauce. Wipe out the skillet with a paper towel and let it cool a minute. Add the butter and minced shallots and allow to cook for a few seconds, taking care that the shallots do not burn. Add the cognac or brandy and the bouillon cubes and stir to dissolve. Stir in the cream and simmer, stirring often, for about 10 minutes until the mixture is reduced to a sauce consistency.

Remove the pan from the heat and allow the mixture to stop

bubbling. Stir in the mustard. Do not cook any further or the sauce may separate. Season to taste.

Large steaks should be sliced diagonally to serve. Pour some of the hot sauce over the steak slices or whole steaks and sprinkle with chopped parsley. Pass any extra sauce at the table.

To Make Ahead: The steaks should be cooked just before serving, but they are *very easy* to prepare, especially if you set out all your ingredients and equipment ahead of time. If time is of the essence, make the sauce in a different pan early in the day, press plastic wrap into the surface to keep a skin from forming, and simply reheat to serve.

TANGY TOMATOES

(6 TO 8 SERVINGS)

These tomatoes are at their very best if made a day or more in advance and reheated before serving. They are unusual and delicious served with almost any meal.

1 stick butter or margarine, melted

3 one-pound twelve-ounce cans solid-pack tomatoes (the kind packed in tomato purée are best, but any will do)

¾ cup brown sugar

3 to 4 tablespoons Worcestershire sauce

Several dashes of Tabasco

Combine all the ingredients in a flameproof casserole that can also go into the oven. Place over medium heat and bring to a boil. Lower the heat and simmer for an hour or more, stirring occasionally and breaking up the tomatoes with a spoon. When the mixture begins to thicken, transfer it to a 250° oven and leave it there for 6 or 8 hours, stirring once in a while. It is done when quite thick and not at all runny.

To Make Ahead: These tomatoes keep beautifully in freezer or refrigerator, but they never last that long at our house!

ROQUEFORT SALAD À LA ROMANOFF

(6 TO 8 SERVINGS)

Oil, for the bowl

Salt, for the bowl (we use coarse
    kosher salt)

1 large clove of garlic, for the
    bowl (optional)

4 ounces good Roquefort cheese

2 heads romaine lettuce

Freshly ground pepper, to taste

DRESSING:

⅓ cup vegetable or olive oil

4 teaspoons red wine vinegar

1 heaping teaspoon Dijon mustard

1½ teaspoons Worcestershire
    sauce, or more to taste

Rinse the salad greens in cold water and shake them out when you bring them home from the market. Wrap the damp greens in several thicknesses of paper towels, then store them in a plastic bag in the refrigerator. When stored in this manner, the greens will keep perfectly for a week.

We prefer a wooden salad bowl for this, but any type will do. Place a little vegetable oil and some coarse salt in the bowl. Rub the inner surface of the bowl with a cut clove of garlic. Place the Roquefort cheese, crumbled, in the bottom of the bowl. Tear the greens into bite-sized pieces and place on top of the cheese. Refrigerate until ready to toss.

Mix all the dressing ingredients together. Cover and leave at room temperature until ready to toss. Set out salt and a pepper grinder.

When ready to serve, move the greens in the bowl to one side to expose the cheese. Pour the dressing over the cheese and mash with a fork until lightly blended. Now, toss thoroughly. Taste for seasoning and toss again. Serve immediately.

To Make Ahead: The dressing is a basic one and may be made ahead, even several weeks ahead, if desired. Store it in the refrigerator, but for best flavor bring it to room temperature before serving. The salad bowl may be seasoned and set in the refrigerator with the cheese and torn greens early in the day. Naturally, the dressing must be added just before serving.

PROFITEROLES AU CHOCOLAT

(6 TO 8 SERVINGS)

CREAM PUFFS:

6 tablespoons (¾ stick) butter,
   cut into small pieces
1 cup water
1 cup unsifted all-purpose flour
Pinch of salt
4 large (possibly 5) eggs, from the
   refrigerator

2 teaspoons granulated sugar
¼ teaspoon orange or lemon
   extract
Butter or margarine, to grease the
   baking sheets
1 egg yolk, beaten with 1 tablespoon cream or half-and-half

FILLING:

1 cup heavy cream
2 tablespoons confectioner's sugar

2 teaspoons vanilla extract

CHOCOLATE SAUCE:

8 ounces semisweet chocolate bits,
   or German sweet chocolate
1 cup heavy cream

1 tablespoon dark rum or cognac
½ teaspoon instant coffee

To make the puffs, place the pieces of butter in a small, heavy saucepan with the water and bring to a rolling boil. The butter will then be completely melted. Remove the pan from the heat and add the flour and salt, beating with a wooden spoon until the mixture looks like mashed potatoes. Return the pan to low heat and continue to beat for 2 minutes. The mixture will become a single mass that follows the spoon and begins to film the bottom of the pan. Remove from the heat.

    Beat in 1 egg at a time. The dough will separate into slippery strands after each addition, but will come back together again as you continue beating. After 4 eggs have been beaten in, look at the dough. It should be smooth and shiny and should fall lazily off the lifted spoon. If it is too thick, beat the fifth egg in a separate bowl and add part of it to the dough. Add more if necessary until you reach the desired shiny consistency. Beat in the sugar and orange or lemon extract.

    Preheat the oven to 450°. Lightly grease two cookie sheets. Use a pastry tube or two spoons to place small mounds of dough, 1½ inches apart, on the sheets. The mounds should be about ¾ inch in diameter—they will double in size when cooked. Brush the top of each puff with the combined yolk and cream to give the finished puffs a lovely glaze.

Bake at 450° for 5 minutes, then lower the heat to 425° and continue baking for about 10 minutes longer. The puffs should be browned and free from moisture on the outside when done. Break one open, and if it is doughy inside, return the puffs to the oven to continue cooking a few minutes longer. When the puffs are done, remove them from the oven and pierce the side of each one with a sharp knife to release the steam. Return them to the turned-off oven for 5 minutes to dry the insides. Let cool. You will have more puffs than you need for this recipe, so freeze the extra ones in a plastic bag for another time.

No more than an hour before serving, beat the cream for the filling until it starts to thicken. Dust the powdered sugar over the cream through a kitchen strainer and continue beating until stiff. Fold in the vanilla.

Cut each puff in half with a sharp knife and fill the lower half with a generous spoonful of the whipped cream. Replace the tops. Refrigerate until serving time.

To make the sauce, simply melt the chocolate with the cream, stirring until smooth, and add the flavoring of your choice—rum or cognac and coffee. This sauce may be made in advance and reheated or kept warm in a double boiler over hot water.

To serve, arrange 3 puffs on each dessert plate. Either spoon the sauce over them or pass the sauce separately at the table. If you prefer, all the puffs may be arranged on a serving plate and sprinkled with powdered sugar, in which case the sauce would be passed separately.

Note: If you prefer, the puffs may be filled with ice cream instead of whipped cream. Frozen puffs can then be served directly from the freezer. They won't have quite the same fresh consistency if served frozen, but no one will notice.

To Make Ahead: The puffs freeze beautifully and need not be defrosted before use. Simply reheat them at 400° for about 10 minutes to freshen them, then cool before filling. The chocolate sauce may be made ahead of time and reheated in a double boiler. The cream should be whipped within 2 hours of serving time, so that it will remain stiff.

A Light, Elegant Luncheon for Six

Cream of Avocado Soup with Condiments

Turban of Sole with Shrimp Mousse and Sauce Aurore

MOSELLE (SPÄTLESE)

Madeline's Salad†

Beautiful Baking Powder Biscuits

Iced Lemon Soufflé with Fresh Berries

*H*ERE IS AN IDEAL MENU for summer entertaining in the garden, though it may, of course, be served anywhere and at anytime of year.

Cream of Avocado Soup has a tantalizing look of misty green velvet that makes it an irresistible companion to the pastel-shaded entrée. A rainbow of condiments will be added at serving time for texture and contrast.

The main course, Turban of Sole, is a glorious crown of fish filets enfolding a delicate pink mousse of fresh shrimp. When garnished with sautéed fresh mushrooms and watercress and topped with sherry-flavored Sauce Aurore it becomes a gourmet's delight. We serve this dish often, not only for luncheons and light suppers, but as the first course for an elaborate dinner. It never fails to delight our guests. A chilled golden Spätlese is divine with it.

In this menu, we again recommend Madeline's Salad (page 77) as a perfect accompaniment to fish because it is so light and simple. It may be served before, during, or after the main course, as you prefer.

We enjoy making Frances Pelham's recipe for biscuits when we have time. They are a lovely example of homemade baking powder biscuits. Served steaming hot and golden from the oven, they require only butter for serving. To save time, you may wish to substitute the canned, ready-to-bake refrigerator biscuits from the supermarket. We have no strong prejudices about the convenience foods available today, and we find that most of the biscuit products are of good quality and have excellent flavor.

Iced Lemon Soufflé is shimmering and elegant—a pale yellow Bavarian cream, heaped high and molded to give the appearance of a soufflé, then garnished with whipped cream, fresh, perfect strawberries, and mint leaves.

We use this menu when we want to show off and hope you will do the same. Your guests will never guess what a breeze it is to prepare (unless you tell them).

TIMETABLE: Much of this menu lends itself to being made in advance.

The Iced Lemon Soufflé may be prepared at your convenience. It will wait patiently in your refrigerator for 2 days and can even be frozen and thawed overnight in the refrigerator before serving.

Assemble the fish and the mousse filling in the ring mold up to 24 hours in advance and refrigerate it. (That is, assuming that the fish you purchased is truly fresh. If you are not sure, do this job within a few hours of cooking.)

The night before the luncheon, blend and chill the avocado soup. All the condiments for the soup, except the bacon, may be placed in serving dishes and covered with plastic wrap at this time. Cook and crumble the bacon and wrap it in foil, to be reheated at serving time. Make the salad dressing and prepare the salad greens. Chill the wine and plan your table setting.

Several hours before serving, whip the half cup of cream and decorate the soufflé. Roll out the biscuits and place them on the baking sheet ready to go in the oven when the fish is through cooking. Chill until serving time.

Sauté the mushrooms briefly and set aside right in the skillet so they may be quickly reheated when the turban is unmolded. Make the Sauce Aurore, cover, and set aside.

About 45 minutes before serving, set your oven to preheat for the turban of sole, placing the open foil package of bacon bits in the oven to crisp. When the bacon is very hot, remove it. Set the boiling water bath in the center of the oven and gently lower the turban of sole into it. Serve the cold soup with the assorted condiments, followed by the salad. This should be a leisurely time for you to enjoy your guests. When the sole has finished cooking, remove it from the oven and immediately raise the temperature to 425° for the biscuits. Unmold the fish as directed and arrange it on a platter. Slide the biscuits into the hot oven. Finish the Sauce Aurore. Cut the turban into serving pieces at the table. The biscuits should be done just as you finish serving. Arrange them in a basket to pass at the table.

The soufflé waits in the refrigerator, all ready to be served, so once you have joined your guests for the main course, you can relax knowing that all you need do is bow to the applause!

CREAM OF AVOCADO SOUP WITH CONDIMENTS
(6 SERVINGS)

The pulp of 1 large or 2 small, ripe avocados
2 cups well-seasoned chicken broth
5 teaspoons red wine vinegar

2 tablespoons fresh lemon juice
1½ teaspoons garlic salt
3 to 4 dashes Tabasco sauce
1 cup heavy cream, or half-and-half

AN ASSORTMENT OF CONDIMENTS:

8 to 10 slices crisp bacon, finely crumbled and warm
¾ cup chopped toasted almonds

2 fresh tomatoes, peeled,* seeded and diced
⅓ cup sliced scallions, or ¼ cup minced chives

Place all the soup ingredients in the container of an electric blender and blend until smooth. Chill thoroughly.

Serve in chilled soup bowls. Either sprinkle each serving with condiments or allow guests to help themselves.

To Make Ahead: This soup will keep in the refrigerator for at least 24 hours without darkening. It may also be frozen, in which case it is best to reblend it when only partially thawed. The bacon for the garnish may be cooked and crumbled several days ahead and stored in the refrigerator wrapped in foil. Before serving, open the foil and reheat in the oven until the bacon is crisp.

* See note, page 25.

TURBAN OF SOLE WITH SHRIMP MOUSSE
AND SAUCE AURORE
(6 LUNCHEON SERVINGS, OR 8 FIRST-COURSE SERVINGS)

8 small to medium filets of sole
1 tablespoon fresh lemon juice

Salt and white pepper
1 tablespoon butter or margarine

A ring mold (5-cup size, measuring about 8½ inches across and 2 inches deep)

MOUSSE FILLING:

¾ pound raw shrimp
1 large egg white
⅞ cup heavy cream
¾ teaspoon salt

2 teaspoons tomato paste*
1 tablespoon chopped parsley
5 teaspoons pale dry sherry

SAUCE AURORE:

¾ cup pale dry sherry
1 tablespoon tomato paste*
6 tablespoons (¾ stick) butter or
   margarine
2 tablespoons minced shallots
6 tablespoons flour

¾ teaspoon salt
1½ cups heavy cream, or half-
   and-half
3 egg yolks
¾ teaspoon Beau Monde seasoning
Several small dashes of cayenne

GARNISH:

½ pound fresh mushrooms
2 tablespoons butter or margarine
A few drops of lemon juice

Salt and pepper
1 bunch fresh watercress (parsley
   may be substituted)

Rinse the fish filets in cold water and dry them. Sprinkle with the lemon juice, salt and white pepper. Butter the mold lightly and line it with the fish filets, arranging them so the dark side is up and the narrow ends point to the center of the mold. Let the ends of the filets hang over the inside and outside rims of the mold.

To make the mousse filling, shell the shrimp. Use a sharp paring knife to make a shallow, lengthwise cut in the backs which will expose the dark intestinal veins. Rinse under cold running water to remove the veins. Drain, then cut the shrimp into chunks. Place them in the con-

* Any unused tomato paste may be frozen for another use.

tainer of an electric blender with the other mousse ingredients and blend for several minutes while forcing the mixture down into the blades with a rubber spatula until it is completely smooth. Fill the fish-lined mold with the mixture, pressing it in compactly to avoid air bubbles. Fold the ends of the filets over the top of the filling. Lay a square of buttered wax paper loosely over the top. If you will not be baking the turban immediately, refrigerate it until needed.

To make the sauce, boil the sherry in a small saucepan until it is reduced to half its original volume (⅜ cup). Remove from the heat and stir in the 1 tablespoon of tomato paste until dissolved. Set aside. In the top of a glass double boiler, over direct heat, melt the butter and sauté the shallots gently for a minute or two, taking care not to burn them. Stir in the flour and salt and cook, stirring, for 2 or 3 minutes. Remove the pan from the heat and stir in the cream—a wire whisk is best for this, though a slotted spoon will suffice. Return the pan to the heat and let cook, stirring constantly, until the mixture boils and thickens. Simmer slowly for a minute, then remove from the heat.

Beat the egg yolks in a small bowl with the same whisk. Quickly beat in about ¼ cup of the hot sauce, then blend the yolk mixture into the sauce in the double boiler and add the reduced sherry mixture, Beau Monde seasoning and cayenne. (If you are making the sauce more than an hour before serving time, set it aside, covered, at this point.)

About 45 minutes before serving, preheat the oven to 350°. Place an oblong pan (about 10 x 14 inches) containing ¾ of an inch of boiling water in the center of a rack set at the middle level of your oven. Place the paper-covered turban in the center of the water bath and bake for 30 minutes.

While the turban of sole is cooking, place the sauce over hot, not boiling, water and let cook until thickened, stirring often. It will become quite thick; however, when you later add the juices from the turban of sole, the sauce will thin to the proper consistency. (*Note:* if by chance you should ever curdle an egg yolk sauce with too much heat, simply beat the curdled sauce gradually into another beaten egg yolk in a mixing bowl. The sauce will return to a velvety smoothness.)

Rinse the mushrooms quickly under cold running water, rubbing away any grit with your fingers. Dry them immediately so they don't absorb water. Slice thickly through the stems and sauté in the 2 tablespoons butter or margarine with a squeeze of lemon juice and a bit of salt and pepper until they are barely tender.

Remove the turban of sole from the oven when it has finished cooking and remove the wax paper. Holding a serving platter on top of the mold, pour off the liquid inside the mold into the warm sauce, then turn the turban out onto the platter. Pour any additional liquid that gathers on the platter into the sauce and blend briskly with a whisk until the sauce is smooth.

To decorate the turban, fill the center with fresh watercress or parsley and surround the outside with the warm sautéed mushrooms. Spoon some of the sauce decoratively over the fish and pass the rest at the table. Each plate should have a sprig of watercress or parsley for color.

To Make Ahead: If the filets of sole are truly fresh, the turban may be assembled in its mold up to 24 hours in advance. Chill until time to bake. The sauce may be made up to 3 hours ahead and set aside at room temperature. The mushrooms should be sautéed within an hour of serving and reheated. Bake the turban of sole and finish the sauce just before serving.

BEAUTIFUL BAKING POWDER BISCUITS
(15 TO 18 2-INCH BISCUITS)

2 cups all-purpose flour
½ teaspoon salt
4 teaspoons baking powder
½ teaspoon cream of tartar
1 tablespoon sugar

½ cup cold vegetable shortening
  (Crisco)
⅔ cup milk
4 tablespoons (½ stick) butter or
  margarine, melted and cooled

Sift the flour, salt, baking powder, cream of tartar and sugar together into a mixing bowl. Using a pastry cutter or two knives, cut the shortening into the dry ingredients until the mixture has the texture of coarse meal. Add the milk all at once and stir just until the dough follows a fork around the bowl.

Turn the dough out onto a lightly floured board or pastry cloth. Knead very lightly with your fingers fifteen times, no more, no less. Pat the dough or roll it gently with a rolling pin to ½-inch thickness and cut into 2-inch circles with a biscuit cutter. Gently knead together the remaining scraps of dough and continue cutting circles until all the dough is used.

Place half the circles, sides touching, on a greased baking sheet. Dip the bottoms of the remaining circles in the melted butter and place on top of the ones on the baking sheet.

Bake at 425° for 15 to 20 minutes. Serve very hot with extra butter.

To Make Ahead: The biscuits may be stored in the refrigerator on the baking sheet for several hours. Bake just before serving. Leftover biscuits may be reheated.

ICED LEMON SOUFFLÉ WITH FRESH BERRIES
(6 TO 8 SERVINGS)

1 ½ tablespoons (1 ½ envelopes)
   unflavored gelatin*
½ cup cold water
6 eggs, separated
¾ cup fresh lemon juice (about 3
   lemons)
1 ½ cups granulated sugar

¾ teaspoon salt
Grated rind (zest, see note, page
   123) of 2 lemons
¼ teaspoon cream of tartar or
   fresh lemon juice
1 ½ cups heavy cream

FOR DECORATION:

½ cup heavy cream, whipped and
   sweetened with 1 tablespoon
   sifted confectioner's sugar

6 to 8 perfect strawberries, if in
   season (or substitute candied
   violets)
Candied or fresh mint leaves

Tear off a length of aluminum foil or wax paper long enough to wrap around a 6-cup soufflé dish to form a collar. Fold it in half lengthwise and oil the inside lightly. Tie it securely around the dish with string.

Sprinkle the gelatin evenly over the cold water and allow it to soften for 5 minutes. Meanwhile, combine the egg yolks, lemon juice, ¾ cup of the sugar and the salt in the top of a glass double boiler. Cook the mixture over simmering water, whisking constantly, until it has the consistency of a thin custard. Remove it from the heat and stir in the softened gelatin and the lemon zest. Continue to stir until the gelatin is completely dissolved. Allow the mixture to cool to room temperature.

Place the egg whites in a clean mixing bowl with the ¼ teaspoon cream of tartar or lemon juice. Beat the whites to soft peaks—the point where they do not slide when the bowl is tilted. Very gradually beat in the remaining ¾ cup of sugar to make a meringue, and continue to

* Please do not add extra gelatin "for good measure." The amount given is sufficient.

beat until the mixture holds stiff, shiny peaks when the beater is lifted. Fold about one-third of the meringue into the custard very thoroughly. Pile the rest on top to wait while you whip the 1½ cups heavy cream in the same mixing bowl you used for the egg whites. When the cream has been whipped to the point where it holds a soft shape, turn off the mixer. Finish folding the meringue into the yolk mixture. Finally, fold in the whipped cream thoroughly and pour the mixture into the collared soufflé dish. Chill for at least 4 hours.

Before serving, remove the collar and decorate the top of the soufflé with puffs of whipped cream topped with whole strawberries or candied violets. Garnish with mint leaves. At the table, spoon the soufflé onto dessert plates or into stemmed glasses.

To Make Ahead: The soufflé will keep for 2 days in the refrigerator or for several weeks in the freezer. If frozen, thaw overnight in the refrigerator before serving.

A Dramatic Chinese
Supper for Six

Crispy Cantonese Chicken Salad

Hot-and-Sour Soup

Almond Soufflé with Orange Sauce
and Toasted Almonds

*W*HEN MARCO POLO RETURNED to Italy in 1295 A.D. from the fabled court of the great Kublai Khan, he brought with him incredible and fantastic tales of an exalted cuisine which was, even then, over three thousand years old. Today in the West we see renewed interest in the cooking of China, where serious attention is given not only to the marriage of subtle flavors and varied textures, but to the artful appearance of the finished dish. Paul believes that "First you eat with your eyes . . ." and for this reason he adores teaching our classes in Chinese cooking. They have become his specialty.

Here is an informal menu that is easy to prepare. Best of all, the ingredients are not so exotic as to be difficult to obtain. Any market that carries even a few Chinese items will have sesame-flavored oil, maifun (rice sticks), light soy sauce, dried Chinese mushrooms and canned bamboo shoots. Everything else called for in the recipes is available at the average supermarket.

The meal begins with an exciting salad which combines crisp deep-fried noodles, shredded chicken and toasted sesame seeds. If you are able to locate some preserved red ginger and add just a touch of that, the dish becomes even more authentic. We love it both ways.

Hot-and-Sour Soup is a delectable main course for supper. It has substance but is not too heavy and is as wonderful to look at as it is to taste.

Loving Chinese food as we do, we are always looking for authentic desserts—a difficult task because Chinese people don't particularly enjoy them and serve them rarely. So Diana invented a hot Almond Soufflé to serve with Chinese food. When we taught this dessert on television there were so many requests for the recipe that the telephone lines at the studio were jammed for an hour! Topped with a rose-colored orange sauce and crisp toasted almonds, this is a very special dessert indeed, and goes well with many menus—so well that we find ourselves serving it more and more often.

Here you have a masterful orchestration of tastes, textures and aromas that will add a touch of oriental adventure to your entertaining.

TIMETABLE: This is truly a simple menu to serve because everything can be prepared in advance. The noodles for the salad may be deep-fried and stored for up to a week. The chicken may be cooked and shredded several days in advance.

Hot-and-Sour Soup can be reheated, if you are careful to do so gently. But liquids thickened with cornstarch tend to "break" or thin out if they are heated too quickly.

Make the base for the soufflé in the morning. Press plastic wrap into the surface and set it out of the way along with the egg whites in their mixing bowl ready to be whipped. Prepare the sauce for the soufflé and leave it at room temperature. Toast the almonds with which the sauce will be garnished.

All of the ingredients for the salad should be set out within easy reach, along with the scallion garnish for the soup.

After setting the table, you will have nothing to do until your guests arrive but relax and read up on some Chinese poetry.

CRISPY CANTONESE CHICKEN SALAD

(6 SERVINGS)

Your guests will be astounded if you cook the maifun noodles while they watch. When the tiny transparent noodles are dropped into hot oil they puff immediately to three times their original size and become crisp morsels of great delicacy.

DRESSING:

1 ½ teaspoons dry mustard	*2 teaspoons sesame-flavored oil**
1 ½ teaspoons cold water	*½ teaspoon salt*
2 tablespoons light soy sauce	

* Sesame-flavored oil is a dark, pungent oil available in markets that carry Chinese ingredients. It should not be confused with sesame oil, which is a salad oil.

SALAD:

1 tablespoon sesame seeds	*4 or 5 scallions*
3 chicken thighs	*½ teaspoon minced preserved red*
Vegetable oil for frying	*ginger (optional)*
½ of a six-ounce package maifun	*¼ head iceburg lettuce, finely*
(Hong Kong rice sticks)	*shredded*

Toast the sesame seeds by placing them on a piece of aluminum foil in a 300° oven for about 5 minutes. Toss them often and remove them as soon as they have turned slightly golden.

To make the salad dressing, combine the dry mustard and water and allow it to stand for at least 20 minutes. Stir in the soy sauce, sesame-flavored oil and salt.

Place the chicken thighs in a small saucepan, cover with water and bring to a boil over medium heat. Lower the heat and allow them to simmer slowly for about 30 minutes or until the meat is tender when pierced with a fork. Remove the chicken from the broth and leave it at room temperature until cool enough to handle. Using your fingers, shred the chicken meat fine.

Heat about 2 inches of vegetable oil in a large, deep pot or a wok. Test the heat of the oil, which should be hot, but not to the point where it is beginning to smoke, by dropping in a thread of maifun. The noodle should puff up, turn white, and become crisp almost instantly. When the oil is the right temperature, drop in a small handful of maifun noodles. As soon as they puff, remove them from the oil with a slotted spoon or strainer and let them drain on absorbent paper towels. The noodles should not be left in the oil long enough to brown. Continue cooking the rest of the noodles in the same manner.

Cut the scallions, including some of the green stems, into 2-inch lengths. Slice them lengthwise into thin slivers. Place the onions in a very large salad bowl with the sesame seeds, shredded chicken meat, crisp maifun noodles, optional red ginger and the lettuce. Pour the dressing over the salad and toss well, breaking up the noodles as you work until everything is well-coated with dressing. Serve immediately.

To Make Ahead: The noodles may be fried up to a week in advance. Store them in an airtight container. The dressing will keep for a week or more on the pantry shelf if tightly covered. Cook the chicken thighs several days ahead and shred them while they are still warm. Toasted sesame seeds may be stored indefinitely in an airtight container.

HOT-AND-SOUR SOUP

(6 SERVINGS)

6 dried Chinese mushrooms, about
   1 ½ inches in diameter
¾ cup canned sliced bamboo
   shoots
6 ounces lean pork
5 cups chicken broth
1 ½ teaspoons salt
5 teaspoons light soy sauce
½ teaspoon white pepper

3 tablespoons white vinegar
6 scallions, sliced fine, including
   some of the green tops
3 tablespoons cornstarch, mixed
   with ¼ cup cold water
1 large egg, lightly beaten
1 tablespoon sesame-flavored oil
   (see note, page 223)

You will need a large, sharp knife or cleaver to prepare this soup because it requires a lot of slicing.

Place the dried mushrooms in a small bowl and cover them with warm water. Allow them to soak for 30 minutes, then discard the water. Cut away and discard the tough mushroom stems. To shred the mushroom caps, place them one at a time on a chopping board, cut into thin horizontal slices and then into thin strips.

Rinse the bamboo shoots in cold water, drain, and shred them as fine as the mushrooms. Trim all of the fat from the pork and shred it in a similar fashion. Have these ingredients, as well as all the other listed ingredients, set out within easy reach before you begin cooking. Almost all the work involved in Chinese cookery is in chopping and slicing. The actual cooking takes only a few minutes.

Place the broth, salt, soy sauce, mushrooms, bamboo shoots and pork in a heavy-bottomed saucepan of at least a 4-quart capacity and bring the mixture to a boil over high heat. Reduce the heat to low, cover the pan and simmer for 3 minutes. Stir in the white pepper, vinegar, and half the sliced scallions and bring the mixture again to a boil. Stir the cornstarch-water mixture until it is smooth and pour it into the boiling soup. Stir constantly until the soup thickens and clears. Slowly pour in the beaten egg while stirring. Taste the soup for seasoning—for "hotter" flavor, add more white pepper.

Pour the soup into a large tureen or other serving bowl. Stir in the sesame-flavored oil and sprinkle the remaining scallions over the top. Serve immediately.

To Make Ahead: This soup may be made several days ahead of time. Reheat it very gently while stirring constantly. Do not freeze.

SECRETS OF A GREAT SOUFFLÉ

The key to making a great soufflé is in the egg whites. It is best to memorize certain rules for beating egg whites and to follow them faithfully.

1. *Egg whites should always be at room temperature (or slightly warm) when they are beaten.* It is easiest to separate the whites from the yolks when the eggs are chilled, because the yolk is less likely to break when it is cold and firm. Set the whites in the bowl in which they are to be beaten and allow them to come to room temperature. If you are in a hurry, set the bowl into a pan of warm water and stir the whites to take the chill off.

2. *The whites, the bowl and the beater(s) must be clean and grease-free.* For this reason plastic bowls do not work well. If you happen to break some yolk into the whites, be sure to remove every trace, as the yolk contains fat which will prevent the whites from absorbing air as they are beaten.

3. *Always add either ¼ teaspoon cream of tartar or an equal amount of fresh lemon juice to the whites before beating.* Either will lend an acidity to the whites which will help them to absorb a maximum volume of air.

4. *Beat the whites for a soufflé only to "soft peaks"—the point where they do not slide when the bowl is tilted.* It does not do any harm to stop beating the whites to test them often. Never beat the whites "stiff"—they will be exhausted and have no strength left to rise in the oven.

5. *Fold one-third to one-half the beaten whites into the soufflé base to "lighten" it.* Do this quickly and thoroughly—there is no need to be gentle at this point. The remaining whites are folded in more carefully.

6. *To fold properly:* Place a portion of the whites on top of the base mixture. Use a large rubber spatula to cut straight down to the bottom of the bowl. Twist your wrist to flatten the spatula against the bottom and pull it toward you and up along the side of the bowl. Some of the base mixture will have "folded" up over the whites on top. Continue cutting and lifting in this manner until all is well blended. Fold the last portion of the whites in gently, just until mixed—a few streaks or puffs of white will not matter. Learn to fold quickly and in a relaxed fashion —cooking is supposed to be fun!

If you take the time to memorize these simple rules, they will spring automatically to mind whenever you are beating whites, be it for soufflés, cakes or meringues.

We recommend that you keep an oven thermometer in your oven at all times to be sure the temperature is accurate. They are available wherever housewares are sold and are not expensive.

You may use any soufflé recipe to make individual soufflés in dishes of 1- to 1½-cup capacity. The small dishes do not require collars. Baking time will be about 20 minutes.

Soufflé recipes may be doubled. Simply use two baking dishes of the same size. Do not attempt to make one very large soufflé, because it will not bake evenly.

Most people think that soufflés must be prepared at the last minute. Actually, the base may be made in advance and left at room temperature. Plastic wrap should be pressed into the surface to prevent the air from forming a skin on top. The dish may be buttered, collared and waiting. The only last-minute preparation is the beating and folding in of the egg whites.

Once you have placed the soufflé in the oven, you must try to be adult about it and not open the door to peek until the soufflé has risen fully, or about 5 minutes before it is done. You are very lucky indeed if you have glass oven doors.

Time the baking of your soufflé so that your guests are waiting for it—create a little suspense. Soufflés wait for no one. They will, however, hold up for several minutes after the collar is removed.

If your oven temperature is not entirely accurate, and your soufflé turns out to be a bit runny in the center, you can always tell your guests that you've done it the French way. The French spoon the runny part over each serving as a sauce. We find, however, that most people prefer a soufflé done all the way through.

We have taught our class on soufflés more than any other throughout the years. Our students are very enthusiastic to find that soufflés are dramatic, exciting, and so much easier to make than they had anticipated. We have an enormous collection of recipes for soufflés of every description and are constantly experimenting with new ones. Someday we will write an entire book on the subject, but in the meantime, these tips will guarantee your success.

ALMOND SOUFFLÉ WITH ORANGE SAUCE
AND TOASTED ALMONDS

(6 SERVINGS)

SAUCE:

1 tablespoon butter or margarine
1½ cups fresh orange juice
1 tablespoon cornstarch
⅓ cup sugar
¼ teaspoon salt
Finely grated rind (zest, see note,
page 123) of 1 medium orange

2 large oranges, peeled and
sectioned with all membranes
removed*
2 tablespoons Cointreau or Triple
Sec
4 drops red food coloring
⅓ cup toasted sliced almonds

SOUFFLÉ:

Butter to coat the soufflé dish and
collar
4 tablespoons (½ stick) butter or
margarine
¼ cup all-purpose flour
1 cup milk
Dash salt

6 large eggs, separated
½ cup sugar, for the base
1 teaspoon almond extract
¼ teaspoon cream of tartar, or
lemon juice
¼ cup sugar, for the whites

Butter the inside of a 6-cup soufflé dish and sprinkle it with sugar. Take a strip of aluminum foil that will reach around the outside of the dish with some to spare, and fold it in half lengthwise. Butter one side of the foil and tie it securely, buttered side in, around the dish to form a collar that stands at least 2 inches above the rim. This will give your soufflé the support it needs to rise high above the dish.

To make the orange sauce, melt the 1 tablespoon butter or margarine in a heavy saucepan. Combine the orange juice, cornstarch, sugar and salt. Mix well and add it to the butter in the saucepan. Stir constantly over medium heat until the sauce becomes thick and transparent. Remove it from the heat and stir in the orange zest, orange sections, liqueur and red food coloring. This sauce should be served warm over the hot soufflé. If making it in advance, cover loosely with plastic wrap and leave it at room temperature. Just before serving, reheat it gently, place in a serving dish, and top with toasted almonds.

For the soufflé, melt the 4 tablespoons of butter in a skillet. Stir in the flour and allow this *roux* to cook, stirring occasionally, for 2 or 3

---

* Navel oranges are easiest because they are seedless.

minutes over very low heat. Take the pan off the heat and add the milk and salt. Stir with a whisk to blend, then return the pan to the heat. Cook, stirring constantly, until the mixture has thickened. Remove it from the heat. Have the egg yolks and sugar in a large mixing bowl. Beat a little of the *roux* into the egg yolks and sugar. Stir briefly, then add the remaining *roux* and beat vigorously until the mixture is blended and smooth. Stir in the almond extract. This is the base of the soufflé. If you will not be using it right away, clean the sides of the bowl with a rubber spatula and press plastic wrap into the surface of the mixture to prevent a skin from forming. Leave it at room temperature until needed.

About 45 minutes before serving the soufflé, preheat the oven to 375°. Beat the whites with the cream of tartar or lemon juice (as directed in "Secrets of a Great Soufflé," page 226), until they do not slide when the bowl is tilted. Then slowly add the remaining ¼ cup of sugar while beating, and continue to beat until the whites hold short, distinct peaks. Fold about one-third of the beaten whites thoroughly into the base. Then gently fold in the rest.

Pour the mixture into the prepared soufflé dish and bake at 375° for 35 to 40 minutes. Uncollar the soufflé and serve it immediately. Spoon some of the sauce and the toasted almonds over each portion.

To Make Ahead: The base for the soufflé and the orange sauce may be made the morning of the party. Cover both as directed and leave at room temperature. Beat and add the egg whites just before baking. Reheat the sauce gently and top it with almonds at serving time.

An Elegant Sit=Down Dinner for Six or Eight VIP's

Very Easy Vichyssoise

AMONTILLADO SHERRY

Boneless Cornish Game Hens
with Wild Rice Stuffing
Sauce Madère

RED BURGUNDY

Carottes Chinoises
Sautéed Cherry Tomatoes
Fresh Buttered Broccoli

Soufflé au Grand Marnier Mimi

$\mathcal{H}$ERE IS A MENU of many virtues, not the least of which is that it is totally unique and will enchant even the most sophisticated of your guests. With its vivid colors, varied textures, rich flavors and tempting aromas, this meal truly provides a sensuous eating experience!

We serve pale yellow Vichyssoise, drizzled with a ribbon of snow-white cream and topped with freshly snipped chives, in abalone-shell soup bowls that we obtained inexpensively in an ordinary shell shop. This cool, smooth potato and leek soup is one of the easiest of cold soups to prepare and has a well-deserved reputation for elegance. No matter what kind of soup bowls you use, you are off to a smashing start, especially if you serve small glasses of a fine Amontillado sherry to sip along with it.

The Cornish Game Hens are boned for ease of eating. Artfully stuffed with *pâté*-flavored wild rice, they have the appearance of whole hens. It is not at all difficult to bone them once you acquire the knack, but simpler yet if you can find a butcher willing to do it for you. Read the description of the boning procedure to him and describe how they will be stuffed. Our own recipe for quick brown sauce is laced with Madeira and spooned over the roasted hens at serving time. A fine red Burgundy provides the perfect accompaniment.

The main course is rich and generous; to prevent it from being overwhelming, we serve three different crisp vegetables with it.

Paul invented the recipe for the Carottes Chinoises while experimenting with a Chinese method of slicing vegetables. Pieces of carrot are cooked until barely tender, then glazed with melted butter, orange marmalade and ginger. Simply fantastic!

Sautéed Cherry Tomatoes go with any meal and couldn't be simpler. They are just heated in butter and seasoned with salt and pepper. Try them any time you want to add a quick splash of color to a menu.

Most of all, we think you will enjoy the very "French" method used for cooking the broccoli. It allows the broccoli to retain its bright green color and can be used for many other kinds of fresh vegetables. Best of all, this method leaves you free of last-minute cooking and timing—the broccoli needs only to be reheated in butter and seasoned.

Mimi, Diana's mother, is a marvelous cook who has a passion for Grand Marnier soufflés. On one occasion, our waiter at the busy La Coupole restaurant in Paris, upon discovering her weakness for the dessert (which did not appear on the menu), disappeared into the kitchen for forty-five minutes to make one for her himself. It mattered little to him that his other customers went unattended—he was creating a masterpiece for "the beautiful American lady." Upon returning from her European tour, Mimi began a search for the perfect recipe for this, her favorite dessert. The result is included here, a marvelous foolproof recipe with detailed instructions for advance preparation. There is no dessert more dramatic: a billowing orange-flavored cloud served with a cold sauce of vanilla and Grand Marnier–flavored cream.

Your guests will need real courage to return your dinner invitation after this romp. We bet they just settle for taking you to a restaurant . . .

TIMETABLE: For a comfortable schedule, begin the food preparation 1 or 2 days before your party. It will, of course, be greatly simplified if you have a supply of Diana's Quick Basic Brown Sauce (page 106) and/or Vichyssoise already on hand in your freezer.

Make the Wild Rice Stuffing and chill it. Bone the hens and chill them. When both are cold, the hens may be stuffed and assembled in the roasting pan ready for the oven. Make the basic brown sauce, if you have none already on hand. Add Madeira to the sauce as described in the recipe and let it cool with plastic wrap pressed into the surface to prevent a skin from forming. Refrigerate until almost serving time, when it will be reheated and quickly finished. Make and chill the Vichyssoise.

With these preparations out of the way, the day of the party should be a relaxed one for you. In the morning, make the base for the soufflé. Set it out of the way with plastic wrap pressed into the surface. Have the egg whites at room temperature in the bowl in which they will be beaten.

Prepare and set out all the vegetables as described in the recipes, ready to be finished at serving time.

Chill the soup bowls for the Vichyssoise. Set the table, providing each guest with one large wine glass for the Burgundy and a small one for the sherry. Mentally rehearse the final assembly of the main course. Put your feet up and read a magazine.

When you are just about to serve dinner, place the hens in the oven and invite your guests to the table. Join them in enjoying the Vichyssoise and sherry.

You will finish preparing the main course while your guests visit at the table. You have invited enough people—they will not lack for attention. Be relaxed about the timing of the soufflé—either excuse your-self during the main course to put it in the oven or wait until dinner is over and put it in then. We enjoy serving soufflés in the living room. However you time it, do tell your guests they are waiting for a soufflé—they will enjoy the anticipation.

VERY EASY VICHYSSOISE
(6 TO 8 SMALL SERVINGS)

2 or 3 leeks	*4 tablespoons chicken stock base*
4 tablespoons (½ stick) butter or	*(Spice Islands)*
margarine	*Salt and white pepper to taste*
2 medium baking potatoes	*1 cup (½ pint) heavy cream*
4 cups water	*3 tablespoons snipped chives*

Cut away most of the green part from each leek and either discard or save it for vegetable soup. Trim away a thin slice from the root end and cut the white part in half lengthwise. Riffle the leek as you would a deck of cards to see where it is dirty, then riffle it again under cold running water to rinse away any sand. Cut the leeks crosswise into ½-inch sections.

Melt the butter or margarine in a heavy saucepan and sauté the leeks over very low heat for about 10 minutes or until they are limp. Peel the potatoes and cut them crosswise into ¼-inch slices. Add the potatoes to the pot along with the water, chicken stock base, and about ¼ teaspoon each salt and white pepper. Bring the mixture to a boil, then lower the heat and simmer for 20 minutes or until the potatoes are tender.

Purée the mixture, a portion at a time, in a blender and transfer it to a glass or stainless-steel bowl to cool. Taste and season again with salt and white pepper. Overseason it, as chilling will dull the seasonings considerably. Press some plastic wrap into the surface of the soup to prevent a skin from forming and chill thoroughly.

Vichyssoise should be served in chilled bowls. Drizzle about 2 tablespoons of cream decoratively over the surface of each portion at serving time and sprinkle with snipped chives.

To Make Ahead: Vichyssoise will keep in the refrigerator for 4 days. It also freezes well. If frozen, thaw it for several hours, then break up the large frozen lumps with a fork and whirr it again in the blender to regain its original smooth consistency.

BONELESS CORNISH GAME HENS WITH WILD RICE STUFFING

(8 SERVINGS)

8 Cornish game hens (about 1 pound each)
4 tablespoons (½ stick) butter or margarine, melted

Salt and pepper
Sauce Madère (page 237)
Chopped parsley to garnish

WILD RICE STUFFING:

8 ounces uncooked wild rice
2 teaspoons salt
4 tablespoons (½ stick) butter or margarine
2 tablespoons minced shallots
2 2¾-ounce cans pâté de foie with truffles (or 5½ to 6 ounces of an equivalent type of canned pâté)

¼ cup cognac or fine brandy
¼ cup minced parsley
2 egg yolks
1½ teaspoons salt
¼ teaspoon ground black pepper

For this recipe the Cornish hens must be boned in a special way. The hens are cut open down the backbone and the wings are removed. Then all of the bones are removed except for the drumsticks. The skin and meat should remain completely intact. This is not as difficult as it may sound. We urge you to follow our instructions and try doing it yourself.

Using poultry shears, cut off the wings completely. Make an incision along the backbone and lay the hen flat, with the legs pointing toward you. It is now possible to remove the breastbone with your index finger. Do this by sliding your finger up along the breastbone and then pulling it out toward you and a little bit to the side. Keep inserting your finger farther up the breastbone and pulling it out toward the side until the meat is completely free from the bone on one side. Repeat the process on the other side of the breast. If you like, you can bone the hens with a small, sharp knife, but by using your finger you will be much less likely to break through the skin. After the breastbone has been removed, use a small knife to scrape the meat from the thigh bone. Cut off the thigh bone. The only bones now remaining are the drumsticks. That's all there is to it. It is not difficult—just get in there and do it!

To make the stuffing, place the wild rice in a strainer and rinse it thoroughly under cold running water. Put it in a 3-quart or larger saucepan with about 8 cups of cold water and the 2 teaspoons salt. Bring to a boil over high heat, then lower the heat and simmer, partially covered, for 25 minutes. Drain.

Melt the butter in a large, heavy skillet. Sauté the shallots for a minute or two. Add the drained rice and stir to coat it well. Add the *pâté* and stir over low heat until the *pâté* is completely dissolved into the rice. Stir in the cognac or brandy and continue cooking over very low heat for about 30 seconds. Place the rice mixture in a mixing bowl and stir in the chopped parsley, egg yolks, salt and ground pepper. Taste for seasoning and add more salt and pepper if needed. Cool completely before using.

To stuff a hen, lay it flat, skin side down, on a work surface, with the legs pointing toward you. Salt and pepper the inside lightly. Place about ½ cup of the cold stuffing in the center. Fold in the sides to cover the stuffing. Bend the breast down between the legs by rolling it toward you until the skin side is up. Tie the legs together with string and have them pointing slightly up toward you. Take a piece of foil— enough to reach around the base of the bird—and fold it into a 1-inch strip. Wrap this strip of foil around the bottom end of the hen to support its shape and to keep the legs pointing slightly upward (see illustration).

Arrange the stuffed hens in a lightly buttered roasting pan large enough to hold them without touching. If desired, refrigerate until an hour or two before baking, but, for accurate timing, bring them to room temperature before putting them in the oven.

About 45 minutes before serving, preheat the oven to 475°. Brush the hens with melted butter and sprinkle them lightly with salt and pepper. Place them in the hot oven and roast them for 25 to 30 minutes, depending on their size, basting them every 10 minutes. If the hens are getting too brown near the end of the cooking time, lower the heat to 350°. If they are not well-browned at the end of the cooking time, there is probably something wrong with your thermostat, and they should be cooked a little longer. We find it a good idea to keep an oven thermometer in the oven at all times.

Remove the foil from the hens before serving, place one in the center of each dinner plate, and arrange the vegetables attractively around them. Pour some of the Sauce Madère decoratively over each hen and sprinkle lightly with chopped parsley. Pass extra Sauce Madère in a sauceboat at the table.

To Make Ahead: The hens may be stuffed 2 days before your party if both the hens and the stuffing are kept thoroughly chilled. Do not freeze.

SAUCE MADÈRE

(1 QUART OR ABOUT 8 SERVINGS)

This is a lovely sauce to use with all roast meats.

1 tablespoon butter or margarine
2 tablespoons chopped shallots
1 cup Madeira
1 quart (4 cups) Diana's Quick
  Basic Brown Sauce (page 106)

1 tablespoon cold *butter*
2 tablespoons cognac or fine
  brandy

Melt 1 tablespoon of butter in a heavy-bottomed saucepan and sauté the shallots gently, taking care not to burn them. Add the Madeira and turn up the heat. Boil it hard until it has reduced to half its original volume (from 1 cup to ½ cup). Stir in the brown sauce and bring the mixture back to a boil. Lower the heat and allow the sauce to simmer uncovered for 15 minutes, stirring often. If the sauce is not to be used immediately, press plastic wrap into its surface to prevent a skin from forming and set it aside or refrigerate until needed.

At serving time, bring the sauce just to a boil. Remove it from the heat and add the cold butter and the cognac. Stir to dissolve the butter— this will give your sauce a lovely gloss—and serve immediately.

To Make Ahead: The sauce will keep beautifully for up to 5 days in the refrigerator or for months in the freezer. Mix in the lump of butter and the cognac just before serving.

CAROTTES CHINOISES

(8 SERVINGS)

About 12 young, medium-size
  carrots
2 tablespoons butter or margarine,
  melted

2 tablespoons orange marmalade
¼ teaspoon powdered ginger

You may cut up or slice the carrots any way you wish. We prefer the Chinese roll-cut (see illustration), which is done in the following manner: Hold a knife or cleaver above the carrot and make a diagonal slice straight down, then roll the carrot a quarter turn and slice again.

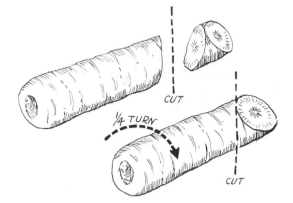

Repeat until all the carrot is used. Cut this way, the carrot sections have a greater surface area to absorb seasoning.

Place the cut carrots in a vegetable steamer over boiling water. Steam just until tender but still somewhat crisp—5 minutes will usually do it for the roll-cut. Have the melted butter, marmalade and powdered ginger ready in a serving bowl. Drain the carrots, if necessary, add them to the bowl, and toss to coat evenly. Serve immediately.

To Make Ahead: The carrots may be cut several hours before cooking. Store them in a plastic bag or right in the steamer. They should be cooked just before serving. It is a good idea to have the serving bowl with the butter, marmalade and ginger waiting on a hot tray to save last-minute fuss.

SAUTÉED CHERRY TOMATOES

(8 SERVINGS)

1 large or 2 small baskets (about 1 quart) firm cherry tomatoes

1 tablespoon butter or margarine
Salt and pepper to taste

Wash, dry, and hull the tomatoes; have them at room temperature. Just before serving, melt the butter or margarine in a heavy skillet. Add the tomatoes and stir over low heat just until they are warm through—don't try to "cook" them. Sprinkle with salt and pepper and serve immediately.

To Make Ahead: The tomatoes may be prepared in advance, but they should be cooked at the last minute. Set out all the necessary equipment early in the day so the whole process will only take a minute.

FRESH BUTTERED BROCCOLI

(8 SERVINGS)

This is a marvelous method for cooking all fresh vegetables.

3 pounds fresh broccoli
1 tablespoon salt
6 tablespoons (¾ stick) butter or
* margarine*

Salt and freshly ground black
* pepper*

Bring 4 to 6 quarts of water to a boil over high heat. Wash the broccoli in cold water. Cut off the flowerettes and set them side. Peel the bottoms of the stalks with a vegetable peeler, then cut them into rather large pieces of equal size. Place the stalks in the rapidly boiling water, followed by the salt. Boil, uncovered, for about 3 minutes, then add the flowerettes and cook 3 minutes longer. Test one of the stems for doneness by piercing it with a sharp knife—it should be almost tender but still give slight resistance. Drain the broccoli, then immerse it in cold water. This process will set and preserve the fresh green color. When the broccoli has cooled, remove it from the cold water and set aside to drain at room temperature.

Just before serving, melt the butter or margarine in a large skillet. Add the broccoli and toss gently to coat each piece. Sprinkle with salt and freshly ground pepper. Continue tossing gently until the broccoli is heated through.

To Make Ahead: The broccoli may be cooked in the morning, cooled, and set aside at room temperature. Have the butter waiting in a skillet, ready to reheat the broccoli just before serving.

SOUFFLÉ AU GRAND MARNIER MIMI

(6 TO 8 SERVINGS)

Before you begin, please read our tips on making soufflés on pages 226–227.

Butter to coat the soufflé dish and
*   collar*
4 tablespoons (½ stick) butter or
*   margarine*
4 tablespoons all-purpose flour
1 cup milk
Pinch of salt
6 large eggs, separated

½ cup sugar (for the base)
Grated rind (zest, see note, page
*   123) of 1 medium orange*
¼ cup Grand Marnier (orange-
*   flavored liqueur)*
¼ teaspoon cream of tartar or
*   lemon juice*
¼ cup sugar (for the whites)

SAUCE:

1 pint French vanilla ice cream,   *Grand Marnier, to taste*
*   softened*

Butter the inside of a 6-cup soufflé dish and sprinkle it with sugar. Take a strip of aluminum foil big enough to reach around the outside of the dish with some to spare and fold it in half lengthwise. Butter one side of it and tie it securely, buttered side in, around the dish to form a collar that stands at least 2 inches above the rim. This will give your soufflé the support it needs to rise high above the dish.

Melt the 4 tablespoons butter or margarine in a skillet—a Teflon one works especially well for this purpose. Stir in the flour and allow this *roux* to cook, stirring occasionally, for 2 or 3 minutes over very low heat. Remove the pan from the heat and add the milk and salt. Stir with a whisk to blend, then return the pan to the heat. Cook, stirring constantly, until the mixture has thickened. Beat a little of the *roux* into the egg yolks. Stir briefly, then add the remainder and beat vigorously until the mixture is thoroughly blended and smooth. Stir in the ½ cup sugar, the zest and ¼ cup Grand Marnier. This is the base of the soufflé. If you are not using it right away, clean the sides of the bowl with a rubber spatula and press plastic wrap into the surface of the mixture to prevent a skin from forming. Leave it at room temperature until needed.

Just before baking, beat the egg whites with the cream of tartar or lemon juice (as directed in "Secrets of a Great Soufflé," page 226) until they do not slide when the bowl is tilted. Slowly add the remaining ¼ cup sugar while beating, and continue to beat until the whites hold short, distinct peaks when the beater is lifted. Fold half the beaten whites thoroughly into the soufflé base, then gently fold in the remaining whites. It will not matter if there are a few streaks of white still showing when the folding process is completed.

Pour the mixture into the prepared soufflé dish and bake at 375° for 35 to 40 minutes.

To make the sauce, simply combine the slightly softened ice cream with enough Grand Marnier to flavor it to your taste.

When the soufflé is done, serve it immediately at the table, spooning the cold sauce over each individual serving.

To Make Ahead: The soufflé base may be prepared in the morning and stored as described above. Have the soufflé dish ready, buttered and collared, so that all you need do after company arrives is to beat and fold in the egg whites.

A Stunning Cold Buffet
for Twenty-four

Curried Flan Ring Garnished

with Fresh Flowers

Harlequin Ham

Sweet Champagne Mustard

Poached Whole Salmon in White Wine Aspic

Green Herbed Mayonnaise

Confetti Salad Vinaigrette

Molded Potato Salad

Chocolate Mousse Pie

ONCE IN A WHILE it's fun to have a large party and impress a lot of people all at once. Here is an elaborate buffet menu that twenty-four enraptured guests will rave about for years. It presents exciting and imaginative proof for Paul's theory that "First you eat with your eyes . . ."

A Curried Flan Ring is a bright yellow crown filled with fresh flowers and surrounded by rounds of French bread. It is served as a spread for guests to make their own canapés and has become a favorite appetizer for our students because it is so easy, and yet so impressive in appearance.

Paul's Harlequin Ham is a masterpiece of design. A boneless canned ham is presliced, then reassembled and held together in its original shape with long skewers which are later removed. It is then smoothly coated with seasoned cream cheese and decorated with paper-thin, diamond-shaped pieces cut from eggplant skin. Surrounded with roses and daisies cut from white turnips, it is a study in black and white. The first sight of this magnificent ham never fails to arouse exclamations of pure amazement. With it we serve Sweet Champagne Mustard, another recipe shared with us by Frances Pelham. The ham is ready to serve in slices as is, or with an assortment of breads and rolls for sandwich-making.

The Poached Whole Salmon in White Wine Aspic is almost as spectacular-looking as the ham. Paul's innovative method of poaching a fish eliminates the need for an expensive fish-poaching pan. And instead of glazing the fish in the classic manner with clarified poaching stock, he uses a lightly sweetened white wine and gelatin glaze, which lends a wonderful flavor to the salmon and also cuts down considerably on the work involved. When it comes to decorating the aspic, give your imagination free rein. Our illustration is only a suggestion. The delicate pink fish is complemented by a misty-green herb-flavored mayonnaise sauce.

Our gay Confetti Salad Vinaigrette is a frivolous combination of vegetables in many colors. It has an unexpected sweet-and-sour flavor that will complement the cold ham.

Molded Potato Salad is encased in a shimmering pickle-juice aspic and studded with carrot flowers and slices of olive—much more interesting than the delicatessen variety.

In this case, the main course does not upstage the finale. Chocolate Mousse Pie is easily the most glamorous recipe in this book. It is irresistible to "Chocoholics" and entices even dieters to throw caution to the winds. The pie consists of a thick, black cookie-crumb crust filled with devastatingly rich chocolate mousse. Dollops of whipped cream encircle the top, along with thin, perfectly formed leaves made of pure chocolate. For a final flourish, three candied violets are placed in the center rosette of cream. Seconds, anyone?

This menu has extraordinary elegance. A word to the wise: Try to make a few small but obvious mistakes in garnishing these dishes, or your guests will not believe that you really did it all yourself!

TIMETABLE: If you are making everything for this party with no assistance, you are going to have your hands full and should begin the food preparation well in advance.

The Sweet Champagne Mustard and the Confetti Salad Vinaigrette may both be made weeks in advance. Carve the turnip roses for the ham and keep them in cold water in the refrigerator or freezer. They will not seem like so much work if you consider that you can use them again and again.

A week before the party, call the market to order the whole salmon. Prepare and chill the Green Herbed Mayonnaise that accompanies the fish.

The fun actually begins 3 days before the party. Mentally plan the serving and make lists to organize everything down to the last detail. Check your serving pieces, glassware, and everything else you will need. Pick up the salmon and do all your other marketing.

The preparation of the Harlequin Ham, which is very time-consuming, may be done 2 days ahead. Once decorated, it should be kept in the refrigerator, covered with plastic wrap and topped with a wet towel. Keep the towel moist to prevent the cream-cheese coating from drying. Poach, chill, glaze and decorate the salmon. Refrigerate it uncovered on its serving platter.

The day before the party, make two Chocolate Mousse Pies by doubling the recipe. Make extra chocolate leaves for decorating the pies, as some may get broken. Children love to make these, so you might be able to enlist some help.

Prepare the Curried Flan Ring and the Molded Potato Salad. After they are completely set, both may be unmolded at your convenience and covered with plastic wrap.

The day of the party should be free of cooking. After all, everything will be served cold. Spend the day garnishing the platters, arranging flowers, and generally getting the house ready. Decorate the pies with whipped cream, leaves and violets no more than 4 hours before serving so the cream will retain its shape.

Everything except the dessert may be placed on the buffet table before guests arrive. When the doorbell rings, you can just relax and enjoy yourself.

CURRIED FLAN RING GARNISHED WITH FRESH FLOWERS

(ABOUT 24 SERVINGS)

1 small onion, chopped fine
1 stalk celery, chopped fine
2 tablespoons butter or margarine
2 tablespoons curry powder

4 teaspoons (1 envelope plus 1 teaspoon) unflavored gelatin
2 cups strong chicken broth
1 cup mayonnaise
3 hard-cooked eggs

To GARNISH THE PLATTER:

Fresh flowers
Sprigs of parsley

Toasted or plain rounds of French bread

You will need an electric blender and a plain ring mold of 5- or 6-cup capacity.

Sauté the chopped onion and celery in the butter over low heat until the onions are transparent. Sprinkle with the curry powder and cook, stirring, for 1 minute longer. Set aside.

Sprinkle the gelatin over ¼ cup cold water and allow it to soften for 5 minutes. Add the chicken broth to the onion-curry mixture and bring to a boil. Remove from the heat and add the softened gelatin, stirring until well dissolved. Chill the mixture for about 30 minutes, or until it starts to thicken, then place it in the container of an electric blender with the mayonnaise and the hard-cooked eggs and blend until completely smooth. Pour the mixture into a cold, wet ring mold and chill until firm.

Before serving, unmold the flan by dipping it quickly into hot water for a few seconds. Hold a wet serving plate over the mold and turn it over to release the flan onto the plate. Repeat this procedure if necessary. Using a wet plate will allow the flan to slide into the proper position.

Before serving, fill the center of the ring with bright, fresh flowers —shocking pink looks especially pretty—and fresh parsley sprigs. Surround it with tiny sprigs of parsley and slices of French bread (the long, thin kind), plain or toasted.

The flan is served with spreaders for guests to make their own canapés.

To Make Ahead: The unmolded flan keeps very well in the refrigerator, tightly covered with plastic wrap, for up to 2 days. Decorate with flowers and parsley within 2 hours of serving. You may wish to freeze some leftover flan—the texture will suffer only slightly.

HARLEQUIN HAM

(AT LEAST 24 SERVINGS)

1 five-pound precooked, canned ham
1½ pounds cream cheese
3 tablespoons bottled horseradish
¼ teaspoon salt

1 tablespoon fresh lemon juice
Skin only of 1 large or 2 small eggplants
Roses and daisies cut from raw turnips, to garnish

Scrape away any excess gelatin from the precooked, canned ham. Place it in a baking dish in a 325° oven for 15 minutes to melt off the remaining juices. Pat it dry with a paper towel and slice as you would like to see it served; then reassemble it, holding the slices together with two long skewers inserted lengthwise. (If you have a friendly butcher, you might ask him to scrape away the gelatin and juice for you. It will not then be necessary to heat the ham at all.) Place the ham on a serving platter and chill it thoroughly.

Combine the cream cheese, horseradish, salt and lemon juice in the bowl of an electric mixer and beat until it is light and very fluffy in appearance.

Spread the seasoned cream cheese ⅛ inch thick over the top and sides of the ham, filling in where necessary to make it symmetrical. Smooth the surface as neatly as possible, using a spatula which is dipped now and again in hot water. Chill just until the cheese topping has hardened, then remove the skewers—the coating will hold the slices together. Cover with a damp cloth to keep it moist.

Remove the skin from the eggplant(s) very carefully with a vegetable peeler. With a single-edged razor or an Exacto knife, cut the skin into diamond shapes that are uniform in size. Use a small, diamond-shaped pattern which you have cut out of cardboard or thin metal. The diamonds should be about 1 inch in length.

Arrange the diamond shapes on top of the cream cheese to create a harlequin effect (as illustrated). Surround the ham on the platter with roses and daisies cut from white turnips (as illustrated).

At serving time, peel down some of the ham slices to demonstrate how guests may help themselves. Serve the Sweet Champagne Mustard (below) next to the ham. You may, if you wish, set out a selection of breads, rolls, whipped cream cheese or butter for guests to make sandwiches.

To Make Ahead: The decorated ham will keep for 2 days in the refrigerator if it is lightly covered with plastic wrap and then with a moist towel. Keep the towel damp to prevent the cream cheese from drying out and cracking. The ham itself will keep for weeks. Turnip flowers will keep indefinitely if immersed in cold water and frozen. Thaw to use again and again. Ham does not freeze well.

SWEET CHAMPAGNE MUSTARD
(24 SERVINGS)

⅔ cup dry mustard
1 cup sugar
3 whole eggs

*⅔ cup white wine or champagne
vinegar*

Mix the mustard and sugar in the top of a glass double boiler. Beat in the eggs, followed by the vinegar. Place over boiling water and beat constantly for 4 to 7 minutes, or until thick and foamy. Pour into a large champagne glass or other dish for serving. Serve with ham or any cold meats.

To Make Ahead: The mustard will keep for up to 1 month in the refrigerator in a glass or plastic container.

POACHED WHOLE SALMON IN WHITE WINE ASPIC

(AT LEAST 24 SERVINGS)

1 four- to five-pound whole
salmon, head, fins and bones
removed

COURT BOUILLON (used to poach the salmon):

3 quarts cold water
1 bay leaf
½ cup chopped carrots
¾ cup chopped celery

1 medium onion, studded with 3
cloves
1 ½ cups dry white wine
1 ½ teaspoons salt
1 medium bunch parsley

WINE ASPIC:

1 ½ envelopes unflavored gelatin
2 cups dry white wine

1 tablespoon sugar

To DECORATE:

The green stem from 1 scallion,
cut into narrow strips
1 hard-cooked egg white, sliced
thin and cut into tiny flower
shapes with an aspic cutter

Sprigs of parsley and fresh daisies
to surround the salmon on the
platter

Combine all the court-bouillon ingredients in a large roasting pan or fish poacher, if you happen to have one. Wrap the salmon in a bath-size Turkish towel, leaving the ends of the towel folded on top of the fish. This will give you something to hold onto when handling the fish during the cooking. Lower the wrapped fish into the liquid and spoon the liquid over the top of the towel to moisten it completely. Bring the liquid to a simmer and allow the fish to cook gently for 20 to 30 minutes, depending upon the size of the salmon.

Wearing rubber gloves to insulate your hands from the heat, lift the fish from the cooking liquid to a flat surface and unwrap it very carefully. Use two pancake turners or spatulas to lift the fish gently onto a serving platter and, while it is hot, peel the skin off with a single-edged razor blade, starting just above the tail and working toward the head. Beneath the skin you will find a pale-grey fatty covering. Still working from tail to head, use a dull table knife to scrape away this fat to reveal the pink salmon meat.

Trim the fish to make it as attractive as possible, cutting away any ragged edges of salmon meat. If there are any holes in the salmon, patch them smoothly with some of the meat you have trimmed away. Chill thoroughly.

To make the aspic, sprinkle the gelatin over ⅓ cup of the wine. Heat the rest of the wine in a saucepan with the sugar until it comes to a boil. Lower the heat and simmer gently for 2 minutes. Remove the pan from the heat and stir in the softened gelatin. Place the saucepan in a bed of ice and stir the mixture slowly for 2 or 3 minutes, until it becomes syrupy. Spoon an even coating of this syrupy liquid over the chilled salmon and set it in the refrigerator until the glaze has set. Remove the pan with the remaining aspic from the ice water to prevent it from setting too much while you wait.

In a few minutes, when the first coat of glaze on the salmon has set, decorate the top of the fish with strips of scallion and lilies of the valley cut from hard-cooked egg white as shown in the illustration. Melt and cool the aspic again to its previous syrupy consistency. Spoon a second coat of glaze over the fish and chill again. Finally, top with a third layer of aspic and chill.

On the buffet table, present the whole salmon to your guests. Serve with Green Herbed Mayonnaise (page 251).

To Make Ahead: The fish may be poached and glazed 2 days before serving. Store, uncovered, in the refrigerator. Do not freeze.

GREEN HERBED MAYONNAISE

(2 CUPS, OR 12 SERVINGS)*

2 egg yolks
1 teaspoon salt
1 teaspoon sugar, or more to taste
1 teaspoon dry mustard
2 scallions, sliced, including part
of the green tops
½ cup minced parsley

Several dashes of cayenne
¼ teaspoon garlic powder
¼ teaspoon dried tarragon
½ teaspoon dried dill weed
3 tablespoons white wine vinegar
1½ cups fine-quality olive oil
2 to 3 drops green food coloring

Combine all the ingredients except the olive oil and food coloring in the large bowl of an electric mixer and beat at high speed for a minute or two. Slowly begin to add the oil *drop by drop* while continuing to beat rapidly. The mixture will begin immediately to emulsify and thicken. Do not be tempted to add the oil more quickly. After half the oil has been added, the remaining oil may be added in a very thin, steady stream. When the mayonnaise is finished, color it as desired with the green food coloring.

If at any point the mixture should separate, start with a clean mixing bowl in which is placed an extra egg yolk. Very gradually beat the separated sauce into the egg yolk to reestablish a smooth consistency.

Cover the mayonnaise with plastic wrap and chill until an hour or so before serving.

To Make Ahead: This sauce will keep for at least a week in the refrigerator. Do not freeze.

* This recipe should not be doubled, so you will have to make it twice for 24 servings. If you are lucky enough to have one of the new Cuisinart food processors, mincing the parsley will take only seconds. All the ingredients should be at room temperature before you begin. If it is raining outside or a storm is threatening, the mayonnaise will not bind, so put off making it until the weather has cleared.

CONFETTI SALAD VINAIGRETTE

(24 SERVINGS)

VEGETABLES:

2 bunches scallions, sliced thin, including part of the green tops
2 green bell peppers, diced fine
4 large raw carrots, diced fine
6 stalks celery, diced fine
¼ cup chopped parsley
2 nine-ounce packages frozen French-style green beans, cooked and drained (or the equivalent of canned beans)

2 ten-ounce packages frozen tiny tender peas, cooked and drained (or the equivalent of canned petits pois)
1 twelve-ounce can white shoe peg corn, drained
1 twelve-ounce can yellow corn
1 four-ounce jar sliced pimientos, chopped fine

DRESSING:

1 cup sugar
2 cups red wine or cider vinegar
¼ cup water

½ cup vegetable oil
Salt, pepper, and garlic salt, to taste

Combine all the vegetables in a large stainless-steel or plastic container. Heat the sugar and vinegar together in a small saucepan over low heat, stirring until the sugar is completely dissolved. Remove from the heat and stir in the water and vegetable oil. Pour the dressing over the vegetables and stir to mix thoroughly. Refrigerate overnight. Then season to taste with salt, pepper and garlic salt. Serve in a crystal bowl with a slotted serving spoon.

To Make Ahead: This salad will keep for weeks in the refrigerator. It is marvelous to have on hand because it goes so well with leftover roasts and cold cuts and is ideal for picnics.

MOLDED POTATO SALAD

(24 SERVINGS)

2½ envelopes unflavored gelatin
½ cup cold water
1¼ cups dill pickle juice
Black and green olives, sliced, to decorate the top

Thin, flower-shaped slices of carrot to decorate the top (as illustrated)
Parsley sprigs to garnish

POTATO SALAD:

9 cups diced, cooked potatoes (6 to 8 medium potatoes) (we use a combination of red or white rose and russet or Idaho)
1¼ cups diced celery
1 medium onion, minced
1 bunch scallions, sliced, including part of the green tops
¾ cup diced pickles (either sweet or dill)

10 hard-cooked eggs, coarsely chopped
2 cups mayonnaise
2 teaspoons celery seed
8 to 10 slices bacon, cooked until crisp, and crumbled
1½ teaspoons salt
¼ teaspoon black pepper
1½ teaspoons dry mustard

Sprinkle the gelatin over ½ cup cold water and let it soften for 5 minutes. Heat the pickle juice just to the boiling point and remove from the heat. Add the softened gelatin and stir until well dissolved. Pour about ¼ inch of this mixture into a 4-quart (or larger) container with a flat bottom, which you are going to use for the mold. Do not use aluminum or tin. Chill for 7 to 10 minutes, or until almost set. Decorate by pressing the sliced olives and carrots into the mixture in an attractive pattern—this will be the top of your potato salad when it is turned out. Chill until completely set.

Meanwhile, combine the potatoes, celery, onions, pickles, scallions, eggs, mayonnaise, celery seed and bacon in a large mixing bowl. Stir the salt, pepper and dry mustard into the remaining pickle juice—gelatin mixture and pour over the salad ingredients. (If the gelatin has begun to set, reheat the mixture gently.) Taste and adjust the seasoning if necessary. Spoon the potato salad over the gelatin layer in the mold and chill until firm—at least 2 hours. Unmold before serving and garnish with sprigs of parsley.

To Make Ahead: Store in the refrigerator for up to 3 days. Do not freeze. The potato salad may be unmolded up to 24 hours before serving. Store, uncovered, in the refrigerator.

CHOCOLATE MOUSSE PIE
(AT LEAST 12 SERVINGS, OR AS MANY AS 16)

We like to make two or three of these at once—a little more work but worth it.

CHOCOLATE CRUST:

¾ of an 8½-ounce package
   Nabisco Famous Chocolate
   Wafers

½ stick butter or margarine,
   melted

CHOCOLATE MOUSSE FILLING:

½ teaspoon dry instant coffee
4 eggs, separated
½ cup granulated sugar
1 teaspoon vanilla extract
⅛ teaspoon salt
2 tablespoons cognac or brandy
1 square (1 ounce) Baker's
   unsweetened chocolate

4 squares (4 ounces) Baker's semisweet chocolate
5 tablespoons butter or margarine
1 square (1 ounce) semisweet
   chocolate, grated
⅛ teaspoon cream of tartar
4 teaspoons granulated sugar
1 cup heavy cream

CHOCOLATE LEAVES:

⅓ *of a six-ounce package of semi-*   *Smooth, fresh leaves, approxi-*
  sweet chocolate bits   *mately 2 inches in length (citrus*
                                                                leaves work well)

TOPPING:

1 cup heavy cream   *Chocolate leaves (directions*
1 teaspoon vanilla extract   *below)*
⅓ *to* ½ *cup confectioner's sugar*   *Candied violets (optional)*

You will need a 10-inch spring-form pan to make this pie. A smaller one may be used, but the dessert will be higher and more difficult to serve!

First, make the crust. Put the chocolate wafers in a heavy plastic bag and crush them with a rolling pin. After they are in small pieces, finish grinding them in a blender, a cupful at a time. Combine the crumbs with the melted butter and pat into the bottom and 1 inch up the sides of your spring-form pan. Bake at 350° for 10 minutes. Chill until needed. You may freeze the crust if you like.

Next, make the filling. Place the ½ teaspoon instant coffee in a measuring cup with 1 tablespoon hot tap water and stir to dissolve. Add cold water to the ⅛ cup mark and set aside. In the top of a glass double boiler over simmering water, beat the egg yolks with ½ cup sugar, the vanilla extract, salt, and cognac or brandy until the mixture becomes thick and pale yellow in color. This will take about 5 minutes, and you should stay with it or the mixture might curdle. (If it should curdle, simply beat it slowly into another egg yolk, using a wire whisk.) As soon as the yolk mixture has finished cooking, pour it into another container to cool a bit.

Melt the 5 squares of the two kinds of chocolate in a large mixing bowl set into a skillet of simmering water. When the chocolate has melted, remove it from the heat and beat in the 5 tablespoons of butter or margarine, a tablespoonful at a time, using a whisk. Then gradually beat in the egg-yolk mixture until it is smooth—the chocolate will thicken and congeal somewhat—don't worry about that. Stir in the coffee.

Grate the remaining square of chocolate on a medium grater and set aside.

Place the egg whites in the clean bowl of your electric mixer with the cream of tartar. If the whites are not at room temperature, set the bowl in some water and stir to take the chill off—if you skip this step the whites will not whip up properly. Now, beat the whites at high speed just to the point where they do not slip when you tip the bowl. Then gradually beat in the 4 teaspoons sugar until the whites form stiff peaks when you lift the beater. Beat approximately 1 cupful of the whites thoroughly into the chocolate mixture to lighten it. Then, using a rubber spatula, scrape the rest of the whites onto the top of the chocolate mixture to wait while you whip the cream in the same mixing bowl (no need to rinse it). The cream should be whipped to the point where it is fairly stiff without being lumpy. Now fold the rest of the whites into the chocolate mixture (as described in "Secrets of a Great Soufflé," page 226). Fold in the cream, followed by the grated chocolate. Pour the mousse into the prepared crust and chill for at least 3 hours or for up to 2 days.

The easiest way to make the chocolate leaves is to melt the chocolate bits in the top of a double boiler. Stir until smooth and remove from the heat. Let cool for a few minutes, stirring occasionally. Use a table knife to spread the chocolate thickly over the backs of clean, fresh leaves. Place the leaves on plates, chocolate side up, in the refrigerator until the chocolate has hardened. Carefully peel the real leaves off the chocolate ones (see illustration).

To make the topping, whip the cream until it holds a shape. Add the vanilla and press the confectioner's sugar through a kitchen strainer into the cream. Whip a little longer until the cream is fairly stiff.

No more than 4 hours before serving decorate the top of the pie with whipped cream and chocolate leaves in any way you like. Usually we press the whipped cream through a pastry tube to form rosettes (see illustration). If you don't wish to bother with a pastry tube, you can simply spoon mounds of whipped cream around the edge of the pie (in which case it will have more of a homemade appearance and your guests are more likely to believe you made it).

Stand the chocolate leaves on their sides in the whipped cream border of the pie, one for each serving. We usually place a few candied

violets on top of a bit of whipped cream in the center of the pie—the color is beautiful with the chocolate.

Brace yourself for cheers and applause at serving time!

To Make Ahead: This dessert is spectacular but time-consuming to make. Therefore, we suggest you make several pies at the same time, 2 days before your party. Freeze the extra pies, undecorated, for another occasion. Leave the spring-form sides of the pan in place until just before serving to protect the pie from injury and cover the top with foil. The pie may be stored, without the whipped cream topping, in the refrigerator for 2 days or in the freezer for 2 weeks. If frozen, thaw overnight in the refrigerator.

Decorate with whipped cream and chocolate leaves no longer than 4 hours before serving. Chocolate leaves may be frozen separately if they are carefully wiped of surface moisture which could cause white spots. They are marvelous to have on hand for dressing up simple desserts and needn't be thawed before serving.

VI

Menus for the Holidays

Our Traditional Turkey Dinner with All the Trimmings

Mulled Wine

Jewel Cheese Ball

Cream of Chestnut Soup

Roast Turkey von Welanetz

MOSELLE (SPÄTLESE)

Baked Petits Pois†

Apricot-Cranberry Sauce with Almonds

Curried Fruit Compote

Marge's Pumpkin Cake

with Brandied Cream-Cheese Icing and Pecans

*T*HIS MENU FOR Thanksgiving or Christmas has provided some of our most stimulating classes—all of our students bring something to taste which has been a traditional holiday favorite in their own homes. Everybody enjoys tasting the others' contributions and sharing their recipes.

In this chapter especially, the method and order of preparation for the entire dinner is highly detailed. We think you'll find our plan eliminates the usual drudgery and last-minute fuss from your big holiday party. Your family and friends will be surprised at the ease with which you handle such a grand undertaking. Holiday *sans* hassle!

Decide which suits your purposes best—a sit-down dinner or a serve-yourself buffet—and set the table accordingly. Our own choice is buffet-style on this occasion. There are so many separate items to serve that the array of delicious foods makes for extra festivity. A beautiful Thanksgiving centerpiece is easily created by arranging dried flowers and leaves in autumn shades of gold and brown. We store ours carefully boxed and labeled, along with our other seasonal decorations, to use again from year to year. For Christmas we like an arrangement of poinsettias, white chrysanthemums and red-berried holly.

If the weather is blustery or snowy, welcome your guests with Mulled Wine. Champagne would be a festive alternate for milder climates. For an appetizer, serve a Jewel Cheese Ball. At Christmastime,

262

roll it in pomegranate seeds or chopped parsley so it will look like an ornament ready to hang on the tree. At other times of the year, we like to roll the ball in chopped pecans or toasted sesame seeds. A cheese ball can be a blessing at holiday time because it requires almost no last-minute attention.

Making the chestnut soup with fresh chestnuts is a true labor of love. The work will be long forgotten, however, if you make it a month or more ahead of time and store it in the freezer. The only difficult task is shelling fresh chestnuts. Your manicure cannot possibly survive, so if you have children available, you would be wise to induce them to do this for you. They'll probably have fun doing what would be a chore for you! It is much, much easier to substitute canned chestnuts—happily, the difference is hardly noticeable. As you might guess, Cream of Chestnut Soup is thick and very rich, so you should serve it in small portions—don't most very good things come in small packages? You might enjoy serving it in soup cups in the living room.

Our method of cooking a turkey is quite unusual—but it's the easiest and quickest way by far. You'll be amazed at the moist, beautiful brown turkey that you will achieve. It will rouse cheers if presented on a platter surrounded by watercress or parsley. Or, even more inviting, fresh, perfect chrysanthemums, the color to suit the season—an exciting and unusual touch! An estate-bottled Moselle (Spätlese), well chilled, will provide the best complement to your turkey.

Some of the stuffing is baked inside the bird, the rest is baked separately. Once again, our Baked Petits Pois (page 131) make a perfect addition to the menu, both for color and simplicity.

And what holiday dinner would be complete without cranberries in some form? Our own Apricot-Cranberry Sauce keeps beautifully for weeks in the refrigerator, to be used as an attractive relish on the table throughout the holidays. We are also including a recipe for an unusual Curried Fruit Compote, delicious with turkey or ham, to use if you require an even more lavish display of food.

Marge, Paul's mother, gave us her recipe for the very moist Pumpkin Cake with Brandied Cream-Cheese Icing and Pecans. This dessert will provide a delightful change from the inevitable pumpkin pie. We especially appreciate the recipe because this cake must be made 2 or 3 days ahead and allowed to age to bring out its full flavor. What an added blessing at this time of year when there are so many last-minute chores.

Why not enjoy the holidays fully this year instead of burdening yourself with unnecessary tasks? It really isn't necessary to spend the whole day in the kitchen. This is a merry menu which we hope will help you and yours have a delightful holiday—together!

Timetable : As far in advance as possible, make the chestnut soup and store it in plastic containers in your freezer. To serve, thaw completely and heat gently—it is quite thick and will burn easily. You may also wish to make the pumpkin cake long in advance. After frosting, let it rest, covered, for 3 days before freezing it, carefully wrapped. Or simply make it 3 days before your party—its flavor is vastly enhanced on standing.

The apricot-cranberry sauce keeps nicely for weeks in the refrigerator in a covered container. To serve, spoon it into a crystal bowl and top decoratively with whole blanched almonds.

Anytime up to 3 days before your party, bake the Curried Fruit Compote. Store it in the refrigerator until the morning of the party. It will require only slight reheating if you have it at room temperature. Make the cheese ball(s), wrap tightly in plastic wrap or foil, and refrigerate. Two hours before serving time, decorate as desired and allow to come to room temperature for ease of spreading. The peas can be arranged in their baking-serving dish and stored in the freezer. You will slide them, still frozen, into a 350° oven an hour before serving.

The day before your party, mix the stuffing according to the directions in the turkey recipe and refrigerate until the next morning. It is not mandatory to do this the day before, but it will make the party day so much easier for you.

Starting on the morning of your party, follow the instructions in the turkey recipe straight through. Our directions for stuffing and roasting the turkey and making the giblet gravy are all given in order of preparation.

Finally, ease your last-minute activities by asking someone to help you by preparing and serving the festive cups of Mulled Wine or glasses of champagne that will welcome your guests to the holiday celebration. Cheers!

MULLED WINE

(12 OR MORE SERVINGS)

1 half-gallon red Burgundy	*12 two-inch pieces stick cinnamon*
1 cup sugar	*1 cup cognac or brandy*
30 whole cloves	*½ cup raisins or currants*

Combine the Burgundy, sugar, cloves and cinnamon pieces in a saucepan. Bring to a boil, then lower heat and simmer for 5 minutes. Stir in the cognac or brandy.

Place some raisins or currants in the bottom of each serving cup. Pour in the Mulled Wine and serve hot. It's potent, so serve it in small portions.

To Make Ahead: Combine the ingredients in the saucepan as directed. Cover and set aside until ready to heat. The mixture should be heated just before serving.

JEWEL CHEESE BALL

(1 LARGE OR 2 SMALL CHEESE BALLS)

1 pound sharp Cheddar cheese, finely grated	*½ cup chopped walnuts or pecans*
3 ounces Roquefort cheese	*1 small clove garlic, pressed*
3 ounces cream cheese	*½ teaspoon Fines Herbes (Spice Islands) or other herb blend*
2 tablespoons butter or margarine, melted	*¼ to ½ teaspoon Beau Monde seasoning (to taste)*
1 four-ounce can pitted, chopped black olives	

DECORATION:

1½ cups fresh pomegranate seeds or chopped pecans, or ¾ cup parsley, chopped fine

Place the Cheddar, Roquefort and cream cheeses in the bowl of an electric mixer and allow them to come to room temperature. Add the other ingredients and beat at low speed until thoroughly blended and smooth. Shape the mixture into 1 or 2 balls. Wrap in plastic wrap or foil and refrigerate.

Two hours before serving, remove the ball(s) from the refrigerator. Roll them in pomegranate seeds, pecans, or parsley, as desired, and place on a serving plate. Leave at room temperature until serving time. Serve with crackers and a spreader.

To Make Ahead: Make the balls up to a week ahead and store, tightly wrapped, in the refrigerator.

CREAM OF CHESTNUT SOUP

(12 SERVINGS)

2 pounds fresh chestnuts in the shell,* or 2 ten-ounce cans whole chestnuts packed in water (not in syrup), drained and rinsed

2 tablespoons vegetable oil (for shelling fresh chestnuts)

4 tablespoons (½ stick) butter or margarine

2 medium onions, chopped

2 large carrots, peeled and chopped fine

1 quart strong chicken or turkey broth (if using canned condensed broth, do not dilute)

1½ cups heavy cream

1 teaspoon sugar

½ cup pale dry sherry

Salt and white pepper, to taste

Chicken stock base, available in jars (optional)

To make the soup you will need a large, heavy-bottomed saucepan or soup pot. In it, melt the butter and sauté the chopped onions until they are lightly browned, being careful not to burn them. Add the peeled or canned chestnuts, carrots and broth. Simmer until the chestnuts are quite soft, about 15 or 20 minutes. Then strain and reserve the liquid in a large saucepan.

* To shell fresh chestnuts, make a cross with a sharp paring knife on the flat side of each chestnut. Place them in a skillet over high heat and drizzle 2 tablespoons of oil over them. Shake them well to coat each one with oil. Place them in a 350° oven for about 20 minutes. At the end of that time, remove one chestnut with a spoon and hold it under cold running water. When it is cool enough to handle, remove the shell and all of the brown membrane. If it does not all come off easily, drop the shelled chestnuts into some boiling water and simmer them for a few minutes, until the skins are easily removed. As we said in the introduction, you are wise to induce any children you have about to do this for you.

Purée the chestnuts and vegetables, a little at a time, with some of the broth, in your blender container until the mixture is completely smooth. Add more broth if necessary to keep the mixture running through the blades. Then strain the puréed mixture into the saucepan containing the remaining broth. Add the cream, sugar and sherry. Heat, without boiling, and season to taste with salt, white pepper and chicken stock base. Be sure to serve this soup in very small portions—it's rich!

To Make Ahead: The soup freezes beautifully, so you can make it several months ahead. To serve, thaw it completely and reheat without boiling.

ROAST TURKEY VON WELANETZ
(Including Stuffing and Giblet Gravy in the Order of Preparation)
(12 SERVINGS WITH LEFTOVERS)

1 turkey (at least 14 pounds), at room temperature
Salt and pepper
¼ cup vegetable oil

½ cup Kitchen Bouquet, or other brown gravy seasoning, for color
Pastry brush
Extra-heavy aluminum foil

STUFFING:

2 eight-ounce packages herb-stuffing mix
2 stalks celery, diced fine
1 large onion, chopped
1 cup chopped parsley
½ pound (2 sticks) butter or margarine

2 cups water
Chopped fresh or dried sage, to taste
Salt and pepper, to taste
1 cup pecan halves

GRAVY:

Turkey giblets, neck, and end
  joints of the wings
1 onion, cut up
6 peppercorns
1 stalk celery or celery leaves, cut
  up

Parsley stems (optional)
2 teaspoons salt
Cold water to cover
½ cup flour
Drippings from the cooked turkey

TO DECORATE THE PLATTER:

2 dozen or so orange chrysanthemums (or any color you like),
  or watercress, or parsley

TIMETABLE
For Foil-Roasted Turkey at 450°

WEIGHT	TIME Stuffed or Unstuffed
7–9 pounds	2¼–2½ hours
10–13 pounds	2¾–3 hours
14–17 pounds	3 –3¼ hours
18–21 pounds	3¼–3½ hours
22–24 pounds	3½–3¾ hours

The day before the party, if you like, put the packaged stuffing mix into a large mixing bowl with the chopped celery, onion and parsley. Melt the butter in the water and pour the mixture slowly over the stuffing mix while tossing it lightly with a fork. Season the stuffing to taste with sage and salt and pepper—it will need a lot. Fold in the pecans and refrigerate until ready to stuff the bird.

The morning of the party, clean and dry the turkey with paper towels. Sprinkle the inside only with salt and pepper. Cut off the end joints of both wings and set these aside with the giblets and neck to use in making the broth for the gravy. Take care that both turkey and stuffing are *cold* so bacteria will not grow. Then stuff both cavities of the turkey very loosely, as stuffing swells while cooking, and skewer the cavities shut. Put the rest of the stuffing in an ovenproof casserole and set it aside. Later you will sprinkle this extra stuffing with broth, cover it with foil, and bake it at 325° for an hour or so. If you won't be needing all of this stuffing the first day, refrigerate this part and bake when needed. It is a good idea to offer both stuffings to your guests, as there are some people who like wet stuffing, and others who prefer it dry. The stuffing from inside the turkey will be very moist!

Set the turkey on a long, wide piece of extra-heavy aluminum foil that will reach around the bird easily with some to spare. You will probably have to connect two pieces together, sealing them with several folds. Mix the vegetable oil with the Kitchen Bouquet (brown gravy seasoning) in a small bowl. Using a pastry brush, brush the turkey all over, even under the wings, until it is completely covered with a brown glaze. This will give the finished turkey a rich, oven-browned color. Wrap the foil up around the turkey, taking care not to tear a hole in the foil with the skewers. Seal the foil on top of the bird to form a loose package. There should be a small hole on top to allow the steam to escape during the cooking, so poke one somewhere around the large cavity with a sharp knife. Place the wrapped turkey on a rack over a roasting pan and set it in the preheated oven to cook at 450° for the time specified on the chart on page 268.

Now put all the giblets except the liver into a 4-quart saucepan with the neck and wing tips, onion, peppercorns, celery, parsley stems, salt and cold water to cover. Bring to a boil, turn down the heat to medium, cover the pot and simmer gently until the giblets can be pierced easily with a cooking fork—this will take 1 to 1½ hours for a large bird. Add the liver and simmer 10 more minutes. Strain the broth into a bowl, skim off the fat, taste for seasoning and set aside. When the neck is cool enough to handle, remove the meat with your fingers. Chop the giblets coarsely and put them with the neck meat into a small bowl with just enough broth to cover and keep it moist; then set aside. Now, sit down somewhere and put your feet up until the turkey is done!

When the turkey is done, remove it from the oven and prick several holes in the bottom side of the foil with a knife, so that the juices will come spurting out into the roasting pan. Place the extra baking dish of stuffing (sprinkled lightly with the strained giblet broth and covered with foil) into the oven at 325° so it will be done when you are ready to serve.

When the juices from the turkey have finished running into the roasting pan, open the foil—be very careful that the steam that will emerge doesn't burn you. Remove the turkey to a platter in a warm spot to rest while you make the gravy. Place a tent of foil over the bird to hold in the heat.

Pour the juices from the roasting pan into a bowl. Spoon the fat off the top and reserve ½ cup. Throw out the rest of the fat (or save it for another purpose). Put the ½ cup of fat into a heavy saucepan with the ½ cup of flour and let this *roux* cook for 2 to 3 minutes. Meanwhile, measure the skimmed turkey drippings and add enough of the reserved broth to make 5 cups of liquid. Stir this into the flour mixture and bring to a simmer. Let simmer for 2 to 3 minutes. If the gravy is too thin, shake a little flour and water together in a sealed jar and stir it immediately into the simmering gravy—this will prevent lumps. Add the reserved giblets to the gravy.

Unskewer the turkey and surround the platter with the flowers, the parsley, or the watercress. Present it to your guests before carving it.

To Make Ahead: The stuffing may be made a day in advance and refrigerated, as may the broth for the gravy. Leftover meat will freeze perfectly, and is nice to have on hand for filling crêpes, making curry, salads, etc. The gravy freezes without any ill effects, as does the stuffing. You might wish to make up your own TV dinners in aluminum-foil pans for simple family fare.

APRICOT-CRANBERRY SAUCE WITH ALMONDS
(4 CUPS, OR 12 SERVINGS)

2 cups sugar
¾ cup cold water
1 pound raw cranberries, washed
  and picked over

½ cup apricot jam
¼ cup fresh lemon juice
½ cup blanched whole almonds,
  for garnish

In a 4-quart saucepan, combine the sugar and cold water and bring to a boil. Cook the mixture for 5 minutes without stirring, then add the cranberries, letting them cook for about 4 more minutes. You will hear a popping noise as the berries begin to burst and become transparent. Remove the saucepan from the heat and stir in the apricot jam. When well blended, add the lemon juice and stir. Chill the sauce thoroughly before serving.

This sauce is most beautifully presented in a crystal bowl with the blanched almonds sprinkled or arranged in a pattern on top just before serving.

To Make Ahead: The sauce will keep for weeks tightly covered in the refrigerator. Top with the almonds just before serving, or the sauce will tint them red and you will lose the lovely contrast of color.

CURRIED FRUIT COMPOTE

(12 OR MORE SERVINGS)

2 twelve-ounce packages mixed, pitted dried fruits
2 twenty-ounce cans pineapple chunks and their syrup

2 twenty-one-ounce cans cherry-pie filling
1 cup dry sherry
1 tablespoon curry powder

Cut the large pieces of dried fruit into halves or quarters. In a 3-quart casserole, combine the dried fruits, pineapple chunks with their liquid, and the cherry-pie filling. Mix together the sherry and curry powder and pour over the fruits. Mix to combine.

Bake the casserole, covered, at 350° for 30 minutes. Uncover and bake 45 minutes longer. Let cool at least 45 minutes before serving.

To Make Ahead: The compote may be baked up to 5 days before serving. Let cool and store it covered in the refrigerator. For best flavor, reheat it to serve slightly warm.

MARGE'S PUMPKIN CAKE WITH BRANDIED CREAM-CHEESE ICING AND PECANS

(12 SERVINGS)

CAKE:

2 cups granulated sugar
4 eggs
1 cup vegetable oil
2 cups (one-pound can) pumpkin
2 cups all-purpose flour

2 teaspoons baking soda
½ teaspoon salt
2 teaspoons ground cloves
2 teaspoons ground cinnamon

Icing:

3 ounces cream cheese
¾ of a fresh (1 pound) box of
   confectioner's sugar

¼ pound (1 stick) butter
1 teaspoon vanilla extract
2 to 3 teaspoons brandy

Decoration:

1 cup chopped pecans

Place the sugar and the eggs in the bowl of an electric mixer and beat until smooth and creamy. Beat in the oil and pumpkin and blend well. Sift together the flour, baking soda, salt, cloves and cinnamon. Add these to the pumpkin mixture and stir until thoroughly combined.

    Pour the batter into an ungreased 10-inch tube pan and bake at 350° for 55 to 60 minutes. Let the cake cool in the pan for 1 hour before turning it out.

    To make the icing, place all the icing ingredients in a bowl and beat them together until smooth. Spread the icing over the cooked pumpkin cake and decorate the top with the chopped pecans.

To Make Ahead: This cake really should be made 2 or 3 days before serving, as the flavor improves vastly on standing. Ice whenever convenient. The cake freezes perfectly, iced or not. It is best to place it in the freezer unwrapped; then, when it is solid, wrap it in foil and seal it tightly. To serve, unwrap and defrost at room temperature for about 8 hours.

USES FOR LEFTOVER TURKEY

TURKEY STOCK

1 turkey carcass
½ teaspoon each *dried marjoram,*
   thyme, and basil
1 onion, coarsely chopped

1 stalk celery, coarsely chopped
1 carrot, coarsely chopped
Parsley stems (optional)
Salt and pepper

Break the turkey carcass into pieces, cracking the large bones. Put into a large stock pot; add all the other ingredients and cold water to cover the carcass. Bring to a boil, let simmer for 5 minutes, then spoon off any scum from the surface. Reduce the heat and simmer, covered, for 3 hours. Strain and refrigerate. Remove the fat from the surface before using.

This stock freezes beautifully and is great to have on hand for soups, gravies, curries, etc.

EASY TURKEY CURRY

(6 TO 8 SERVINGS)

6 tablespoons (¾ stick) butter
1 tart apple, peeled and chopped fine
1 onion, chopped fine
1 clove garlic, pressed
2 tablespoons curry powder

2 tablespoons flour
2 cups turkey stock made from the carcass
Cayenne pepper to taste (optional)
4 cups cooked turkey meat, diced

Melt the butter and add the apple, onion, garlic and curry powder. Cook until the onion is transparent. Add the flour and cook 2 to 3 minutes longer. Add the stock while stirring and bring to a boil. Stir constantly until the sauce thickens. Season to taste with cayenne. Add the turkey meat and heat until the meat is hot through. Serve with your favorite curry condiments—fresh pineapple is delicious here So are toasted coconut, peanuts and chives. This curry freezes very nicely.

TURKEY CURRY SALAD

(10 OR MORE SERVINGS)

An exotic recipe from our dear friend, Susie Gross.

8 cups coarsely cut cooked turkey
1 twenty-ounce can water chestnuts, cut into quarters
2 pounds seedless grapes
2 cups celery, chopped
2 cups sliced and toasted almonds

3 cups mayonnaise
1 tablespoon curry powder
2 tablespoons soy sauce
1 large can lichee nuts, drained (optional)

Mix all ingredients except the lichee nuts and chill. Serve on a platter surrounded with lichee nuts.

To Make Ahead: Store in the refrigerator for up to 48 hours.

A Festive and Formal Holiday Buffet

French 75

Roquefort Mousse

Butter-Roasted Pecans

French Asparagus Salad

Cornish Game Hens with

Black Cherry Sauce

SPARKLING VOUVRAY or ASTI SPUMANTE

Orange Halves Filled with Wild Rice–Sausage Casserole

Frances Pelham's Flaming Rum-Plum Pudding

with Hard Sauce

*T*HIS HOLIDAY SEASON BUFFET is a knockout and provides a welcome escape from the usual turkey and ham. It is a
very exciting menu because few of these dishes could ever be found
in even the most illustrious restaurants.

It is really not a dinner that guests can balance on their laps because the 'Cornish hens, even though served partially boned, require a
bit of manipulation. Card tables might be set up just before serving to
provide extra seating for a large number of guests. Candlelight would
be especially flattering on this occasion, to both your food and your
guests.

A French 75 is a celebration in itself. Our version of this cocktail,
combining champagne and brandy, is much less potent than the
standard recipe. It is easy to make and will solve the usual problem of
drink-mixing if you don't have a bartender on hand for the evening.
Set out several small bowls of Butter-Roasted Pecans for your guests to
nibble on during the cocktail hour, and serve a molded Roquefort
Mousse, the lightest and most elegant hors d'oeuvre spread ever, surrounded by parsley sprigs for decoration and crackers for spreading.
This concoction always inspires raves and requests for the recipe.

The main course is even more spectacular than the hors d'oeuvre.
Gay individual packages of marinated asparagus spears are tied with
long parsley stems and topped with a cauliflowerette. These salads are
arranged on a platter so guests can serve themselves. Halves of Cornish

Game Hens are topped with a zesty Black Cherry Sauce and whole black cherries. They are surrounded on the platter by hollowed orange halves filled with a spicy wild rice–sausage mixture. Complete the main course with a well-chilled sparkling Vouvray or Asti Spumante.

Because your guests will be so sated after consuming this magnificent entrée, in order to reclaim their attention dessert must be the most dramatic course of all. Frances Pelham's Flaming Rum-Plum Pudding is the only holiday dessert we know that can do the trick. It is made of a combination of spices and plums (not with suet, as is traditional in England) and served with the fluffiest, most velvety Rum Hard Sauce ever devised. Be sure to lower the lights and flame the warm pudding with rum or brandy in front of your guests. It is rich, so serve it in very small slices. There is no point in wasting it, because it will keep indefinitely. Serve seconds on request.

TIMETABLE: The Plum Pudding is the most flexible of desserts at holiday time. It can be made months ahead of time and stored in refrigerator or freezer. We make several to give as gifts right in the molds, and we include the recipe. Hard Sauce is at its best when made on serving day.

Butter-Roasted Pecans keep for weeks in the refrigerator. We like to reheat them slightly before serving to bring out their flavor.

The Wild Rice–Sausage Casserole will keep for at least 5 days in the refrigerator and for a month or more in the freezer. The Roquefort Mousse will be at its finest if made within 2 days of serving and stored in its mold in the refrigerator.

Cook the vegetables for the salad and cover them with marinade the day before serving.

The morning of your party, cook the hens and prepare their sauce. Hollow the orange shells for the wild rice, and be sure to thaw any frozen items you will be needing. Pour the cognac, and place orange slices in the champagne glasses. Cover until just before your guests arrive to prevent evaporation. Arrange the salads on a large platter and store in the refrigerator.

Unmold and garnish the Roquefort Mousse. Keep chilled until serving.

The rest of the dinner requires only reheating.

FRENCH 75

(12 SERVINGS)

It is not necessary to buy an expensive imported champagne for this purpose. Use any domestic champagne that you like. Our own favorite is Korbel Naturel.

A French 75 is most often made with 1 part champagne to 1 part brandy, or 1 part brandy to 2 parts champagne. Needless to say, it is a highly potent drink and should be served with discretion. We prefer our own version of 1 tablespoon brandy to a glass of champagne, garnished with an orange slice. This drink is ideally served in tall, tulip-shaped glasses filled two-thirds full.

2 fifths champagne　　　　　　*12 thin slices orange (1 small orange)*
¾ cup brandy or cognac

Place 1 tablespoon brandy or cognac in each glass, along with an orange slice. Add champagne and serve immediately.

To Make Ahead: Place brandy or cognac, along with the orange slices, in the glasses early in the day. Cover with a flat tray to prevent evaporation. Add the champagne as your guests arrive.

ROQUEFORT MOUSSE

(12 OR MORE SERVINGS)

6 egg yolks　　　　　　　　　*¾ pound good Roquefort cheese,*
3 egg whites　　　　　　　　　　*at room temperature*
2 cups heavy cream　　　　　　*½ teaspoon lemon juice*
1½ tablespoons (1½ envelopes)　*Parsley or watercress sprigs to*
　unflavored gelatin　　　　　　*decorate*
¼ cup cold water　　　　　　　*Sesame melba rounds for serving*

Carefully separate the eggs and set 3 of the whites aside in the bowl of an electric mixer to come to room temperature. The other 3 whites may be frozen or stored in the refrigerator for another use. The Roquefort cheese should be at room temperature.

Place the 6 egg yolks and ½ cup of the cream in a heavy saucepan over low heat and beat with a whisk until the mixture is creamy. Pour the remaining 1½ cups of cream into a mixing bowl and chill in the refrigerator until you are ready to beat it. Sprinkle the gelatin over the ¼ cup of cold water and allow it to soften for 5 minutes or so, then set the container of gelatin into a pan of hot water and stir until the mixture becomes liquid. Stir it into the warm yolk and cream mixture and pour into the container of an electric blender. Turn the blender to low speed and add the cut-up Roquefort cheese. Blend until smooth, forcing the mixture down into the blades with a rubber spatula. If you don't have a blender, press the Roquefort through a sieve into a mixing bowl and stir the gelatin mixture into it. Let the mixture cool to room temperature in a mixing bowl—only a few minutes are necessary for this.

Beat the egg whites in a clean mixing bowl with the lemon juice until they do not slide when the bowl is tilted. Remove the whites to another container and, in the same bowl, beat the remaining cream until it holds its shape. Fold the whipped cream into the cheese mixture and then fold in the beaten egg whites, in two parts.

Oil a 7- or 8-cup mold, or several smaller molds, and pour the mixture into them. Chill for an hour or longer.

Before serving, loosen the mousse around the edges of the mold. Dip the mold into hot water for just a second, then turn the mousse out onto a serving plate. Decorate as desired with sprigs of parsley or watercress (and perhaps some red pimiento at Christmastime). Serve with plain or sesame melba rounds and several small spreaders so guests can help themselves.

To Make Ahead: The mousse will keep nicely for up to 2 days in the refrigerator. Plastic wrap should be pressed into the exposed surface to prevent a skin from forming. It also freezes beautifully.

BUTTER-ROASTED PECANS

(12 SERVINGS)

We make these in large quantities to give as hostess presents in attractive glass canisters. They make a delicious nibble for people on a low-carbohydrate diet.

4 cups pecan halves
½ stick butter, melted
2 teaspoons coarse salt (kosher salt
  is perfect)

¼ teaspoon freshly ground black
  pepper (or more to taste)

Heat the oven to 350°. Toss the pecan halves in the melted butter and place them in a single layer in a shallow baking pan. Roast them in the oven for 15 to 20 minutes, stirring often to prevent burning. They must be watched carefully toward the end of the cooking time.

Remove from the oven and transfer the nuts with a slotted spoon to a large, brown grocery bag. Save any butter remaining in the pan to flavor vegetables. Shake the nuts in the bag to remove the excess butter. Sprinkle the salt and pepper over them in the bag and shake again to coat them evenly. These are at their best served warm or at room temperature.

To Make Ahead: The roasted nuts will keep for weeks if stored in an airtight container in the refrigerator, or they may be frozen. Serve at room temperature or slightly warm.

FRENCH ASPARAGUS SALAD

(12 INDIVIDUAL SALADS)

60 to 84 fresh or frozen asparagus
  spears (5 to 7 per person)

½ head cauliflower
½ bunch long-stemmed parsley

DRESSING:

2 tablespoons red wine vinegar
1 tablespoon Dijon mustard
  (Poupon)
6 tablespoons fine-quality olive oil

¾ teaspoon Worcestershire sauce
½ teaspoon cut chives, fresh,
  frozen, or dried
1 teaspoon minced parsley

*Salt and freshly ground black
  pepper*

Simmer or steam the asparagus and the cauliflower separately until they are barely tender. Break the cauliflower into flowerettes. Drain and place the vegetables in separate glass or china dishes.

Blend together the vinegar and the mustard and add the other dressing ingredients. Pour the dressing over the cooked vegetables and marinate in the refrigerator for up to 24 hours. Any cooked, leftover vegetables are delicious when marinated in this dressing.

This salad is most attractive served as small bundles of asparagus tied around the center with a long stem of parsley and topped with a cauliflowerette (see illustration). Arrange the salads on a platter or individual salad plates. Refrigerate until 2 hours before serving, then, for finest flavor, allow to come to room temperature.

To Make Ahead: It is best to prepare this salad no sooner than the night before your party. The vegetables lose their fresh quality if marinated more than 24 hours.

CORNISH GAME HENS WITH BLACK CHERRY SAUCE
(8 LARGE SERVINGS, OR 16 SMALLER SERVINGS)

*8 fresh or frozen Cornish game
  hens, thawed
4 tablespoons (½ stick) butter or
  margarine, melted
Salt and pepper*

*1½ cups chicken stock (home-
  made or canned)
1 cup dry white wine
½ cup Madeira
2 bunches fresh watercress to
  garnish the platter*

Sauce:

¼ cup drippings, from browning the hens	2 bay leaves
	2 one-pound cans pitted dark cherries in syrup
2 tablespoons sugar	
1 cup fresh or frozen orange juice	2 tablespoons cornstarch
2 tablespoons red wine vinegar	½ cup cold water
2 tablespoons fresh lemon juice	Grated rind (zest, see note,
2 tablespoons each red currant jelly and orange marmalade	page 123) of 2 oranges
	¼ cup cognac or brandy
1 cup red Burgundy	

Wash the hens with cold water and dry them well with paper towels. Preheat broiler. Place the hens breast down in a metal pan that will hold them snugly, and arrange the giblets around them. Brush the backs with half the melted butter or margarine and sprinkle generously with salt and pepper. Broil the hens 4 or 5 inches from the heat for 3 to 5 minutes or until browned. Turn them on their sides (using tongs or a cooking spoon so you don't pierce the skin) and brown both sides in the same fashion. Finally, turn them breast up, brush with the remaining butter, and brown the breasts. Reserve the drippings for the sauce.

While you are browning the hens, bring the combined chicken stock, white wine, and Madeira to a boil in a small saucepan. Let it cook over medium-high heat for about 45 minutes until it is reduced to ¾ cup (or one-quarter the original volume).

Preheat the oven to 350°. Place the browned hens and their giblets in a pan that can go into the oven. Pour the reduced stock around the hens. Cover tightly with a lid or with aluminum foil and bake for 45 minutes.

Place 4 tablespoons of the drippings from browning the hens into a heavy-bottomed saucepan, and set over medium-high heat. Stir in the sugar and continue stirring until the mixture seems to brown a little and is slightly thickened. Stir in the orange juice, vinegar, lemon juice, currant jelly, marmalade, Burgundy, bay leaves and half the juice from the cans of black cherries. Reserve the other half of the juice for later. Let simmer for 30 minutes. Strain this sauce into another pan and set aside.

When the hens are done, remove them to a warm platter where they can cool a bit before you cut them into halves. Pour the juices in which they were cooked through a strainer into the pan of reserved sauce. Bring the mixture to a boil and thicken with 2 tablespoons cornstarch mixed with ½ cup cold water. Stir in the reserved cherries along with the remaining cherry juice and half the orange zest. Bring the sauce to a boil once more, and if it does not seem thick enough, add a little more cornstarch and cold water and bring to a boil once more. Remove from the heat and stir in the ¼ cup cognac or brandy.

The hens will have cooled a bit by now, so they will be easier to handle. Using poultry or kitchen shears, cut them neatly down the breastbone and the backbone into halves. You will find it very easy to remove the breast and rib bones with your fingers—we always do this because it makes the eating so much easier. You may reheat the hens now if they have cooled. Cover them with foil and reheat at 350° for about 10 minutes before serving.

To serve, arrange the hens on a large platter surrounded by watercress and the oranges filled with Wild Rice Casserole. Pour some of the sauce and cherries decoratively over the birds. Sprinkle with the remaining orange zest.

To Make Ahead: Most of the work for this dish may be done in the morning. Brown the birds and partially make the sauce. If desired, the hens may be cooked and the sauce completed 2 hours before serving. Reheat the hens as directed above. Save any leftover sauce to serve with other poultry.

ORANGE HALVES FILLED WITH WILD RICE–SAUSAGE CASSEROLE

(12 OR MORE SERVINGS)

This casserole does not have to be served in orange shells—it is delicious served as a side dish with any poultry or game.

1½ cups uncooked wild rice
1 tablespoon salt
2 one-pound fourteen-ounce cans solid-pack tomatoes with their liquid
1 medium onion, chopped fine
2 teaspoons salt
1 tablespoon sugar
1½ pounds bulk pork sausage

Sausage seasonings, if necessary (see page 284)
1 pound fresh mushrooms
2 tablespoons butter or margarine
Juice of ⅛ lemon
6 or more large, firm, thick-skinned oranges
1 four-ounce package sliced almonds
½ cup parsley, chopped fine

Place the wild rice in a kitchen strainer and rinse under cold running water until the water runs clean. Place the rice in a pot and cover by 2 inches with cold water. Add the 1 tablespoon salt. Bring to a boil and simmer for about 30 minutes, or until the rice is tender. Meanwhile, place the tomatoes and their liquid in a large saucepan and, using a kitchen spoon, chop them coarsely against the side of the pan. Add the chopped onion, 2 teaspoons salt and sugar, and simmer, uncovered, for 30 minutes. Set aside until needed.

Cook the sausage in a skillet, breaking it up as it cooks, until brown and crumbly (no pink should remain). Taste it now, and if the sausage you have purchased is not well-seasoned, add just a pinch of each of the following: marjoram, sage, summer savory, thyme and black pepper. Set aside until needed.

Wash the mushrooms quickly under cold running water, rubbing off any sand with your fingers. Dry them immediately and slice them through the stem. Melt 2 tablespoons butter or margarine in a skillet and add the mushrooms. Sprinkle with salt and the juice of ⅛ lemon and sauté over medium-high heat, covered, for 2 to 3 minutes, until the mushrooms give off some of their moisture. Uncover the pan and continue cooking for 2 or 3 minutes longer, until almost all the moisture in the pan has evaporated. Remove from the heat and set aside.

In a 3- or 4-quart casserole, combine the cooked wild rice, tomato mixture, sausage and sautéed mushrooms and set aside.

To make the orange shells, cut the oranges in half crosswise. Remove the pulp and all the white membrane with your fingers. For eye appeal, notch the edges of the shells, using a pair of kitchen shears. Refrigerate, or even freeze the shells, but allow time for them to reach room temperature before filling them with the wild-rice mixture at serving time.

Toast the almonds in a 350° oven, watching carefully and stirring often, until they are lightly browned. Set them aside until serving time, along with some chopped parsley for decoration.

To serve, heat the casserole, covered, at 300° to 350° for about 20 minutes or until it is very hot (use whatever temperature is convenient). Spoon the mixture into the prepared orange shells and top each serving with toasted almonds and chopped parsley.

To Make Ahead: The casserole may be made well ahead of time and frozen, or refrigerated for up to 3 days. The oranges may be prepared and frozen if desired—bring them back to shape under warm running water. The almonds may be toasted and kept for several days at room temperature. Fill the orange shells just before serving.

FRANCES PELHAM'S FLAMING RUM-PLUM PUDDING WITH HARD SAUCE

(12 OR MORE SERVINGS)

½ cup sifted all-purpose flour
½ teaspoon baking soda
1 teaspoon ground cinnamon
½ teaspoon ground cloves
¼ teaspoon salt
¾ cup fine, dry bread crumbs, or Zwieback or melba crumbs
½ cup (1 stick) butter or margarine
¾ cup firmly packed light-brown sugar

3 eggs
2 one-pound cans purple plums, drained, pitted and chopped
1 tablespoon grated orange rind
1 eight-ounce package pitted dates, cut up
1 cup seedless raisins
8 ounces mixed, chopped candied fruits
1 cup chopped pecans
½ cup currants

RUM HARD SAUCE:

1½ cups confectioner's sugar
¼ pound (1 stick) soft butter

2 tablespoons dark Jamaican rum

TO SERVE:

6 candied cherries (optional)
12 leaves cut from angelica or citron (optional)

⅛ cup cognac, brandy, or dark rum to flame the pudding

You will need a steamed-pudding mold (see illustration). The one we use measures 7 cups to the top. Frances either uses an 8-cup mold or makes 1½ times the recipe to fill a 12-cup mold.

Make the pudding at least 1 day in advance for best flavor and texture. Sift the flour, baking soda, cinnamon, cloves and salt into a small bowl, then stir in the bread crumbs. In a large bowl, cream the butter or margarine until fluffy and light. Gradually add the brown sugar and continue beating until the mixture is very light. Beat in the eggs, one at a time, beating well after each addition. Stir in the chopped plums and orange rind. Blend in the flour mixture, then fold in the dates, raisins, candied fruits, pecans and currants.

Grease the pudding mold, lid and all, very heavily with solid vegetable shortening, then dust with granulated sugar. Spoon the pudding mixture into the mold, and tie the lid on with string to hold it tightly during the cooking.

Place the mold in a large kettle on a rack or trivet or some other object to hold it off the bottom. Pour in boiling water to half the depth of the mold and cover the kettle tightly. Bring to a boil, lower the heat to keep the water simmering, and steam the pudding for 4½ hours, or until it is firm to the touch and a long skewer inserted into the center comes out clean. Keep the water boiling gently during the cooking time, adding more boiling water as necessary.

Cool the pudding in the mold for 5 minutes. Loosen around the edge with a knife and invert onto a serving platter.

To make the Rum Hard Sauce, sift the sugar through a kitchen strainer at least 5 times. Beat in the soft butter and rum. Continue to beat until the sauce is fluffy and light.

Before serving, garnish the pudding with red cherries and with leaves cut from candied angelica or citron if you like. Frances surrounds it with fresh holly, which must be removed before the pudding is flamed. Heat cognac, brandy, or dark rum in a ladle in front of your guests. Ignite and pour over the pudding. When the flames die, cut the pudding into small portions (it is very rich!), top with Rum Hard Sauce, and serve immediately.

To Make Ahead: The pudding may be made months in advance. Wrap it in cheesecloth which has been soaked in cognac, brandy, or rum, then wrap it tightly in foil and store in the refrigerator. It may be reheated in the oven (rewrap in foil after removing the cheesecloth) or resteamed in its mold. Either way, allow about 20 minutes. The Hard Sauce is at its best if served the day it is made, though it may be made ahead of time for convenience. Store at room temperature for up to 5 days or in the refrigerator for a longer period of time.

Index

Index

*Diana von Welanetz was born and raised in Beverly
Hills, California, where she began swapping recipes for
mud soufflés at the age of six. Her credentials in haute
cuisine include classes at the Cordon Bleu in Paris and
five years' further study with renowned chef Gregoire
Le Balch. Paul, a talented painter and sculptor as well as
a lover of fine food, is also a dedicated traveler and a
hopeless romantic. Together the von Welanetzes have
traveled the world collecting recipes for this book and
for their own highly acclaimed cooking classes.*